MEMPHIS HOOPS

MEMPHIS HOOPS

Race and Basketball in the Bluff City, 1968–1997

KEITH B. WOOD

Sport and Popular Culture
Brian M. Ingrassia, SERIES EDITOR

The University of Tennessee Press / Knoxville

The Sport and Popular Culture series is designed to promote critical, innovative research in the history of sport through a wide spectrum of works— monographs, edited volumes, biographies, and reprints of classics.

Copyright © 2021 by The University of Tennessee Press / Knoxville.
All Rights Reserved. Manufactured in the United States of America.
Hardcover: 1st printing, 2021.
Paper: 1st printing, 2023.

Library of Congress Cataloging-in-Publication Data

Names: Wood, Keith B., author.
Title: Memphis hoops : race and basketball in the Bluff City, 1968–1997 / Keith B. Wood.
Other titles: Sport and popular culture.
Description: First edition. | Knoxville : The University of Tennessee Press, 2021. | Series: Sport and popular culture | Includes bibliographical references and index. | Summary: "This book considers the role of collegiate basketball in Memphis following the 1968 assassination of Martin Luther King Jr. Keith B. Wood analyzes the racial dynamics in the city through the lens of one of the city's iconic sports figures, Larry Finch, a Memphis native and the first black player signed by Memphis State. Finch helped Memphis State make the NCAA championship game his senior year, but the team lost to UCLA. Finch was then drafted by the Lakers in 1973 but decided to stay home and play for the American Basketball Association's Memphis Tams. After two years of playing semi-professionally, Finch returned to the sidelines as a coach and would eventually become the head coach of Memphis State. Finch was championed as a symbol of the racial healing power of basketball that helped counteract the racial turbulence ongoing in the city, but for decades the city's racial strife continued off the basketball court"— Provided by publisher.
Identifiers: LCCN 2020056672 (print) | LCCN 2020056673 (ebook) | ISBN 9781621906681 (hardcover) | ISBN 9781621906698 (adobe pdf) | ISBN 9781621908579 (paperback)
Subjects: LCSH: Finch, Larry. | Memphis Tigers (Basketball team)—History. | African American basketball players—Tennessee—Memphis. | African American basketball coaches—Tennessee—Memphis. | African Americans—Tennessee—Memphis. | Memphis (Tenn.)—Race relations—History—20th century.
Classification: LCC GV884.F55 W66 2021 (print) | LCC GV884.F55 (ebook) | DDC 796.323/630976819—dc23
LC record available at https://lccn.loc.gov/2020056672
LC ebook record available at https://lccn.loc.gov/2020056673

To Coach Tony Delgado,

Thank you for seeing more in me.

—K.W.

Contents

Illustrations

Foreword

Founded in 1819 on the Fourth Chickasaw Bluff overlooking the mighty Mississippi, Memphis has faced its share of triumphs and challenges throughout more than two centuries of history. Before the Civil War, it was a quickly growing rail hub, cotton shipping center, and slave trading market. During postwar Reconstruction, the city witnessed a tragic race riot in which a white mob destroyed an African American neighborhood and massacred nearly fifty black Memphians. In the 1870s, yellow fever epidemics ravaged the city, killing thousands and causing its charter to be revoked. Early-1900s Memphis was dominated by the political machine of Boss Crump, whose reign ended just as the national civil rights movement gained steam. By the late-twentieth century, despite the prosperity and prominence brought by major corporations like FedEx, the Mid-South region confronted challenges more like those of Rust Belt cities than of the emerging Sun Belt. Memphis, says sociologist Wanda Rushing, is a place of paradoxes: "an interesting southern city with a turbulent past positioning itself for a promising future."[1]

Of course, one of the most notorious and troubling events in Memphis's turbulent history was the 1968 assassination of civil rights icon Martin Luther King, Jr., at the Lorraine Motel. The murder dashed so many Americans' hopes of nonviolent progress toward racial justice. King's room was immediately sealed off and eventually became a museum exhibit, with some people banking the city's future at least partly on its rich yet troubled past. As Keith Wood convincingly argues in *Memphis Hoops: Race and Basketball in the Bluff City, 1968–1997*, basketball ostensibly united Memphis in the years following King's murder, yet it is all too clear that the hardwood was never the easiest place to unify a city long divided by racial inequality.

At the heart of this gripping story is Larry Finch (1951–2011), the local kid from Orange Mound and hoops phenom at Melrose High School who shunned offers to play big-time basketball at other universities so he could instead stay close to home. Not all members of Memphis's black community endorsed Finch's decision to play for Memphis State—a university that was segregated until the late 1950s—but he thrived there. In March 1973, Finch even led the Tigers to their first Final Four appearance in St, Louis, where they battled John Wooden, Bill Walton, and the seemingly unstoppable UCLA Bruins in the national championship game.

Wood shows us that the court was a place where Memphians navigated the fast-break changes brought about by the end of Jim Crow. It is telling that in January 1973, exactly two months before that famous game against UCLA, the *New York Times* said Memphis had never welcomed change—yet, somewhat paradoxically, the article then went on to describe big changes happening in the city, from school desegregation to the abandonment of antiquated temperance laws.[2] We now know 1973 was a year of inflection, even disruption, and that was certainly the case in the Mid-South. Even as Finch and company brought Memphis into the national limelight, the Bluff City continued to struggle with its past, present, and future.

When professional basketball briefly came to Memphis in the 1970s, Larry Finch again chose to stay close to home, starring for the Memphis Tams of the American Basketball Association (ABA). His style of play never quite fit with the pros, though, and he only lasted two seasons. Progress—in sport, as well as equality—came in fits and starts. Many white Memphians cheered Finch's Tigers in 1973, but they virtually ignored the basketball championship won by the Magicians of historically black LeMoyne-Owen College two years later. Finch became Memphis State's head coach in 1986 and served until 1997 when, despite a solid coaching record, he was forced to resign from the top basketball job at what was then called the University of Memphis. Yet as Wood astutely illustrates, if we focus on Finch's coaching career—in the era of black icons like Michael Jordan and Oprah Winfrey—we obscure the significant story of his mentor, Verties Sails Jr., whose head-coach ambitions were thwarted a decade earlier, at a time when basketball had already supposedly, if not actually, augured a post-racial city.

Woven throughout *Memphis Hoops* are essential personalities and places of the Bluff City: Isaac Hayes and Stax Records; the Mid-South Coliseum and the Great American Pyramid. By the early twenty-first century, pro basketball was back in Memphis with the arrival of the NBA Grizzlies and, not long after that, the opening of the FedEx Forum at the edge of Beale Street—the historic African American neighborhood and entertainment district that most clearly captures Memphis's attempts to move into the future by looking back to its past.

This is a compelling book about a sport and a city and the complicated dance between the two. Memphis has had plenty of hoops through which to jump—and getting past them was never as easy as it may have seemed to casual observers. Wood has done historians and readers a tremendous service in untangling the story of race and basketball in the Bluff City.

Brian M. Ingrassia
West Texas A&M University

NOTES

1. Wanda Rushing, *Memphis and the Paradox of Place: Globalization in the American South* (Chapel Hill: University of North Carolina Press, 2009), 5.

2. Jim Nordheimer, "Memphis: A City That Wants Never to Change," *New York Times*, January 26, 1973, 37.

Introduction

With 2:51 remaining on the clock in the 1973 NCAA national championship basketball game, Bill Walton of UCLA sprained his ankle. Memphis State's Larry Finch helped carry Walton off the floor to the sidelines. Finch showed humility and humanity as the crowd cheered Walton's performance. Walton's 44 points catapulted the Bruins to their seventh straight national championship. Even though Memphis State lost, the team drew attention and highlighted sports as an arena of racial discussion. At the center of this story stands Larry Finch, whose basketball career spanned a period of profound change in the city of Memphis. Finch was a local schoolboy hero from Orange Mound's Melrose High School who became the first African American head coach at Memphis State University. His career provides a frame to examine how race and sport intersected in the city during a turbulent era.

To many Memphians, the 1973 Tigers told a story of racial progress. They believed basketball allowed for an assertion of racial equity on the court and an opportunity to unite the city off the court. Basketball, as a social function, recast black identity in a positive light following the turbulent times that preceded this era. It provided a cultural counterpoint for black people to the grim experiences of working and living in a city marked by inequality. Players such as Finch became positive black male models of identity to both black and white communities. Basketball also served as a forum for symbolic political assertion. Through competition with white people, basketball gave the black community in Memphis a heightened sense of black consciousness and self-esteem. Even many white Memphians touted a language of racial unity thanks to the 1973 Tigers.

In an era when colleges in the South began to integrate their college basketball programs, the city of Memphis embraced its flagship university's shift in that direction. For Memphis State University, Larry Finch became a symbol of possibility in integrated athletics. Just as Jackie Robinson's stellar play catapulted the Brooklyn Dodgers to the World Series, Larry Finch carried the Tigers to the National Collegiate Athletic Association (NCAA) finals. Outside of the Mid-South Coliseum, however, the city of Memphis was divided. The 1968 Sanitation Workers Strike, which brought Dr. Martin Luther King Jr. to the city, was evidence of the problems the city faced. King's assassination was a nadir in the city's history. The city's predominately white police force deemed itself a target after King's assassination. This led the Memphis Police Department to request more helicopters, mace, and riot helmets. The tension came to a head in October of 1971 when sixteen-year-old Elton Hayes was beaten to death by white police officers after he tried to evade them in a speeding car. Following the Hayes incident, the city broke into riots for ten days before twenty-three police officers were suspended.[1] Two years after Hayes's and five years after King's assassination, many in the establishment were exalting Finch as a racial unifier. Finch welcomed the characterization, which mirrored his personal belief that "if the world were like an athletic program—a winning team—it would be a lot better."[2]

Yet basketball also told a story of continued racial inequality. The inequities faced by black male basketball players and coaches in the city during this era mirrored the racial animus in the city. Even as the Tigers marched toward the 1973 NCAA basketball championship game, the city remained torn over a court-ordered busing plan. White flight to the suburbs and the exponential growth of private schools in the city reflected a racially polarized city, driven by white prejudice. Mayor Wyeth Chandler proclaimed that the Tigers "unified the city like it's never been unified before. Black and white, rich and poor, old and young are all caught up in their success. Memphis is a better city now, thanks to the Memphis State basketball team."[3] But that same year, Chandler, amid a political struggle over the forced desegregation of Memphis City Schools through busing, also said, "I cannot and will not urge any parent to send his child into a ghetto school."[4] These quotes, parallel together, reflect how basketball in Memphis simultaneously asserted racial equality and exploited its black athletes.[5]

Just as sports can reflect the dominant ideas of our society, they can also reflect the struggle.[6] Sports can be a vehicle for racial integration. The stories of Joe Louis and Jackie Robinson are stories of hope for black Americans. Their athletic feats placed them at the top of the pantheon of American sports heroes from the country's two most popular sports. However, throughout their careers, the issues of race and nationalism vexed them, as they had all black Americans for more than one hundred and fifty years.[7] When these men confronted racial animus through sport, they demonstrated the possibilities of racial uplift.[8] They functioned as racial ambassadors, appeasing white people while inspiring black people.

Yet sports have also provided arenas for many black athletes to challenge racial norms and air their grievances. Muhammad Ali, for instance, forced the professional boxing world and the United States to confront the issues of racism and war. His courage in the face of racism allowed other black Americans to overcome their fears.[9] Ali's celebration of black culture challenged the existing social order because it helped eliminate the negative self-image prevalent that centuries of white oppression instilled among some black people and encouraged black consciousness.[10] When Tommie Smith and John Carlos raised their fists on the medal stand during the 1968 Mexico City Olympics, they became symbols of the revolt of the black athlete. In the 1960s, sociologist Harry Edwards challenged the theory that athletics brought men of all races together on equal footing. His Olympic Project for Human Rights was the catalyst that led Smith and Carlos to revolt against the racism that black Americans faced openly.[11]

Black athletes in the 1970s transformed the game with their performance of the black aesthetic found in inner-city basketball.[12] By the 1970s, as academic integration became a reality on southern campuses, athletic departments in conferences such as the Atlantic Coast Conference (ACC) and Southeastern Conference (SEC) resisted integration. In basketball, as opposed to football where players are covered from head to toe with pads, the athlete is exposed for the fans to see in shorts and a tank top. Basketball players are a more visible symbol of blackness. Because basketball is the most intimate of major team sports, and games occur in enclosed spaces, black basketball players faced racial animus in a more personal way. Yet basketball, with its smaller squads, offered a greater likelihood of an immediate competitive return with the addition of a single player for universities.[13] *Memphis Hoops* studies the intersection of basketball and race in Memphis. As the South inched slowly toward integration, basketball allowed the city of Memphis to showcase its growth and erase the national perception of a racist Memphis established following Dr. King's assassination, even as basketball revealed the city's enduring racial divide. By analyzing high school, collegiate, and professional basketball, this book seeks to provide a balanced portrayal of how sport shaped racial change in Memphis during the thirty years following King's death.

The Memphis NAACP had been challenging segregation on campus at Memphis State University since 1956. In 1957, Maxine Smith and Laurie Sugarmon attempted to enroll in the graduate program. Two years later, in 1959, the university admitted eight students who became known as the "Memphis State 8."[14] These students were an isolated minority. There were no black professors. No classes taught black history, and no events or clubs on campus allowed black students to express their pride in being black.

Starting in 1966, a group of black male students initiated the Black Student Association to integrate Memphis State students without sacrificing black identity.[15] In April 1969, the BSA confronted Memphis State president Cecil Humphrey in his office. They requested student government funding, representation, campus jobs, an end to all forms of discrimination on campus, active recruitment of black personnel at all levels, development of a Black Studies Program, the hire of a black administrator, and more black athletes.[16] Memphis State refused to budge. The administration enlisted the Memphis Police Department to arrest 109 protesting students.[17] These students were released and allowed to continue their studies for the remainder of the semester on a probationary status. The BSA initiatives eventually led to the hiring of Laurie Sugarmon as the first black professor, the hiring of Ernest Davis as the first black administrator, and the election of Maybelline Forbes as the first African American homecoming queen in the school's history.[18] The BSA helped challenge the university's racial patterns and allowed the university to move from desegregation to integration.[19]

South of campus, on the other side of the railroad tracks, the schoolboy heroics of Larry Finch and his Melrose Wildcat teammates were garnering the attention of Memphis State head men's basketball coach Moe Iba. *Memphis Hoops* begins with the story of how Larry Finch led his Melrose High Golden Wildcats to the MIAA City Championship against Overton High's Johnny Neumann in front of a sellout crowd at the Mid-South Coliseum. This game spotlighted the optimism of city leaders that basketball could serve as a healing salve while exposing racial tensions. This chapter also introduces us to Coach Verties Sails, whose role as a mentor and father figure helped to create star basketball players in the city, and seeks to highlight his importance to the city's basketball iconography. The next chapter chronicles Finch's senior year at Memphis State, where he guided his team to the 1973 NCAA finals against UCLA. As the city united behind the team, race relations off the court became heated when the federal courts mandated busing to integrate the city's schools. Although white political officials proclaimed Finch as a unifying symbol, they ardently opposed school desegregation. Finch's personality endeared him to the university's fan base, and his myth continued to grow.

The third chapter shifts the focus from collegiate to professional basketball. If college basketball created a myth of racial unity, then the ABA's failure in Memphis debunks that same myth. Following his stellar collegiate career at Memphis State, Finch played for two seasons in the ABA in Memphis in front of minuscule crowds. If basketball truly unified the city in the 1970s, where were the same crowds for ABA games? The fourth chapter returns to collegiate basketball with an examination of the city's historically black college, LeMoyne-Owen College. In 1975, LeMoyne-Owen captured the NCAA men's Division III National Championship. However, LeMoyne-Owen's play was unknown to most white Memphians. Chapter five returns to Memphis State with an analysis of the school's first black assistant coach, Verties Sails. Following his playing career at LeMoyne-Owen College, a brief tenure as an assistant at Melrose High, and a successful stint as Melrose's head basketball coach, Sails earned the opportunity to become the first full-time black assistant in the South. Black basketball players were now acceptable at the university, but the racial animus that Sails faced as a coach mirrored the issues that black people continued to face in the city.

Chapter six focuses on the underlying racial tension behind one of the most turbulent periods in Memphis State men's basketball history. Finch returned to Memphis State as an assistant under Dana Kirk. The scandals under Kirk stemmed from the exploitation of black players, exposing the underlying racial animus that remained in the city during the 1980s. The final chapter analyzes Finch's tenure as Memphis State's first black head coach. He returned the program to respectability but continuously had his competence questioned, which suggested enduring racial prejudices. Finch's time as a head coach did not happen in a vacuum. During Finch's tenure as head coach, the city witnessed a shift in its political paradigm when it elected its first black mayor in the controversial 1991 election. Finally, in a unique twist, when Finch was fired in 1997, he received praise and adoration from the university, its fan base, and the city, even as they were discrediting the school's most treasured commodity.

Basketball historian Stanley Cohen notes that "what once burned bright in memory recedes into the more remote pockets of recollection. We treat the past as if it were a vault in which events can be stored and preserved against the incursions of time. But time stakes its claim. Memory is an untrustworthy guide. The tale, cast each time anew, becomes transformed in the telling. The facts, of course, are always the same; it is the way we see them and feel about them that changes."[20] In the era after the assassination of Martin Luther King Jr., the city promoted a collective memory of racial unity through basketball. The reality is more complicated. Basketball served as both an arena of prejudice and as a vehicle of racial liberation. Finch himself was both the myth that needs to be questioned and a reflection of black aspirations for genuine equality. In *Memphis Hoops*, Finch is, at times, the main character. At other times, he is on the periphery or even absent. Nevertheless, he remains a complicated symbol through which to understand Memphis basketball.

Memphis Is My Home

Under the guise of high school athletics, a few progressive-minded athletic directors and coaches attempted to use sports as a conduit to improve race relations in the city in the 1960s. The first integrated high school football game in the city took place on September 15, 1965, between all-white Catholic High and all-black Father Bertrand High at Crump Stadium in front of close to 7,000 fans.[1] The following spring, the Tennessee Secondary Schools Athletic Association held its first integrated state basketball championship. All-black Pearl High of Nashville defeated all-white Treadwell High of Memphis on the campus of Vanderbilt University in the state's first integrated basketball championship. That very same night, in College Park, Maryland, the Texas Western Miners were taking on Adolph Rupp's Kentucky Wildcats for the NCAA championship.[2] When Texas Western's Don Haskins started an all-black line-up, the Miners broke another racial barrier. Their win against Kentucky changed the course of college basketball. The following school year, schools across the city began to schedule integrated athletic events. Historian Jules Tygiel coined the phrase "baseball's great experiment" to describe the affect that Jackie Robinson had on the integration of major league baseball. Robinson's integration into professional baseball set a precedent for other institutions to provide some of the social justice that had long been denied to the black community. Sport ultimately played into the civil rights movement in richly symbolic terms. Black athletes on the baseball diamond, football gridiron, and in the basketball arena reinforced race pride and established role models for African Americans who believed that the time had come to assert their claims to full participation in the life of the nation.[3] In the fall of 1967, a group of coaches and athletic directors mapped out a plan to integrate athletics in high school sports under the umbrella of the Memphis Interscholastic Athletic Association (MIAA).

The MIAA provided the foundation for the integration of high school basketball in Memphis as well as a platform to introduce the city to Larry Finch. Following the 1954 *Brown v. Board* decision by the United States Supreme Court, Memphis began the political struggle over the desegregation of public schools. Memphis City Schools began the process in 1960 when they enrolled thirteen first graders in all-white Bruce, Gordon, Rozelle, and Springdale elementary schools.[4] But by the fall of 1967, the schools in the city remained predominately segregated. Coaches and athletic directors attempted to use the athletic arena to show Memphians that the black and white communities could share common ground. From these initial steps emerged the MIAA city basketball championship games at the Mid-South Coliseum. These games became the showcase for high school basketball in the city, as black and white teams competed for a championship that placed them atop the city's basketball hierarchy.

Hampered by inclement weather, the inaugural 1968 MIAA basketball championship was only a glimpse into what could be. The following year, the 1969 MIAA basketball championship game featured the city's two best players when Larry Finch's all-black Melrose High School squared off against Johnny Neumann's all-white Overton High School. One year removed from the assassination of Dr. King, school integration was a politically and socially explosive issue. Local media coverage openly avoided any racial undertones, but underneath the façade of racial indifference was a community torn apart by race. The sellout crowd at the Mid-South Coliseum pointed to its importance in both the black and white communities. The Coliseum was the place where white and black fans of the Tiger basketball program came together in Memphis to heal the wounds of the city, according to the myth surrounding Finch. Emotionally, the building holds a special place in the hearts of the Tiger faithful who have promulgated this narrative. Players, fans, and coaches who participated in this game have all looked back with a sense of civic pride because of the lack of any violence surrounding the game. The 1969 MIAA City Championship basketball game both transcended and exposed the racial tension in Memphis. A peaceful, unifying narrative became a foundational stone for unifying the city behind basketball, even as the city suffered from racial division.

For the decade preceding the MIAA's decision to desegregate high school athletics, the city juggled varying philosophies, strategies, and legal remedies to limit school desegregation. High school athletics remained segregated. Before 1967, white athletes played in the Prep League or Shelby County League, and black athletes played in the Negro Leagues. Local coaches and athletic directors began to defy cultural norms and cross-racial boundaries in 1965 when Catholic High played Father Bertrand in football. The courage of Catholic's Ollie Keller and Father Bertrand's W.P. Porter personified the ideals of social justice that Catholic schools taught.[5] These same ideals were not as prevalent with the leadership governing the Memphis City Schools. Nevertheless, over the next two years, integrated high school athletics became less contentious as teams continued to cross racial lines to play. These initial contests preceded the desegregation of high school athletics in the summer of 1967.[6]

In June of 1964, the Tennessee Secondary Schools Athletic Association (TSSAA) Board of Control members voted to allow black schools into TSSAA as affiliate members, which allowed them to schedule basketball games with white schools. In March of 1966, Pearl High of Nashville became one of three black schools to compete in the TSSAA state basketball champions. They defeated Memphis Treadwell High at Vanderbilt's Memorial Coliseum to become the state's first African American state champion.[7] That summer, Dean Ehlers joined the Memphis City Schools as head of athletics after four years as the basketball coach at Memphis State. Basketball became more of a priority in the city with Ehlers directing athletics. Treadwell's basketball coach Bill McClain was joined by John Clayton (Frayser High), William Collins (Melrose High), and Lloyd Williams (Hamilton High), among others, in a fight for equal standing with football. They sought "open gym" time so their players could practice outside of the season with their school, and so that they could coach their boys in local summer leagues. After losing the state championship game to all-black Pearl, Treadwell's McClain also believed it was time for schools in Memphis to begin integrating play.[8] Getting this approved by TSSAA, Ehlers, and local principals became the biggest hurdle.

The egalitarian nature of competitive athletics proscribes that teams seek out the best competition to assert their prominence, and so basketball coaches in the city united across racial lines for the betterment of their players. This was the first step toward integrating play. When the TSSAA accepted interracial games in 1964, the foundation the Memphis coaches needed to address the topic was already in place on the state level. Getting past the cultural norms in Memphis held by principals and other administrators was the greatest challenge. Charles Williams, head of the Health and Physical Education department with the City Schools, was the crucial liaison between the coaches and administrators across the city in the push for an integrated MIAA. Ehlers remained firm in his conviction that a democratic process was the only means to achieve integration in city athletics. Athletic integration was initially defeated in 1966 when the white school's coaches, who were in the majority, voted together to maintain segregated play. The following summer, many of the white coaches, led by Treadwell's McClain, banned together with the city's black coaches in a moment of racial unity to form an integrated MIAA and allow for integrated athletics in the city.[9] Although the schools in Memphis remained segregated, the city's coaches used the athletic arena to show Memphians that the black and white communities could share common ground. An integrated MIAA became a reality in the fall of 1967, and the city's first integrated basketball city championship was on schedule for February 1968. These games would help catapult basketball as the preeminent sport in the city.

The integrated MIAA gave birth to the city's most important prep game of the year, the city championship basketball game. For years, the city's best white basketball teams assumed they were the best, and the black basketball teams assumed the same. Jim Crow laws denied the city's best players, on both sides, the opportunity to compete against each other for their respective high schools. Very few white players crossed racial boundaries into black neighborhoods, such as Orange Mound, to compete against the city's best black basketball players.[10] Black players who went to find games in white neighborhoods quickly found themselves halted by Jim Crow. Thus, the best basketball players in the city were kept away from each other except on the rare occasions when white players sought out games in black neighborhoods. The creation of an integrated basketball city championship provided players an opportunity to openly compete against each other, even while segregation continued to divide the city. Playing in the city's prime sports arena, black and white players in town were given a platform to showcase their abilities.

Built in 1963, the Mid-South Coliseum became the home of the Memphis State Tiger basketball program in 1964 and the MIAA Basketball City Championships in 1968. Located on Early Maxwell Boulevard, the Mid-South Coliseum sits on the southern edge of the Memphis Fairgrounds. It became a space where Memphis's black and white communities could meet under one roof and unify in some small way behind sport. Played in front of a sold-out Mid-South Coliseum crowd, the 1969 MIAA city basketball championship game foreshadowed Finch's success in bringing the city together behind basketball. The Coliseum became one of the few places where Memphians could meet, despite their racial differences, for the common cause of cheering good basketball. Yet even as they met in the Mid-South Coliseum for MIAA high school championship games, Jim Crow norms remained intact—white people sat on one side to cheer their team and black people on the other side to cheer on their team. Outside of the Mid-South Coliseum, the political paradigm was changing, and racial strife in the city led many to believe the city was on the precipice of exploding. For the short time that the city gathered in the Mid-South Coliseum, these issues became secondary to the excitement transpiring on the hardwood floor. During the regular season, the MIAA held games on both black and white campuses, but they played the city semifinals and championship games at the Mid-South Coliseum. The Coliseum provided a ray of hope for integration by hosting fans from both black and white schools. However, it maintained segregation by having white fans on one side and black fans on the other; the Coliseum's oval design made segregating more significant numbers of fans plausible. Outside of the Coliseum in 1968, the city's segregation pattern was being challenged during the Memphis Sanitation Workers Strike.

The coaches, athletic directors, and school administrators who created the MIAA could not have anticipated the political events that surrounded the first MIAA city championships in February of 1968. Weeks before this game, sanitation workers Echol Cole and Robert Walker were killed on the job by the hydraulic ram of their garbage packer on Colonial Street.[11] Their deaths sparked black resistance in the city that culminated in the Memphis Sanitation Workers Strike. For sixty-three days, the workers marched, held daily rallies at United Rubber Workers union hall, and joined mass meetings at black churches. They challenged Mayor Loeb's patent refusal to acknowledge their union with signs that read "I am a Man." The strike was an assertion of self-determination in the face of racism and paternalistic labor relations by Loeb.[12]

On Thursday morning, February 23, the day before the inaugural MIAA City Championship game, the AFSCME leadership and the city's sanitation workers gathered in the city council's chambers and participated in a sit-in. Numerous black preachers led the group in song and prayer. The *Commercial*

Appeal reported that the NAACP's Jesse Turner Sr. had urged the black men in Memphis to "call a friend and have him bring a bucket of garbage."[13] The *Commercial Appeal* claimed that Turner's request was an invitation to "desecrate city hall, the symbol of authority of the people of Memphis."[14] The local NAACP, led by Turner, continued to push for union recognition and dues check-off as the critical issues in the strike. On February 23, the same day the editorials attacking Turner appeared in the *Commercial Appeal*, the City Council voted 9–4 to reject the strikers' demands.[15]

Mayor Henry Loeb stood firm against the sanitation workers. He agreed to recognize the union, but not their right to collect dues. The sanitation workers were allowed a union amongst themselves, but not one with outside influences. Loeb told the strikers, "the city does not have contracts with other unions."[16] The moment harkened back to "Boss" E.H. Crump, who vehemently opposed unions in the city in 1940. "We aren't going to have any C.I.O. nigger unions in Memphis," he decried, "They can do what they want in Detroit, Chicago, and New York City, but we aren't going to have it here in Memphis."[17] Historian Roger Biles argues that the white establishment in Memphis remained committed to the plantation mentality in which benevolent owners took care of their grateful laborers, and opposed any "radical" notions such as the closed shop and collective bargaining.[18] Loeb's political ideology was firmly entrenched in maintaining the status quo established by Crump. Loeb viewed the sanitation workers as his "boys"—a disparaging way to refer to black men that arose on plantations. Meanwhile, many of the forward-thinking coaches and athletic directors in the city were devising a way to bring the city's youth together in the gyms and on the playing fields across the city.

▲ ▼ ▲

To avoid segregated divisions and to distribute the schools evenly, Memphis area high school athletic directors could not construct leagues based solely upon geography. The MIAA created two separate divisions of schools that each had two conferences within them: a red division and a blue division.[19] During the 1967–68 high school basketball season, teams throughout the city came together in gyms across the city in athletic competition. Although racial tensions were present, there were no significant incidents reported from these games.

The 1968 MIAA City Championship game was the type of matchup that the founding administrators hoped to create when they birthed the new integrated format. Before the integration of athletics in the city, Frayser High dominated the all-white versions of the city championship and Carver High dominated Negro League play.[20] They represented two communities: the Frayser community was a predominately white, blue-collar, working-class neighborhood in northwest Memphis. Carver High, located in the Riverview section of South Memphis where residents worked in the industrial sector, served its all-black community.

Riverview is one of several neighborhoods in the South Memphis community, and Carver High served proudly as a symbol of its community. The neighborhood encompasses a two-mile square area south of downtown bounded by South Parkway Avenue, Florida Avenue, Mallory Avenue, and McKellar Lake. It has been part of Memphis since the 1800s and was the home to many of the city's prominent black middle class. South Memphis, in the 1960s, was a large manufacturing and distribution base. More than two-thirds of construction for the Riverview neighborhood took place between 1940–1970.[21] Most of the homes are small single-family units. Defined by strong familial ties and powerful connections with the community's churches.[22]

Carver High was opened in 1957, three years after *Brown v. Board,* in the Riverview section of South Memphis to ensure that white and black students in South Memphis would remain segregated. Local NAACP activist and Memphis City School Board member Maxine Smith called the opening of all-black Carver a shameful ploy to keep black students out of all-white Southside High.[23] By 1968, students and parents in the Riverview community charged that the school was overcrowded, understaffed, and lacked necessary equipment—equipment that was given to comparable white schools in the district.[24] Nevertheless, teachers at Carver built pride in their students for the Carver community through tough lessons that went beyond the curriculum and prepared them for life.[25]

Carver coach L.C. Gordon was no stranger to breaking racial barriers. A 1957 graduate of Memphis's Booker T. Washington High School, Gordon was the first black basketball player at Oklahoma State University. For years Blair T. Hunt, principal at Booker T. Washington High, believed in racial assimilation. Hunt worked behind the scenes as a liaison between the black community and E.H. Crump's administration. Many in the black community criticized him for trading support for favors, but he kept the voices of the black community alive.[26] Gordon was a defensive stalwart at Booker T. Washington High who caught the eye of Memphis State coach Bob Vanatta. Instead of attempting to break Jim Crow norms in the city by inviting Gordon to join the Memphis State team, Vanatta suggested Gordon to Hank Iba, head basketball coach at Oklahoma State.[27] Unlike Finch, Gordon left the city of Memphis to play for a predominately white college. His choices to play major collegiate basketball were limited to leaving Memphis and the South or playing for a lesser known historically black college. Yet, stories like Gordon's foreshadowed a time when black players would be welcome on the Memphis State's campus.

Gordon accepted the scholarship to Oklahoma State sight unseen. Following graduation from Washington High, Gordon enrolled at Oklahoma State University and became the school's first black basketball player.[28] As the school's first black player, Gordon was not allowed to live in the same dorms as his teammates, eat in the same cafeteria, or go to the movies in any of the same places as his white teammates. Traveling to road games and playing in hostile gyms subjected Gordon to racial slurs and ugly epithets.[29] Gordon persevered through these trials and graduated with a bachelor's degree. After graduation, Gordon returned home to Memphis and began a career teaching and coaching basketball at Carver High School. Gordon's return to the city to coach high school basketball echoed many black players before him who left and then returned to coach in the city. It also foreshadowed Finch's career.

L.C. Gordon quietly broke the color barrier at Oklahoma State in 1958. Ten years later, he quietly guided his all-black players from Carver into the city's first integrated championship basketball game. Gordon's Carver team squared off against Coach John Clayton and his Frayser High Rams, a perennial white basketball power in the late 1960s, in the city's first integrated MIAA city championship.

Frayser started as a community built around the Illinois Central Railroad in the mid-19th century. It was primarily a passenger railroad stop between Memphis and Covington, Tennessee.[30] In the mid-20th century, commercial and industrial growth led to population growth and its eventual annexation in 1958 by the City of Memphis.[31] Frayser's blue-collar community allowed Clayton to build a respected, hardnosed program. The Rams competed for city championships in the five seasons before the creation of the MIAA city championship. They returned to the city basketball finals in 1968, after winning the all-white Prep League the year before.[32]

On a blustery Friday night in February, with a dusting of snow on the ground, the Mid-South Coliseum welcomed 3,914 fans to watch the inaugural MIAA City Championship game. The Carver High Cobras held a decisive height advantage over the Rams; their tallest player was only 6'2", while the Carver front line included one 6'4" wing player and two 6'6" post players.[33] From the onset, the Carver defense stifled the much smaller Ram offense. Coach L.C. Gordon's demands for defensive intensity from his charges overwhelmed the smaller Rams for three quarters. Frayser fought back in the fourth quarter and cut the lead to one. The Cobras' size and defensive presence ensured the victory and their first MIAA city championship.[34] The game was a success for those who created the MIAA. No overt political issues surrounded the game. For a fleeting moment, both the black and white communities came together under one roof to watch basketball. Although each community sat on one side of the Mid-South Coliseum, they did gather in one place peacefully. For the moment, basketball drew the city's attention away from the racial animus surrounding the sanitation workers' strike.

In the months that followed the inaugural MIAA city championship, the city witnessed the final civil rights battle of Martin Luther King Jr.'s life. James Lawson's invitation to join the AFSCME's struggle against Mayor Loeb brought King to Memphis. On March 18, King called for a general strike of black workers and students in the city during a speech at the Mason Temple Church of God in Christ. He claimed that to deprive people of jobs and income is "murder, psychologically." He went on to tell the audience that men like Loeb were depriving millions of "life, liberty, and the pursuit of happiness."[35] King reminded the nation that "it is a crime for people to live in this rich nation and receive starvation wages."[36] When King returned on March 28, the march disintegrated into window breaking and looting. A police riot followed that injured many of the protesters. Loeb then requested the governor send in the National Guard to squelch the violence.[37]

Troubled by the violence associated with the march, King vowed to return to restore the peaceful nature of the movement in Memphis. When King returned on April 3, Judge Bailey Brown issued an injunction against King participating in any marches in Memphis. King declared, "We are not going to be stopped by mace or injunctions. We stand on the First Amendment. In the past, based on conscience, we have had to break injunctions, and if necessary, we may do it [here]."[38] On Wednesday, April 3, King gave the final speech of his life at the Mason Temple COGIC, "I've Been to the Mountaintop." The speech elicited transcendent hope for those in attendance and called upon a city to face the injustices Loeb imposed upon the black sanitation workers. King charged America to "be true to what you said on paper."[39] The next day King was assassinated on the balcony of the Lorraine Motel. Following his death, the sanitation workers and the city came to an agreement. They recognized the union, provided raises for the sanitation workers, and based future promotions on competency and seniority.[40] Loeb remained vigilant in his refusal to budge and was allowed to escape direct responsibility for the agreement by allowing the City Council to sign the agreement with the union, thereby disavowing personal responsibility for the agreement.[41]

The strike and its aftermath marked the beginning of massive white flight from the city and the end of Loeb's political career.[42] In Memphis, like in other cities throughout the country, white people left the city for the suburbs in droves following King's assassination, and the public schools in the city integrated the remaining white students and black students. The push factors behind this white flight became visible following Dr. King's assassination. These perceived factors included deteriorating city services, rising taxes, accelerating blight, mounting crime rates, racial mixing of neighborhoods, and the fear of court-ordered busing.[43] A research analyst for the Tennessee legislature's claimed that parents in Memphis confessed, privately, that they moved their children to private schools. Parents asserted, "their apprehension over placing their children in an atmosphere of potential racial conflict."[44]

By the fall of 1968, the issue of busing in the city had stalled in the federal district court. The May 1968 Supreme Court Case *Green v. County School Board* noted that the "freedom of choice" plan could not be accepted as a sufficient step to bring about a transition to a unitary system. The *Green Case* identified six factors to determine if the vestiges of a dual educational system were present in public school districts. These factors became known as the Green factors and are essential to understanding court-ordered public school desegregation. The Green factors are student assignments, faculty assignments, staff assignments, facilities, transportation, and extracurricular activities.[45] Using the Green factors, the NAACP urged federal court Judge Bailey Brown to desegregate the district's faculty completely. He denied that motion. Transferred to Judge Robert McRae in November 1968, the case became a conduit for further racial polarity in the city. McRae ordered the Memphis City Schools to conduct and file a facilities survey.[46]

While arguments were heard over the issue of school desegregation and busing in the federal courts, the city's high schools were completing another year of integrated athletics. Following a productive junior year at Melrose High in 1967–1968, Larry Finch honed his skills on the hardwood floors of recreational centers and playgrounds across the city as he prepared for his senior season. Finch came from a long line of basketball prodigies from Orange Mound. Located in the eastern section of Memphis, Orange Mound is considered by its residents to be the preeminent black community in the United States behind Harlem, New York. The community was founded three years after the all-black town of Mound Bayou, Mississippi, in 1890. Unlike Mound Bayou, which was founded by African Americans, Orange Mound was established by white real estate developer Elzey E. Meachem for the black community in Memphis.[47] According to sociologist Charles Williams, Orange Mound became a symbol of stability for the black residents of the community and the surrounding white communities. He describes the community as one that developed complex and enduring relationships based on kinship, friendship, church membership, class recognition, love, security, unity, community involvement, and community identification.[48] By the post-World War II era, Orange Mound was self-sufficient. It had stores, a theater, a high school, a swimming pool, and a park, making it the second-largest black community in the country.[49]

Finch's mother, Maple West, grew up on Carnes Avenue after moving to Memphis with her mother, Willie Mae West, from Barton, Mississippi.[50] Finch's grandmother divorced her husband, Willie Irvin, before Maple turned five, which precipitated their move to Memphis. Maple grew up in a single-parent household with a strong black woman as the head. When she married Harry James Finch in 1949 after his discharge from the Navy, she hoped to provide her children with a two-parent household. Harry, better known as James, was a cook in the Navy during World War II and was discharged as a petty officer third class.[51] The military had long been a tool of respectability in the black community. James Finch's successful service in World War II made him hope for a better life when he returned home to Memphis. The Finches continued to live in South Memphis after their marriage. James worked for Shelby Electric, where he repaired electric motors. Maple gave birth to Larry in 1951, and over the next nine years the family grew to include eight children.

When Larry was ten, his father passed away from complications incurred from his service in World War II. Maple suddenly became the head of a household with eight young children, so she went to work as a domestic in private white homes to support her family.[52] As a single black mother, Maple turned to the community to help her raise her family. She also allowed Larry to be a guide and leader for his younger siblings. When Maple went to work, Larry was in charge.[53] Government cheese became a staple at the Finch household, so much so that Larry refused to eat anything with cheese on it for the remainder of his adult life. Although the times were tough, Maple taught her children to take care of each other and never speak ill of family.[54]

Maple moved her family to Select Street just as Larry was finishing elementary school. The median income in Orange Mound was half that of nearby white neighborhoods in Memphis, but the community bonded together and ensured its sons and daughters went on to college.[55] Her move to Select Street signaled her independence as the head of her household. Maple made $5.50 a day as a domestic—the two quarters paid for her bus fare.[56] Like black women throughout the urban South in the postwar era, her role as a parent obligated her to accept discriminatory wages, but it did not keep her from combatting institutional racism by instilling a belief in her children of the transformative value of a college education. Maple maintained a level of dignity that influenced her children and laid the foundation for her children's work ethic. Although she relied upon community assistance for help, she always asked if visitors wanted anything to eat when they walked in the door.[57]

Within Orange Mound, churches further connected the community. The black church created a spirit of self-help that developed into benevolent and mutual aid societies. Maple made sure that her children attended every service with her at Park Avenue Church of Christ.[58] Maple provided a solid Christian foundation for Larry that grounded him in knowing right from wrong. The family walked to church, and young Larry knew that regardless of the weather, he would be in a pew with his family. Park Avenue Church of Christ provided the primary space for social activity and stability for Maple's family. In Orange Mound, the black church was also the biggest proponent of education through its support of church-run daycares and financial support for Dunbar Elementary and Melrose High.[59]

For Finch, family also included men in the community, such as Leonard Draper. He was a pivotal figure in Larry's youth. Draper ran a summer league at Gaston Community Center in South Memphis, where Larry's grandmother still lived.[60] Larry began playing at Gaston when he was fourteen. Draper mentored Finch during the car rides home from Gaston to Select Street. Only eleven years older than Finch, Draper was a big brother figure and helped Larry find a summer job at the Triangle Meat Market on Lamar Avenue.[61] Larry, as the oldest, was eager to help his mother in any way that he could. Ever cognizant of his basketball future, he quit his job at the Triangle Meat Market after he saw a worker lose a finger while slicing meat.[62] Larry's relationship with

Draper was emblematic of what some refer to as his "old soul." Larry always felt comfortable around older men so that he could learn more. Larry was quiet. He studied people first before extending his friendship. Once he made friends, those friends became friends for life. His loyalty to his friends was one of the strengths of his character.[63]

One of the strengths of Orange Mound, despite its poverty level, was the pride that the community had in its schools. Next to the family, and then the church, the schools in Orange Mound directly touched the lives of its citizens. Finch attended both Dunbar Elementary and Melrose High in Orange Mound. Dunbar Elementary, right down Select Street from the Finch residence, was named for Paul Lawrence Dunbar, the famous black poet, and was opened in 1958.[64] Melrose High was the pride of the community. As a cohesive unit in the community, Melrose High brought together people of different denominational backgrounds, socioeconomic classes, and genders. It also had a degree of integration—a few white teachers and assistant principals worked there over the years.[65] Floyd Campbell was the principal of Melrose during Finch's time there. Campbell ran a disciplined school. It was common for him to ring a bell in the hallway, which signaled to all students to stop what they were doing and freeze. He would ring the bell again and the girls would be allowed to go into class first, then the boys would follow.[66] These lessons were vital for Melrose students, who would leave the safety of its halls and enter a city governed by Jim Crow laws.

Finch was one of the better students in his class at Melrose. He had an uncanny knack for remembering whatever the teacher was talking about during class and a near-photographic memory. Accelerated classes filled his schedule. If basketball had not worked out, he would have still attended college on his academic ability. His godmother Mildred Turner, an English teacher at the school, always made sure that his writing and communication skills were competent enough that when he left Melrose, he would be successful.[67] While at Melrose, a friend of Finch's introduced him to his cousin, Vickie Stephens. Vickie was one of nine children, and her older brother Eddie lettered in basketball at Melrose. She was in the tenth grade when they met and recalled their first meeting: "I didn't know who he [Finch] was."[68] Finch, as was his norm, studied Vickie and became friends with her before they started dating. Because of his ability to communicate with older folks, he was able to convince Vickie's father to attend one of his games at Melrose. Finch bought Vickie's father two tickets to his next game to gain his respect. The irony was that her father had never attended one of Eddie's games because he worked nights, but Finch convinced him to attend one of his games.[69] Finch's charm worked with Vickie's dad, and his athletic physique garnered her attention. Walking through the gym one day after school, she saw Larry shooting while wearing tight cutoff jeans and told him, "Boy, you got some pretty legs."[70] She had been captured by his smile and his huge heart, too. Leonard Draper described the two as inseparable during their high school years.[71]

Student life at Melrose mirrored the family atmosphere of the Orange Mound community. Students expressed themselves, but they were also mentored and nurtured in a fashion that prepared them for the world outside of Orange Mound. Pep rallies at Melrose were rare occasions for the student body to let loose. It was here that Mr. Campbell allowed the students to express themselves and their support for the football and basketball teams. Basketball games at Melrose were standing room only as the entire community came out to support the team. The games created an atmosphere of pride for the student body and the community.[72] Although Larry shined as an All-American guard on the basketball team, he also ran track for the Golden Wildcats, belonged to the ROTC, was the chaplain of the Student Council, and was elected Most Versatile Male by his senior class.[73] Verties Sails mentored Finch as Melrose's assistant basketball coach. Sails was a father figure who made sure that the boys on the team completed their homework and acted right in class. If they needed food, he made sure they had something to eat.[74] Sails was another example of how the community took care of its own.

Basketball allowed Finch to maneuver through racial boundaries that others in the city feared. While in high school, Larry developed a friendship with Johnny Neumann, the white prep star from Overton High. Much of white Memphis viewed Neumann as the "white hope," but to Finch, he was a friend who loved the game of basketball as much as he did.[75] Finch and Neumann solidified their relationship on the courts of South Memphis and Orange Mound. Larry's competitive drive led him to play games in black neighborhoods throughout the city. Although he became an iconic figure in the Orange Mound community, he developed his game in gyms throughout black Memphis. Finch's closest friend was Ronnie Robinson. The two played pickup games regularly and in summer leagues together. The common denominator with these relationships was the love of the game. For these young basketball players, the game provided a shared ground to test their skills and develop friendships. Basketball was the vehicle that brought them together across racial lines. However, the reality remained that after the games were over, Finch and Robinson returned to black Orange Mound and Neumann to white East Memphis.

Orange Mound was a unique place in an era when Jim Crow laws reigned. Its black citizens felt as if they had their rights. Surrounded by black home-owners, black-owned stores, a post office, and a black-owned strip mall, they felt safe. In the few stores that were owned by white people, black people were treated with respect. Black children tended not to feel threatened by Jim Crow, at least inside the confines of Orange Mound.[76] Orange Mound gave Finch a deep sense of who he was. Later in life, Finch looked back with pride. "This is my heart right here, Orange Mound, Tennessee," said Finch. "There will never be a place like Orange Mound. Everything in this city starts and ends right here in Orange Mound."[77] This space allowed the community to protect the next generation. Because of how the community fostered a young Finch, he remained loyal throughout his life.

▲ ▼ ▲

The style of play in American cities varied along racial lines. *Press-Scimitar* columnist George Lapides explained the success of basketball in inner-city Memphis, "In the poverty areas of the city basketball is cheaper to play. All you need is a rim and a ball."[78] Basketball in inner-city Memphis was played with a unique style that was flashy, creative, and required self-confidence. Like the New York Knicks' guard Walt Frazier, black players around the country in the late 1960s wore bushy afros, goatees, thick headbands, and wrist bands. They played the game with a style that personified a unique black cultural aesthetic.[79] Basketball played across the tracks in black neighborhoods developed its own unique style. Black players in Memphis were no different from black players in other major cities like New York when it came to the variance in styles. "In your face" became the defiant way in which black players verbally and physically as-saulted their opponents on the court. Originally the jump shot, Finch's weapon of choice, was the black player's assertion of physical superiority.[80] Finch's abil-ity to elevate over defenders and shoot the jump shot made him one of the most highly recruited players in the city. The jump shot was later eclipsed in the black basketball lexicon by the slam dunk, but both were frowned upon by bas-ketball traditionalists.[81] White traditionalists preferred fundamental basketball that was readily identifiable by a series of passes, back door cuts, and screens set to create a shot for a teammate. For years the set shot was the favored way to shoot the basketball. The jump-shot and the dunk were considered flashy and part of the inner-city game. In Memphis, as throughout the rest of the country, the style of play diverged along racial lines.

Basketball is a city game. Its battlegrounds are strips of asphalt between tattered wire fences or crumbling buildings; its rhythm grows from the uneven thump of a ball against hard surfaces. Pete Axthelm describes basketball as more than a game—it is "a major part of the fabric of life." He describes the city game as pretty simple: "kids develop 'moves.' Other young athletes may learn basketball, but city kids live it."[82] New York City had the Rucker Tournament, and Philadelphia had the Baker League to showcase this brand of stylish and innovative basketball.[83] By 1969, the Rucker and the Baker tournament had been pipelining players from Philly and New York to major colleges throughout the country. Memphis did not have anything comparable to these showcases. The city's black players either played at historically black colleges and universities (HBCUs) in the South or at schools in the Mid-West and North, where Jim Crow laws were already eroding.

Finch's emergence, along with Ronnie Robinson's dominance in the post, signaled the return of Melrose High basketball to prominence under Coach William Collins. In his eight years at the helm, Collins produced Harlem Globetrotter Jewel Reed, Tulsa star Bobby Smith, Ronnie Robinson, and Finch. Bobby "Bingo" Smith was considered by many to be one of the most talented basketball players to ever come out of the city. He began his varsity career in eighth grade, and by the time he graduated, he was the city's all-time leading scorer.[84] Smith was initially offered a scholarship by Memphis State Coach Dean Ehlers to play for the hometown Tigers. When Ehlers rescinded the scholarship offer in the late summer of 1965, Smith was forced, like so many other black basketball players before him, to leave Memphis to play major college basketball.[85] As a school in the South, Memphis State was not ready for its first black basketball player when Smith graduated in 1965. As Finch's notoriety grew, Orange Mound remained skeptical that Memphis State would offer one of its own a scholarship.

In the second edition of the MIAA city championship, Finch's Melrose team faced Johnny Neumann's Overton Wolverines. Carl John Neumann was born in Cincinnati, Ohio, on September 11, 1951, the second of two sons to Robert and Margaret Neumann. Robert and Margaret met in Cleveland, where they both grew up, before moving to Cincinnati. Robert's mother passed away when he was four, and he was raised by his maternal grandparents. Robert joined the United States Navy in 1942 and served as an aviation ordinance officer. He settled his family in the upper-middle-class neighborhood of Rosewood, located on the northern outskirts of Cincinnati.[86] In 1948, the Gardens, home to the NBA's Cincinnati Royals, opened to fanfare as a new type of suburban arena.[87] Neumann's older brother Bob brought Johnny to games at the Gardens to watch Oscar Robertson play. During these games, the brothers kept a notebook of the moves Robertson made, along with subtleties in Robertson's game that they could recreate in their games.[88] Taking these lessons to heart, Bob developed his game enough to sign scholarship papers with Memphis State in the spring of 1960. Their father uprooted the family and moved them to Memphis in the fall of 1961, so they could watch Bob play for Dean Ehler's Tigers squad. The Navy's base in Millington, Tennessee, allowed Robert Sr. to transfer to the Memphis area and remain on active duty. Johnny was only in fourth grade when the family moved to Memphis, but his brother's play instilled in the younger Neumann a love for the game.

Bob Neumann Jr. developed into one of the stars of the Memphis State program under Bob Vanatta and Dean Ehlers. Bob Jr. was an integral part of the Tigers 1962 NCAA tournament team. Although he missed all but eight games during his junior year with an injury, he returned his senior year to lead the Tigers in scoring.[89] While his older brother was starring for the Tigers, Johnny entered middle school at Colonial Middle School in East Memphis. His coach at Colonial, Bob Yancey, recalled that Johnny continued to mimic Oscar Robertson in drills.[90] Schools in the city remained strictly segregated, as did the basketball courts. The younger Neumann gained entrance into pickup games at the Roane Field House by tagging along with his brother. Johnny's game continued to develop, and as it did, he continued to look for more significant challenges. When he emerged as a star at all-white Overton High in East Memphis, Neumann was dominating white high school players and wanted to test himself against the city's best black high school players. Local prep reporter George Lapides described how Neumann crossed the color line to play in Orange Mound and at Gaston Community Center to his readers: "He [Johnny] wanted to go to play where the players were good enough to play against him."[91] Neumann claimed that "this is where you made your name, on the playground. You earned respect."[92] Neumann was not a native of the city and placed his love for basketball in front of any cultural norms associated with Jim Crow. Young Neumann crossed over racial boundaries into black neighborhoods to test his skills against some of the city's best black talent. His desire to compete against the best talent in the city transcended the prescribed racial boundaries in the city. Yet, his reputation as the best basketball player in the city was a source of pride for white Memphians.

Overton High opened in 1959 to accommodate the growing white population in East Memphis and endeared itself to a white population with a "Lost Cause" mindset by adopting the moniker Rebels as their mascot. Overton High, one of the Memphis City Board of Education's most significant projects in the late 1950s, accommodated the growing populations in the Colonial and Sherwood neighborhoods. It opened with modern amenities that made the East Memphis school one of the best in the district. Within ten years, the school went from 250 students to over 1,500.[93] Neumann played for Bob Miller, a "boyishly looking, exuberant coach," who was enjoying the benefits of one of the South's top recruits on his team.[94] Neumann possessed a remarkable combination of athleticism, hoop intelligence, and on-court showmanship.[95] He was an All-American that SEC schools coveted more than any other local player, including Finch. Adolph Rupp's recruitment of Neumann for the University of Kentucky legitimized him as the preeminent white player in the city. Rupp had long been a powerful symbol of segregation in the SEC, refusing to recruit black players to Kentucky.[96] Rupp's recruitment further ingrained the perception that Neumann was the great white hope. Challenged by the city's racial climate, white Memphians were in search of a "white hope." By the late 1960s, black athletes were beginning to dominate the game of basketball on a national level. Black players now dominated the NBA, and Bill Rusell, the Celtics' black star, coached them to a world championship.[97] Black basketball star Lew Alcindor led UCLA's domination of the college game. When the city of Memphis began to desegregate its athletic events in 1968, white Memphians became fearful that the racial dynamics taking place on a national level were capturing their city as well. Neumann's presence signified a sense of counter-resistance for the white community from the burgeoning dominance of black basketball players in the city.

Overton's Johnny Neumann was not a stereotypical white basketball player. He was eccentric. He displayed a flair that was usually associated with black players. Neumann's game drew comparisons to LSU's flashy guard "Pistol" Pete Maravich. Maravich played the game in a fashion that many felt was cultural appropriation. Black players were chastised and deemed selfish for flashy play, but white players like Maravich were idolized for it. Neumann's aptitude on the court resembled the game played by black people, it centered on improvisation.

Johnny patterned his game after Pete Maravich of the LSU Tigers, as well as Oscar Robertson. An inch and a half taller than Maravich, Neumann muscled in shots in the post with a flair akin to Maravich's.[98] Neumann secured his reputation during his junior year at Overton when he was named second-team all-state by the AP and led the city in scoring at 26.6 points per game.[99]

The 1969 MIAA City Basketball Championship brought together the city's two premier prep basketball players and their respective communities in the highly anticipated matchup between all-black Melrose High and all-white Overton High. The Melrose community was excited after years of being denied an opportunity to play the best white schools. The creation of the MIAA meant that white schools were now willing to play black schools.[100] The build-up to the game included media coverage worthy of the biggest basketball game in the city. The Memphis State Tigers, under Moe Iba, had struggled throughout the season, so fans turned to this high school basketball game in hopes of seeing the next generation of Tiger stars.[101] Finch's Melrose team was a more balanced unit, but his sweet shooting touch made him the second most sought-after recruit in the city behind Neumann. William Collins likened Finch to Bingo Smith, the ex-Melrose star who was jilted by Memphis State, because of his shooting range and his ability to take the ball to the basket.[102] Before the season the local prognosticators had predicted that Neumann and Finch would meet in the city championship, and neither disappointed.[103]

The Mid-South Coliseum expected over 9,000 people to watch. Two local AM stations and one FM station brought the game to those who could not get a ticket to get into the game.[104] Many fans, like Paul Finebaum, sat outside in their cars before the game, fearing that the line would be so long they would not get into the game.[105] Finebaum made it in, but at 7:15 pm the Mid-South Coliseum ticket windows hung signs that read "SOLD OUT" as over 10,000 fans packed into the Coliseum.[106] Once inside the Mid-South Coliseum, the city remained segregated. The Melrose community and its black fans sat on one side, and Overton's white fans sat on the other side. Finch and the Wildcats set the tone in the first three minutes of the game. By the time the first quarter ended, Melrose was ahead 27–13. It never looked back. Finch played like he was on a mission to prove that he was the best player in the city. He scored 16 of his 21 points in the first quarter.

Neumann and his teammates were no match for Melrose. The Rebels had no answer for 6'6" Ronnie Robinson, who was a force in the paint. Melrose held a 45–37 half-time advantage, and Coach Collins credited the Wildcat bench's depth for the lead.[107] Although Finch was the face of the Melrose program, the play of Robinson and the rest of the Golden Wildcat team also gave them a decided advantage. Mid-way through the first half, Neumann broke his hand going for a loose ball. On the way down, he hit his hand on Robinson's knee brace. Neumann told the manager to wrap his hand and "don't tell my dad."[108] He understood that physical toughness was a requirement to win, especially against Melrose. He continued to play and finished with 34 points; he exhibited a toughness that equaled his talent.[109] Foul trouble plagued Neumann throughout the night. Each time Neumann went to the bench, his teammates struggled against the bigger and faster Wildcats. With 3:16 left in the fourth quarter, Neumann committed his fifth personal foul, and the game fell out of reach for the Rebels. Melrose triumphed, 76–65.[110] After the game, Finch told reporters, "we just made up our mind to win a championship."[111] Finch understood, as well as Neumann, that winning this game gave Finch and Robinson bragging rights on the playgrounds throughout the city for the next year. The friendship molded on the playground between Finch and Neumann further elevated the intensity of these two stars in leading their teams.

Neumann alone was no match for the depth of talent that Melrose possessed, and Overton suffered its first defeat of the year at the hands of Finch and his Golden Wildcat teammates. Coach Miller commended his Overton group for playing hard and with tenacity.[112] Melrose's win secured the first two MIAA city championships for all-black schools. The popularity of the MIAA city basketball championship elevated the city's love affair with basketball. It provided, for a moment, space where the black and white communities could gather to cheer on their favorite basketball teams. Players around the city began to see this game every winter as the apex of the local prep basketball season. Hamilton High junior Clint Jackson described the impact of the MIAA city championship on Memphis prep basketball: "The state tournament to us was not as prestigious as being in the city championship game. Everybody wanted to make it to the Coliseum, that was our Madison Square Garden."[113] The 1969 game set the standard by which all MIAA city championship games would be judged moving forward.

The 1969 MIAA City Basketball Championship game became the prologue for the relationship between the city of Memphis and Larry Finch. Finch's star shone bright enough to bring an array of major college basketball coaches to Orange Mound to recruit him, from John McLeod of Oklahoma to John Wooden of UCLA. As coaches from across the country came through attempting to lure him away, Memphis State remained his top choice, but Coach Collins was still disgruntled by Memphis State's treatment of Bingo Smith four years earlier. Collins believed that it would be in Finch's best interest was to follow the same path as Smith and attend Tulsa. Nevertheless, Finch wanted to stay home and play for Memphis State. As the oldest of eight children, he felt a responsibility to be there for his mother, and the only place that she would be able see him play was Memphis State.[114] Leonard Draper, Finch's mentor and director at the Gaston Community Center, helped convince Finch that Memphis State would take care of him. Maple Finch also turned to Draper for advice for her oldest son. After years of mentoring Finch, Draper was a trusted family friend. He helped assure Finch's mother that Memphis State would keep its word and take care of her son. Draper recalls Maple Finch turning toward him and saying, "I'm turning my son over to you."[115]

When Finch announced his intentions to sign with Memphis State, the divide within the Orange Mound community became even more apparent. Finch consulted with Melrose's assistant, Verties Sails, about his decision to stay home and sign with the Tigers. Sails offered his support without reservation. When it came time for signing day, fellow Golden Wildcat Ed Bell recalled "a lot of tension in the room" when Finch signed.[116] In an open sign of protest of Finch's decision, Coach Collins did not attend. Instead, Sails stood behind Finch and his mother Maple as he signed. It took years for many in the Orange Mound community to forgive both Sails and Draper for standing behind Finch's decision to sign with Memphis State. Many in Memphis's black community referred to these men as "Uncle Toms" for influencing Finch's decision to attend Memphis State.[117] This act secured the relationship between Sails and Finch. Not only was Sails a father figure and mentor to young Larry, but this selfless act also solidified a bond between the two for the remainder of Finch's life. Collins left Melrose High that spring and moved to Tech High School, which left an opening for Sails to become the next head basketball coach at Melrose.

Following the 1969 season, Tiger's Coach Moe Iba had still not signed Robinson, until Sails stepped in. Convinced that Robinson was too thin to play in the Missouri Valley Conference, Iba wavered on bringing Robinson to Memphis State along with Finch. Sails reminded Iba of Robinson's stats against the high level competition that Melrose had faced on a nightly basis. He also predicted that Robinson would gain 25 pounds once he ate at the college training table three times a day. That summer, Robinson underwent knee surgery and spent eight days in the hospital, where they served three meals a day. When they released him, Robinson's pants were too small because he had put on 20 pounds. Sails sent him over to see Coach Iba that afternoon. Iba was convinced, and Robinson signed with Memphis State shortly after that. Just as Sails stood behind Finch when much of Orange Mound and Coach Collins refused to, Sails stood up for Robinson because he knew what Robinson could do if given the opportunity he deserved.[118] Sails continued to jump through hoops as a black basketball coach at a time when his opinion as a black man mattered less than that of his white peers. Nonetheless, he continued to stand up for and fight for opportunities for players like Finch and Robinson.

Overton's Neumann signed with the University of Mississippi, leaving Tiger fans to wonder how good the Tigers could have been with Neumann and Finch in the backcourt. Neumann's recruitment to Ole Miss was a source of controversy in the city. Neumann later confirmed in divorce proceedings that the Ole Miss athletic department paid for his living expenses while he was in Oxford, Mississippi.[119] Neumann averaged 38.4 points per game on the freshman team and then averaged 40.1 points per game to lead the nation in scoring during his only season of varsity competition as a sophomore.[120] Neumann left Ole Miss with two games remaining in his sophomore season when he signed a five-year, $2 million-dollar contract with the Memphis Pros of the ABA. During his ABA career, he became once again the "white hope" when he was traded from the Virginia Squires to the Kentucky Colonels to increase the number of white players on a Colonels team that was predominately black.[121] Neumann's collegiate and professional careers were marred by stereotypes that defined his style on the court as part of the "black aesthetic" while being unfairly labeled as the "great white hope."

▲▼▲

Memphis was always Larry Finch's home, and following his success in the 1969 MIAA City Championship game, the city became infatuated by his persona. Finch became part of the social fabric of the city. Basketball courts were some of the few spaces in the city where black and white people could meet without confrontation. The relationships that Finch developed as a young man in Orange Mound helped form the young black man that Memphis State fans rallied around to rejuvenate their basketball program. Finch's high school and collegiate careers occurred as the city was at a crossroads in its history. Earlier generations of black athletes from Orange Mound accepted segregation or left the South. Finch stayed home and played at Memphis State. After his collegiate playing career, he returned to Memphis State as an assistant coach and then was hired as the school's first African American head coach. Sociologist Zandria Robinson refers to this period as the post-soul era, an era that signified the cultural shift from past to present and back again.[122] Finch carved out a new identity of being black, of being southern, and of being a southern black man in this era that immediately followed King's assassination in Memphis. Finch followed in the footsteps of black basketball players, like L.C. Gordon and Bingo Smith, who grew up on the playgrounds of black Memphis, but they had to go elsewhere to play college basketball. As Finch etched a new path for the city's best black basketball players, it was men like Verties Sails who stood behind him and allowed him to break through the fear and distrust that many in the black community held for white Memphians. As he broke through and jumped through the hoops in his path, he brought with him his best friend from the neighborhood, Ronnie Robinson. Finch's impact on both black and white Memphis changed the trajectory of the Memphis State basketball program.

In 1979, ten years after the Melrose/Overton city championship game, Magic Johnson and Larry Bird met in the NCAA championship game. According to Nielsen Media Research, that game received a 24.1 rating, which meant that nearly a quarter of the television sets in America were tuned in to the game that night.[123] The game between Michigan State and Indiana State generated so much national interest that it brought the NCAA's March Madness to a new level.[124] College basketball in the late 1970s was sitting on the precipice of becoming one of the country's most celebrated sporting events of the year. Former coach and NCAA champion Al McGuire described it as "being on the launching pad in 1979. Then Bird and Magic came along and pushed the button."[125] The 1969 MIAA championship game held that same level of excitement and impact on the city of Memphis. Melrose's assistant Verties Sails proclaimed that "the city championship game was more important than the state championship. Those were bragging rights!"[126] In only its second year of existence, the city flocked to the Mid-South Coliseum to watch Finch and Neumann compete. One year after the assassination of Dr. King, this game defied the suggestion that black and white people could not come together on common ground in Memphis. Following the 1969 MIAA City Championship, the MIAA became part of the continuing battle over desegregation in the city when school busing divided the city once again. By 1974, the Memphis Christian Athletic Association was declaring its own city champion from among the white private schools that were established after the busing program began.

In 1973, Earvin Johnson attended predominately white Everett High as part of the forced integration in East Lansing, Michigan. Racial tensions were high as white kids did not want black kids there, and black kids like Johnson wanted to remain at black schools.[127] Basketball became a way for people in East Lansing to sort out racial conflicts. Johnson went on to become a McDonald's All-American at Everett as the white community embraced their 6'9" point guard from the other side of town. George Fox, Johnson's high school coach, claimed that by attending Everett High, Johnson "learned how to deal with racial problems. He mingled with white kids, he dated white girls, if truth be known, and nobody seemed to mind."[128] The same political push for integration through busing that impacted East Lansing, Michigan, divided the city of Memphis. Neumann and Finch missed the racial conundrum of busing in Memphis by several years. In Memphis in 1969, basketball reconciled racial problems for a moment, but once the game was over, the racial schism remained as strong as before. White Memphians accepted the integrated MIAA city championship as long as the schools remained predominately segregated.

Like Bird and Johnson, Neumann and Finch were rivals and friends, and their relationship was full of racial symbolism. For two hours, fans from white East Memphis and black Orange Mound gathered with other fans from around the city to decide a city champion. The Mid-South Coliseum brought the city together in one place, even if that place remained segregated. Black fans stayed on the Melrose side of the arena, and white fans stayed on Overton's side of the arena. For the city, this was a step forward, but the reality is that the racial divides that existed outside of the Mid-South Coliseum remained during the game. Basketball gave the people a temporary common ground where the hopes of white and black people were played out in front of them. Outside of the Mid-South Coliseum, the white political establishment struggled to find common ground with the black community. The game did not solve the city's poverty rate, the economic disparity between the two communities, or the disparity between white schools and black schools. It only provided a brief reprieve from the realities of life outside of the arena of sport.

The 1969 MIAA City Championship game became emblematic of the myth that basketball healed the wounds of the city. The next chapter will explore how the myth of basketball as a racial healing trope became fully embedded in the consciences of the Memphis State faithful during the team's run to the 1973

NCAA finals. The Tigers' games became one of the few places where white and black people came together on common ground. As the city united behind the Tigers' run through the NCAA tournament, Larry Finch and his teammates became symbols of hope for racial reconciliation in the city. This myth, that sport healed the racial issues present in the city, was promulgated by both local sports reporters and politicians to shroud the underlying racial problems faced by the city.

2

To Bring This Town Together

The Tigers' run to the NCAA championship game against UCLA in 1973 was used to create a myth. This myth described how a young, charismatic black athlete from the "other" side of the Belt Line healed the city's racial wounds. Larry Finch became the focal point of the Tigers' rise to national prominence during his three-year career at Memphis State. Before the Tigers improbable run to the NCAA finals, the nation had last focused on Memphis during the 1968 Sanitation Workers Strike and Dr. King's assassination. Since that tumultuous time, the city was in search of a healing salve. When Finch and Ronnie Robinson from Melrose High signed with Memphis State in 1969, this marked a shift in the program's fortunes. Before Finch, the Tigers were a regional program that received minimal attention from national media. Defeated in the NCAA's first round in each of the three previous seasons before 1973, the Tigers lacked national recognition.[1] The 1973 run placed the Tigers on the national map at the right time. NBC's new $1.165 million contracts created more interest in March Madness when it moved the NCAA finals to prime time on Monday night.[2] Memphis politicians corralled the spirit created by Finch and his Tiger teammates to help them navigate the shifting racial atmosphere in the city. Shepherded by the local media and the Memphis fan base, this narrative of racial unity became part of the lore surrounding Finch and his Tigers.

Before Finch's arrival, black athletes from the city had no choice but to leave the city to find universities where they could compete in intercollegiate athletics. The Tigers were white Memphis's team. For the black community, cheering for the Tigers before Finch was a somewhat foreign concept. When

Herb Hilliard walked on to the Tigers basketball team in 1967, he became the first African American to play at Memphis State. Hilliard was a graduate from Woodstock High School in Millington, Tennessee, and was therefore not considered a Memphian by most black people in the city.[3] When Finch arrived on campus with Ronnie Robinson, black Memphians had a reason to cheer for the Tigers. There was an underlying racial tension that permeated campus when Finch and Robinson arrived as students in the fall of 1969. Student Harold Byrd described MSU's campus in 1970 as a place where "you could cut the racial tension on campus with a knife." He added that "it was like a war and people were thrown together."[4] In this racial cauldron, Finch and Robinson began their careers. Coach Moe Iba hoped that the duo from Melrose would help turn the program around and that they could make basketball a unifying tool on campus and in the city. After watching Finch play in the 1969 MIAA City Championship game, the city's basketball fans waited in anticipation for Finch to become part of the Tigers' varsity team.

Throughout the South, the 1960s ushered in a new era in collegiate basketball, an era of integration. In the ACC, Billy Jones broke the color line when he enrolled at the University of Maryland in the fall of 1964 and played in his first varsity contest during the 1965–1966 season. Jones was followed in the ACC by C.B. Claiborne at Duke and Pete Johnson at Maryland the following season. The SEC began desegregation when Perry Wallace suited up for Vanderbilt's varsity during the 1967–1968 season.[5] Wallace, a native of Nashville, began his journey on the freshman team at Vanderbilt with fellow black teammate and Detroit native Godfrey Dillard. Only Wallace survived the travails of play in the South to suit up for the Commodores on the varsity level. Godfrey injured his knee during pre-season practice as a sophomore and missed the entire 1967–1968 season. The following season, after recovering, he was demoted to the B-team and was never given a chance to compete in the SEC.[6] Dillard became, like so many other black athletes at predominately white universities in this era, an example of how white people dilute, divide, and push back against black achievement to maintain power.[7]

Back in the ACC, the University of North Carolina welcomed its first black player, Charles Scott, in the 1967–1968 varsity season. ACC fans often remember Scott, who became a perennial all-conference and All-American player for the Tar Heels, as the first to break the color barrier because of his success.[8] As Finch was completing his senior season at Melrose High, Al Heartley became the first black player at North Carolina State. Two years later, while Finch was a sophomore at Memphis State, five schools in the ACC and SEC added their first black players. Another six schools followed suit in 1971–1972, including the University of Virginia's Al Drummond. When Drummond suited up for the Cavaliers in 1971, all schools in the ACC had black players. While the University of Tennessee and Mississippi State integrated their basketball teams for the 1972–1973 season, Finch led the Tigers to their first NCAA Final Four appearance.[9] Finch's playing career did not break any color barriers for Memphis State. Yet, its trajectory shadowed the ever-changing racial composition of collegiate basketball in the South. Finch's arrival on the freshman team invigorated the team with a style of play that brought excitement to the game, which invigorated the Memphis State fan base. Fans began to pour into the Mid-South Coliseum before the varsity games to see Finch and Robinson play in the freshmen games.

As the 1970 collegiate basketball season kicked off, Reverend James Netters noted that racial divisions remained a constant in the city. Netters told the *Commercial Appeal*, "There is as much polarization at the grassroots level as ever. . . One serious event, one big event, could ignite it again (like in 1968)."[10] Poverty in the black community remained as endemic as ever. The only discernible change for black people in the city was that Mayor Loeb was gone and in his place was Wyeth Chandler. However, Chandler's election in 1971 only continued the plantation mentality that defined black subjugation and poverty in the city. Netters's fears materialized when federal judge Robert McCrae Jr. issued his 1972 court order to desegregate Memphis schools through busing. The Supreme Court's 1971 ruling in *Swann v. Charlotte-Mecklenburg* aided McCrae's efforts to desegregate the schools in the city. The Charlotte desegregation plan restructured school attendance zones and used busing to bring black students to formerly segregated schools. *Swann* also reaffirmed the use of race-based numerical guidelines to determine what constitutes a racially integrated public school system.[11] McCrae similarly applied these guidelines within the Memphis City Schools. Busing was to be the central vehicle for school desegregation in the city.

Busing became the central piece in the struggle for racial equality in the city and further divided the city along racial lines. During his three years on campus, Finch provided a distraction from political issues as he and Ronnie Robinson reinvigorated the Tiger basketball program. Two or three times a week, the Tigers' basketball team provided an opportunity for black and white people to come together, united behind a desegregated basketball team. In the confines of the Mid-South Coliseum, desegregation worked and brought the city together. However, the white establishment used the team's success as a political tool to divert attention from the racially divided reality that existed outside of the arena.

Sports journalism following World War II could serve as an advocate for social justice. Wendell Smith of the *Pittsburgh Courier* led the movement to force Major League Baseball to give black people the same opportunity offered to white players. At a time when few white people thought of racial issues, Smith and his fellow black sportswriters injected the integration controversy into the broader public arena.[12] Just as Smith advocated for Jackie Robinson, George Lapides of the *Press-Scimitar* promoted the narrative of Finch and of the Tigers healing the city. Lapides's unique position as the sports editor at the *Press-Scimitar* gave him a platform to describe Finch in this fashion. Four years earlier, Rabbi James Wax helped to resolve the impasse between Loeb and the sanitation workers. Lapides, a Jewish sportswriter, created the bridge between the white and black communities through basketball. The *Press-Scimitar,* the afternoon paper, historically defended issues of social justice for the black community.

As a lifelong Memphian, Lapides understood the complex racial dynamics in the city. A 1957 graduate of White Station High, Lapides spent his youth working at his father's wholesale dry goods store, J. Lapides and Sons. At 12 years old, Lapides began attending every Tiger home basketball game. His love for journalism began shortly after that when a local printer in the neighborhood brought him once a week to watch the printing press. Lapides was hooked. After graduating from White Station, he enrolled in a journalism program at the University of Tennessee, Knoxville. A bout with hepatitis forced him to give up his role as sports editor of the *Daily Beacon,* UTK's student newspaper, and return home to enroll at Memphis State. Not long after, Lapides began writing for the *Press-Scimitar* while maintaining his studies at Memphis State.[13] Back home in Memphis, he was able to continue his love affair with the Tigers and now add his voice to discussions surrounding the Tigers. Memphis sports fans knew that although the *Commercial Appeal* was the morning paper, Lapides and the *Press-Scimitar* had the real scoop on sports in the city.[14] Lapides became a fixture in the city's sports media just as Finch emerged on the city's basketball radar. His stories crafted narratives of Finch that brought to life the realities of being a black athlete from Orange Mound for many Memphians. He introduced the city to Finch's charm and love for the city. Lapides's narratives carefully crafted a persona that the people of the city found endearing. By initiating this narrative, Lapides made it possible for basketball fans, politicians, and others to believe that the city's wounds after the assassination of Dr. King could be healed through basketball.

The first time that Lapides framed Finch as the city's unifying persona was after the Tigers 1972 loss to the University of Louisville in the MVC championship: "The Tigers have done more to unify this city than anything else that has been done or undone previously." This one byline became the impetus for the myth that made Finch the central figure of the healing trope in Memphis. Lapides added that "most white [people], I think, give it no thought that Finch, Robinson, and Fred Horton are black, and most black [people], I also think, care less that Don Holcomb and Bill Laurie are white."[15] Lapides interviewed Mayor Chandler, who was using the late February basketball game as an opportunity to improve his perception in the community, and questioned Chandler on his position regarding the Tigers. Chandler, a prudent politician and close friend of Lapides, carried that same message to the media. Chandler told the *Appeal* after the Tigers' loss that "the unified support of Memphis for the Tigers was a great example of how a common cause can unite all segments of the city into one gigantic cheering section."[16] Lapides had placed this narrative in Chandler's lap. He reminded his audience that "MSU has an integrated basketball team with black stars, and white and black [people] alike have been pulling for the Tigers."[17]

Only ten days earlier, Chandler had met with a group of white parents and students from Westwood High to discuss the racial issues confronting them because of the increasing black population in the southwest Memphis neighborhood school. The white students claimed that "troubles started after some black boys insulted some white girls."[18] Chandler's disregard for the opinions of the black students alienated him from the black community. The tension in the Westwood community became emblematic of the racial friction throughout the city. As litigation in the courts consumed many Memphians, basketball provided an escape from the racial discord. Tiger basketball provided an opportunity for Chandler to get away from the tension in his city. The Tigers' 1972 MVC championship game in Nashville allowed Chandler to promote Finch and the Tigers as the city's healing salve. The 200 miles between Memphis and Nashville safely separated Chandler from the racial animus brewing back in Memphis over busing. For his part, Lapides continued to build this healing narrative for Memphians in his articles, chronicling Finch's and the Tigers' rise to national prominence.

Chandler displayed two personas as mayor of the city over the next year. First, he celebrated the Tigers' unifying spirit. Then, Chandler reinforced his commitment to the segregation of the city's public schools. He used Finch to shield the white political establishment from the attacks his administration was taking from the black community over busing. As the son of former Mayor Walter Chandler, Wyeth, was a product of the city's white political establishment. Name recognition gave him entrance into the city's political establishment. When Chandler ran for mayor in 1971, he relied heavily upon support from Loeb's white constituencies. Ninety percent of white people in the city voted for Chandler in 1971, and he never garnered more than three percent of the city's black votes in any of the elections he won. He was indifferent toward the black community during his tenure as mayor because his voting base was white Memphis.[19] For white Memphis, Larry Finch made them feel like they were allowing black people to integrate Memphis, even as little changed.

When Coach Gene Bartow arrived at Memphis State at the start of Finch's sophomore year, he changed the team's tactics. Coach Moe Iba had relied on a deliberate offense, backed by solid defense. Bartow immediately redesigned the offense with an emphasis on fast-break basketball. Coach Bartow's new approach allowed Finch to flourish. Ten seconds into the opening night of the Bartow era, Finch drilled a twenty-foot jumper that propelled the Tigers to a 99–79 victory over the University of California at Davis. Finch sat out most of the first half in foul trouble, but he scored twenty-one points in the second half to finish with 24 points for the game.[20] That night, Larry Finch emerged as a star for Memphis State. Bill Laurie, the point guard for the 1973 Tigers, described Finch as "confident in his abilities, which allowed him to make players around him better, with encouragement, not by screaming at people."[21] Finch became the star player that Bartow built around in his quest to bring the Tigers to national prominence. The Tigers completed Finch's first varsity season 18–8, a twelve-game improvement from the previous year.[22]

Finch's success on the hardwood at Memphis State drove the resurgence of the Tiger basketball program and elevated the Tigers from a regional program to one with a national profile. Following his sophomore season, he was named the Missouri Valley Conference's Player of the Year. The *Commercial Appeal* celebrated Finch's sophomore campaign as the most exceptional individual effort in Tiger basketball history.[23] The smiling picture of Finch that accompanied the article painted him as a fun-loving, good-natured, young, black man who represented the university well. His smile hid the hard truth and the hoops he was forced to jump through to find success.

Finch and Bartow's relationship was a quintessential father-son relationship. Coaches are parental figures to their charges. Strong, solid, and secure individuals who act as role models to their players, teaching them the skills and work ethic necessary to become responsible and successful citizens.[24] This sense of paternalism under Bartow endeared Finch to white Memphians in the Tiger's fan base. Bartow's up-tempo style of play allowed Finch to flourish as a player. Finch grew into the leader on and off the court that Bartow needed to rejuvenate the Tiger basketball program. Finch worked as hard or harder than his teammates, and never took a day off. This work ethic carried over to the classroom, where he never missed a class. Like his mother Maple, who went to work every day, Larry's work ethic was contagious and spread throughout the team. In return, Bartow relied on Finch to be his leader on and off the floor. Walk-on Tom Miller remembered that "if there was a message to the team, he used Larry to convey it. Even when there were older guys on the team, he used Larry." Miller also added that Finch "was never one of those attitude guys, even to the walk-ons."[25] Finch's charisma captivated the Tiger fan base. Fred Horton, who had a reputation for tough physical play, did not endear himself to the Tiger faithful as Finch did. Finch was not soft, but after fouling an opposing player, he reached his hand up and helped his opponent to his feet. Finch's sense of decency and sportsmanship alleviated many of the fears white Memphians had that black males were overly aggressive people who failed to follow sport decorum.

By the end of his junior year, Finch led the conference in scoring, smashed the Memphis State single-season scoring record, and won the Missouri Valley Conference player of the year award.[26] Denny Crum, Louisville's head coach, respected Finch's game and what he was doing for Tiger basketball. He described Finch as one of the best all-around guards in the country in all phases of the game.[27] At the time, the Tigers' biggest rival was Louisville, and in 1972, Finch beat out Louisville's Jim Price for the Missouri Valley's most valuable player award. Finch turned the Louisville series into a rivalry. Because of that, he forever endeared himself to the Memphis faithful. When the Tigers lost the 1972 MVC title to Louisville in a one-game playoff, they were forced to accept an NIT bid. The NCAA took one team from each league into its tournament. Disappointment followed after the loss to Louisville, and the Tigers played lethargically in their first-round loss to Oral Roberts in the NIT. Sitting on the edge of the national recognition that comes with playing in the NCAA tournament, Finch and his teammates sharpened their focus and honed their skills heading into his senior season. His senior year on the hardwood floors of the Coliseum paralleled a tumultuous season in the city's classrooms.

Entrenched in a bitter struggle over school desegregation, Memphis was a city divided as the Tigers returned to campus in the fall of 1972. Federal judge Robert McRae Jr. ruled that Memphis could no longer maintain a system of single-race schools. He issued a plan to bus 13,000 of the 145,581 Memphis City Schools students in order to achieve racial balance.[28] McRae became the face of busing in Memphis. A graduate of Memphis's Central High, he believed that it was time for black Memphians to have the same opportunities that he once had. White people in Memphis opposed to busing echoed the feelings of former mayor Henry Loeb, who rolled down his window at an intersection in the city to holler at Judge McRae, "Hey, you son-of-a-bitch, quit integratin' those schools," and then grinned and sped away.[29] An organization of white parents opposed to busing emerged, calling themselves Citizens Against Busing (CAB). Their resistance methods included burying a school bus and protesting with placards that read, "Here lies a school bus. No mourning for us. No more fuming. May this be the end of busing."[30] Most white Memphians were content with the status quo.

At the heart of this issue was the de facto segregation in the city schools. For years the white establishment avoided adhering to the Supreme Court's 1954 *Brown v. Board* ruling by offering small concessions to the black community. White Memphians on the school board justified their position by convincing themselves that black people did not want to go to school with white people any more than white people wanted to go to school with black people.[31] By 1972, the local branch of the NAACP, led by Maxine Smith, had led several protests speaking out against the inequalities in the segregated school system. The NAACP found an ally when McRae replaced Marion Boyd on the federal district court in Memphis. In March 1972, the MCS school board offered two plans to McRae for his approval: Plan A was a minimal busing and maximum pairing of schools. Plan B called for busing to all schools, creating a 30% minority minimum at each school. The Memphis branch of the NAACP suggested a third plan that bussed 61,000 students, twice as many as the MCS's Plan B.[32] In April of 1972, McRae approved Plan A, which called for minimal busing. McRae's ruling escalated the white community's angst. For some, it was all-out panic. For white people, having African Americans attending white schools was distasteful, but sending their children to black schools was an abomination.[33]

Mayor Wyeth Chandler banded together with CAB groups in the city and pushed for an amendment to the City Charter to block city tax dollars from being used to pay for busing students in the city schools.[34] Chandler began to actively campaign against busing, making appearances with CAB groups at both Hillcrest and East High Schools. He threw his support behind their intent to boycott, saying he was, "100 percent behind their efforts to fight this busing." If this boycott stopped the busing, "the loss of two days to a child's education would be insignificant."[35] Chandler's impassioned support of CAB demonstrated his position against desegregation. The Mid-South Coliseum was an acceptable space for racial mingling and unity, but schools were not. Chandler and many within the white establishment drew a line in the sand before school busing.

As the beginning of the school year approached, the status of Plan A remained in legal limbo. In June 1972, an appeal to the *Northcross v. BOE Memphis City Schools* (1961), the original federal desegregation case in Memphis, forced a stay on Judge McRae's ruling to implement Plan A. By August, McCrae's ruling was reinstated with instructions to institute Plan A in January 1973.[36] Students all over the city would start school in August in one building, and then, after having developed relationships with their teachers and peers, they would start all over at a new school in the middle of the year. White parents throughout the city feared the worst and began to seek other options for their children. Designed to maintain neighborhood schools, zoning maintained the city's de facto segregation. McRae's court order implementing Plan A nullified zoning and thereby nullified the accepted racial norm of neighborhood schools.

White parents responded by moving their children to private schools in the city—creating one of the largest private school networks in the nation. White churches throughout the city decided to pre-empt the forced desegregation of public schools in the city by opening schools in the hallways of their churches. Sunday school classrooms became classrooms for many white children whose parents opposed bussing in the public schools. White Memphians veiled their exodus by claiming to seek a Christian environment for their children. Two and a half weeks before the implementation of Plan A in January 1973, East Park Baptist Church recommended "the establishment of a private, church-sponsored school that would provide academic excellence within a Christian environment."[37] Pastor Peyton Allen placed his sister Pat Allen, a Memphis City

Schools teacher, in charge of the committee to open Briarcrest Christian School in East Memphis.[38] On the other side of town, ten Southern Baptist churches in the Whitehaven community met in April 1972 at a local restaurant to discuss a vision for a Christian school. The Southern Baptist Educational Center (SBEC) purchased a thirty-six-acre lot at the corner of Holmes and Tulane for the school. The school's plans called for the school to have grades 1–12 and to open in the fall of 1973. In the interim, the elementary school used Broadway Baptist Church's facilities, and the high school used Graceland Baptist Church.[39] Within three years, white Memphians in neighborhoods throughout the city had opened over 85 private Christian or CAB schools and took with them over 35,000 students.[40]

While lawyers and politicians struggled with the issue of busing in the city's schools, the Memphis State campus prepared for its last season with Finch. As the 1972–73 Memphis State basketball season approached, the *Daily Helmsman* lauded Finch's role in the city as a unifier. The school's newspaper proclaimed that Finch "stole the hearts of Memphis basketball fans, and racism is no longer quite so popular in the city as it once was."[41] The Tiger faithful who attended games at the Mid-South Coliseum viewed Finch as a "calm, friendly and self-assured young man," according to the *Helmsman*.[42] Finch and his running mate Ronnie Robinson made a pact between themselves to bring Memphis State to the national championship game of the NCAA tournament. Finch knew that he had to live up to the preseason hype that went with being labeled one of the best guards in the country. Ladell Anderson, head coach of the Utah Stars of the American Basketball Association, described Finch as the best senior guard in the entire nation.[43] On top of all the preseason hype from the media, the Tiger faithful had been requesting season tickets since the 1972 season ended in April.[44]

Racial tensions made their way to campus at the beginning of the season. The anti-war and the Black Power movements brought protests to Memphis State's campus, like so many other campuses around the country. Basketball games became a visible arena in which the black Student Association at Memphis State could make political statements.[45] Throughout the season, the BSA protested American racism and imperialism by sitting down during the Star-Spangled Banner. This display of resistance by the BSA led to increased racial friction on campus. A letter to the editor in the school's newspaper demonstrated the racial divide on campus. The letter claimed that, "rather than bringing ourselves closer together, actions such as these (by the black students) only serve to further polarize the races in the City of Good Abode."[46] The *Helmsman's* sports editor referred to the complaint in the letter as an example of the "redneck ethic of control over the conduct of others that is dangerous."[47] Finch could more easily assimilate at the university because of his status as a star basketball player. But for other black students who were not in the limelight, the cultural shock of attending Memphis State created challenges. Finch's high school sweetheart Vickie Stephens followed Finch to Memphis State but remembers feeling like a "fly in buttermilk."[48] The language, the behavior, and the mannerisms that black students attending Memphis State had to adopt were new and forced many to feel out of place. They also felt prejudice from white teachers and white students. For many black Memphis State students, this was their first experience being in the minority. Black students on campus in the early 1970s had grown up in predominately black neighborhoods before coming to Memphis State. In their neighborhoods, they only saw a limited number of white people within their communities. As the Tigers began to win, these tensions seemed to move to the back pages and did not appear as prevalent as they had when the season opened. The old sports adage that "winning cures everything" was one of the ingredients in the recipe for the racial healing trope of 1973.

The lack of acceptance on campus for black students points to the difficulties faced by black people on campus who were not athletes. But black athletes also faced challenges. For black athletes at white universities, any relationships with white co-eds were fraught with danger, especially in the South. Coaches at white universities who were recruiting black athletes to star on their campuses told these players to "stay away from white women." Perry Wallace, the first black basketball player in the SEC at Vanderbilt, dated a black co-ed during his time on campus, thus avoiding the increased stress of challenging another racial boundary. Wallace recalled that the fear of "having to always look over your shoulder was simply not peaceful."[49] When Vickie Stephens followed Finch to Memphis State in the fall of 1969, this alleviated the fear that Finch would possibly date a white co-ed student. Finch maintained his steady relationship with Stephens during their four years together at Memphis State. Stephens, however, had not always planned on attending Memphis State with Finch.

During their senior year at Melrose, Finch told Stephens he was going to Memphis State and that she would go with him. Stephens had planned to move to Los Angeles with her older sisters. When he informed her of his plan, Finch told Stephens, "you are going to Memphis State with me." She replied, "I am?" He said, "yes, you are."[50] Finch understood the complexities of attending Memphis State on a level that belied his years. By bringing Ronnie Robinson, he brought not only his best friend but also another black teammate from Orange Mound. By bringing his high school sweetheart to Memphis State, he brought another piece of Orange Mound with him. Out of the spotlight, Stephens often faced the daily stresses of being black on the Memphis State campus on her own, whereas Finch received a pass. She remembers her first semester on campus as "a shock to me. I'd been around black people my whole life in my community. I hadn't really corresponded with any white [people] [before attending Memphis State] at all unless I went downtown." Many of Stephens's black classmates confronted these same issues when they arrived on campus at a predominately white Memphis State in the fall of 1969. She remembers having to make many adjustments to life on campus. Stephens recalled getting to know some of her white classmates and finding out that some of her professors showed prejudice toward her in grading her assignments. Finch provided something tangible for the Memphis State community on the court, and his support group at Melrose prepared him to confront its academic rigors. Stephens did not receive the same affection from professors that Finch received because of his athletic glory. She recalled that the white people on campus "weren't mean. You just felt uncomfortable being the only one (or in the minority)."[51]

The arrival of Larry Kenon, a 6'9" junior college All-American from Amarillo College in Texas, heightened the championship hopes of the Tigers in the fall of 1972. He seemed to be the missing piece in the post that the Tigers needed to advance through the NCAA tournament bracket. Kenon, a Birmingham native, was so athletic that he could dunk two basketballs at the same time. Finch remained the hometown hero who received the accolades, but without Kenon, the Tigers would not have reached the same heights. The 1972–73 Tiger roster featured four black starters and one white starter, Bill Laurie. Bartow's starting five would have caused problems for the university only a few years earlier. Gene Haskins's all-black starting five in the 1966 NCAA championship game for Texas Western against Kentucky was a recent memory and something that was still a problem in the South. By making Laurie point guard, Bartow was putting a white player in what many believed to be the most intellectual position on the floor.[52]

The high expectations for the Tigers were deflated early in December when the team started the season 2–3. The team faced chemistry issues when Kenon joined the starting unit, which caused their early season woes. Kenon believed that Finch and Robinson did not particularly enjoy sharing the spotlight with the newcomer.[53] His perspective changed after he saw teammate Billy Buford cry after losing to Texas 80–79 in early December. He was profoundly impacted by the moment and decided to place his issues aside. Kenon marked that moment as the one where he gained an understanding of how important winning was to these Tigers.[54] By January, the Tigers had found their way. Finch's 34 points against Florida Tech in mid-January made him the all-time leading scorer in the school's history.[55] Also that night, Ronnie Robinson became the all-time leading rebounder in school history. Ten days later, Finch once again wowed the Tiger faithful with a 48 point performance against St. Joseph's of Indiana. The *Commercial Appeal* described Finch as "simply amazing" and "the heartbeat of Memphis State basketball."[56] Kenon's emergence, the continued excellence from Finch and Robinson, and the improving team chemistry allowed the Tigers to go on a fourteen-game win streak starting in late December. Memphis State student Sheila Davis recalls that the winning streak "was overwhelming and that the campus and city were on fire with excitement."[57] As the Tigers heated up on the court, the tension in the city peaked when busses began to initiate Judge McCrae's plan for desegregating Memphis' schools.

On January 22, 1973, during the Tigers' win streak, buses rolled down the streets of Memphis for the first time in the fight to bring educational equality to the city. Forty thousand students were truant from school on the first day of busing. Within the next few weeks, students began to trickle back into the city schools.[58] Buses brought white kids into predominately black schools. Buses brought black kids into predominately white schools. Skepticism surrounded both sides of the racial divide. The organization of Reverend Billy Kyles, People United to Save Humanity, was present at black bus stops to protect black students and bus drivers. Years of racial distrust led Kyle to urge black men to protect their women and families from those opposed to busing. He also attacked Mayor Chandler's membership in CAB and questioned his resolve to enforce the federal court's order to begin busing.[59] While many white people kept their children out of school in protest, many black people prepared for the worst. The racial climate recalled Reverend Netters's premonition that the city was a powder keg awaiting one match to explode into racial chaos. The federal courts, the Memphis City School Board, the NAACP, and the Citizens Against Busing created one of the largest educational exoduses in the history of public education. Busing did not create the suburbs in Memphis, but it expedited the process. The only thing that slowed white flight eastward was the annexation of East Memphis, Frayser, Parkway Village, and Oakhaven in the years preceding Plan A, which slowed the loss of white people inside city limits.[60]

The cost of white flight to the city school system was disconnectedness. Neighborhoods that had previously held strong communal bonds around their school slowly lost that communal feel. As white flight became the norm, students migrated from Sheffield High School to Wooddale High, and then to Kirby High, each time moving toward the outer boundaries of the city limits. Shelby County continued to build the infrastructure necessary to escape east. Contractors continued to build bigger and more luxurious houses to make white Memphians feel comfortable and achieve the kind of racial balance that was the norm before school busing. Five years after the first desegregated basketball city championship in 1968, the politicians and citizens of the city returned Memphis to an even more segregated state. The growing division in the city was countered by the unity and cohesiveness of the Tigers' team as the season wound to its completion.

The Tigers dropped a road game late in mid-February to rival Louisville that ended hopes of an undefeated MVC regular season.[61] In the next to last game of the season, the Tigers defeated New Mexico State 54–53 and secured the NCAA tournament bid from the MVC. As the Missouri Valley Conference champion, the Tigers received a bye into the Sweet 16 of the 25–team NCAA tournament. After a one-sided victory over West Texas State on Senior Night, Larry Finch hugged his long-time friend and running mate Ronnie Robinson at half court of the Coliseum. Robinson and Finch received a three-minute standing ovation from the home crowd when Bartow subbed for them with 1:10 left in the game.[62] Sportswriter George Lapides defined the moment as one "that will live forever."[63] Lapides lauded Finch and Robinson as special heroes who were adopted by most Memphians. Their actions off the court thrilled Memphians as much as their actions on the court. Finch and Robinson were both named to the all-conference first team for the MVC. Finch was named an honorable mention All-American by the United Press.[64] Inside the Coliseum, the city's racial discord seemed miles away. Here in this space, two kids from Orange Mound lifted the Tigers from the doldrums of the MVC. Over the next month, the Tigers began a journey that further entrenched Finch as a healing factor in the city.

The Tigers wrapped up a championship season, and the fans cherished one last chance to see Finch and Robinson in blue and gray. Six miles away at city hall, the racial tension reached new levels. On February 6, John Ford, the newly elected councilman, became embroiled in a heated public discussion with the white chairman of the city council, Thomas Todd. Ken Keele, president of CAB, had requested city council funding for CAB schools. Ford asked Todd, "Why don't you just shut the hell up?" when Todd repeatedly denied Ford's demands to speak against the CAB schools' request. The following week Harold Ford, Reverend Kyles, and about one hundred other followers demanded a voice against funding CAB schools. Todd once again denied the Ford entourage the opportunity to speak. When the crowd became unruly, he chided Ford's followers: "Mob rule does not get us anywhere, and I feel you are trying to intimidate this council or me." Todd was on the defensive as the racial tension grew in the chambers of City Hall. Harold Ford chastised black councilmen J.O. Patterson and Fred Davis for siding with their white colleagues to keep the black folks present in the city council chambers from speaking.[65] The city's political patterns were shifting in favor of African Americans as Ford's political machine emerged. John Ford's presence on the council assured black Memphians that attempts by CAB proponents to fund segregated schools using tax dollars would not happen. As Ford continued to push for the voice of his black constituents to be heard, Finch pushed forward with his Tiger teammates toward their goal—a national championship.

The Tigers opened their 1973 NCAA tournament in a region that included four teams ranked in the top 13 in the nation. Memphis State won its first two games against South Carolina and Kansas State by a combined total of 36 points.[66] In the game against South Carolina, Larry Kenon led the team with 34 points and 20 rebounds, but it was Larry Finch who delivered the "killing blows to the Gamecocks."[67] Kenon's play in the NCAA regionals solidified his position as a top draft pick, but Finch's play remained the focal point of the Tiger fanbase. Finch's 32-point shooting performance against Kansas State two days later further captivated Memphians. Finch later proclaimed, "That's my favorite game because it put us in the Final Four."[68]

As the team arrived at the Memphis International Airport from Houston after their quarterfinal victory, the pilot came over the intercom and said, "Congratulations to the Memphis State Tigers." He said, "I understand there is quite a mob at the airport waiting to bring y'all back home." A crowd estimated at over 5,000 awaited the Tigers at 12:20 am bearing signs that read: "UCLA— The Memphis State of the West."[69] The *Helmsman* described the atmosphere at the airport as pandemonium: "People covered the floor, people were sitting on reservation counters, on a car put there by some unsuspecting car dealer, everywhere."[70] The *Tri-State Defender*, Memphis's black newspaper, joined the jubilation and supported the city's newfound unity behind the Tigers. *The Defender* highlighted Finch's 57 points over the weekend and his status as regional MVP as it exalted Finch.[71] The next stop for the Tigers was St. Louis for the Final Four, where Providence, Indiana, and UCLA awaited them.

The Tigers made their way north to St Louis for the program's first Final Four appearance. Finch offered his Temptations tape, and Billy Buford added, "and naturally, we've got to have that *Shaft* tape."[72] The Tigers looked to Stax recording artist Isaac Hayes as their good luck charm, the definition of 1970s black manhood, to inspire them to break the Tigers losing streak in St. Louis. Hayes, from Memphis, was the first black artist to sell a million dollars' worth of records. His deep penetrating voice rapped with the audience and drew them in, similar to the way in which Finch's jump-shot excited fans. Hayes was a man of fashion who made a statement when he stepped on stage. He wore unique, colorful combinations of tights, a pair of boots, and a chain that wrapped around his waist and neck. Chains have historically represented bondage to black men. In the 1970s, they became a symbol of black power. With his gold chains, bald head, beard, and shades, Isaac Hayes became a symbol of black militancy.[73] Black women fell for Hayes's expression of black sexuality, and black men dug the lyrics. Hayes' soundtrack from the 1971 movie *Shaft*, enthralled Finch and his teammates. Hayes, the leading artist for Memphis's Stax studios, announced a shift from the soulful sound that emanated from the black church to a more militant black funk sound prevalent in the 1970s.[74] *Shaft* itself was part of the new genre of blaxploitation, films dedicated to "all the Brothers and Sisters who had enough of the man."[75] Finch, the proclaimed leader of the 1973 Tigers, announced a shift from Memphis State's all-white "Dixie Darlings" to the predominately black team that brought Memphis to its first Final Four. In 1969, Nina Simone covered Bob Dylan's iconic classic, "The Times They Are a Changin'," which expresses Finch's impact on the city of Memphis and Tiger basketball—the times they were changing.

The Tigers' semifinal opponent, Providence, was 27–2 and ranked number four in the country. Providence College is a small Catholic college run by the Dominican Fathers. Like the Memphis State faithful, the Providence fan base provided enthusiastic support for their hometown Friars. Lenny Wilkens from Brooklyn, John Thompson from D.C., and Johnny Egan from Hartford had led Providence's previous teams. Marvin Barnes and Ernie Degragario, two local products from Providence, led the 1972–1973 Friars.[76] Like Finch and Robinson, the two local products restored faith in their hometown basketball program. Unlike Finch and Robinson, who both came from Orange Mound, Barnes and DiGregorio came from two different worlds. The six-foot-tall DiGregorio came from North Providence's Italian community, which was enjoying the economic successes of post-war America. DiGregorio's family lived in a split-level colonial home where Sunday dinners resembled the typical sizeable Italian family gathering. Opposite DiGregorio was 6'9" Marvin Barnes from black West Providence. When Barnes arrived on campus in the fall of 1971, he was not thrilled about playing with "Ernie D": "First of all, he was white, which wasn't exactly my favorite color. Secondly, he was way too cocky." Eventually, the teammates from two different worlds grew to not only like each other, but to lead their team to the Final Four. DiGregorio described the two's newfound friendship as one grounded in similar interests and in the goal of playing professionally. Throughout Barnes' freshman season, during which he was forced by NCAA rules to play on the freshman team, Ernie D and Barnes both came to practice early and stayed late, working on ways to capitalize on each other's strengths. Before the end of Barnes's freshman season, he became a regular at the DiGregorio Sunday night family dinners, and Ernie D. was playing pickup games in West Providence on its asphalt courts. Ernie D. also described the unique nature of their friendship, "In Providence, being best friends with someone of a different race just wasn't done. There was a 'stick with your own kind' type of attitude. Marvin and me, we didn't pay any attention to that color barrier bullshit."[77] Throughout their run to the Final Four, their wins brought together Italians from along Atwell Avenue in North Providence and black people from West Providence to cheer for the Friars.[78]

The Tigers were familiar with the St. Louis Arena, but the unfavorable results from previous NCAA games there haunted them. They held an 0–7 record in NCAA tournament games played in St. Louis and set themselves to breaking the jinx that the city held over them in tournament play. When the game tipped off, the city of Memphis all but shut down to watch or listen to the game. WMC estimated that 250,000 television sets tuned into NBC's signal. Another 100,000 radios tuned in to WMC-790 to hear Jack Eaton call Saturday's semifinal game with Providence.[79] Finch's matchup with DiGregorio gave Finch another opportunity to prove he was as good or better than anybody else.[80]

Barnes was arguably one of the most talented players in the Final Four. Unlike Finch, who knew that he always wanted to stay home and play for Memphis

State, Barnes almost became a Cincinnati Bearcat after his stellar prep career at Providence's Central High School. Barnes's recruiting visit to Cincinnati was his first plane trip, and it was so turbulent that his plane diverted to Baltimore. Barnes, visibly shaken, took a Greyhound bus back to Providence.[81] Barnes was more willing to accept Providence coach Dave Gavitt's pitch for the hometown after his turbulent attempt to visit Cincinnati. Barnes grew up in West Providence federal housing and, like Finch, was an example a black player from the "other" side of town playing for a predominately white college. Barnes faced isolation on Providence's campus as one of only thirty-eight African Americans enrolled at the school. He described how white students treated black students on campus as if "we had some highly contagious disease." A priest on campus once told Barnes that he needed to "start smiling because he was scaring the preppie types on campus, with their crew cuts, Izod shirts, Irish wool sweaters, and tasseled penny loafers."[82]

In contrast to the perception of white students at Providence that Barnes was angry, Finch was seen by Memphis State's white students as personable and approachable. Tigers team photographer Phyllis Dibell, a white co-ed, described Finch as someone who was "fabulous. He talked to you, made you feel good. He was cute."[83] Finch's personality endeared him to the Tigers' predominately white student body. In contrast, Barnes was seen as a troubled black youth from inner-city Providence. Barnes's character was damaged further before 1972–1973 season when he accepted a plea bargain in a case filed by Larry Ketvirtis, Providence College's 6'10" backup center. Ketvirtis accused Barnes of hitting him in the mouth with a tire iron.[84] In Memphis, wealthy white boosters invited Finch to their houses for post-game parties with their families, and he signed autographs for young white Tiger fans after games.[85] Finch became a beloved figure on campus and among the predominately white Tiger fan base, whereas Marvin Barnes became known as "Bad News."

The Friars had reeled off 17 straight wins heading into the national semifinal game, including six over ranked teams.[86] In the first eight minutes of the game Barnes controlled the boards, Ernie D made a behind the back pass between two Tiger defenders to guard Kevin Stacum for a wide-open lay-up, and the Friars were in control. DiGregorio's inspired play gave the Tigers fits and led the Friars to a 49–40 lead at the half.[87] The Tigers' dream season looked over. Nat Holman, the legendary former CCNY coach who had won both the NCAA and NIT tournaments in 1950, called the Friars' inspired play, "the best eight minutes of basketball I've ever seen."[88] The Tigers caught a break when Barnes collided with Ronnie Robinson and banged his knee with Providence leading 24–18.[89] Without Barnes in the lineup, Bartow instructed his charges to feed Larry Kenon, the ball inside. Without Barnes to offer any resistance, Kenon responded with 28 points and 22 rebounds. Barnes reentered the game with 5:51 remaining in the second half. He pulled the Friars to within one point on a flat-footed layup. Following the layup, Gavitt pulled Barnes out as his knee had completely locked up. The Tigers went on a 13–1 run after Barnes left the game to secure the 98–85 victory.[90] Finch told reporters after the game that the initial push by Providence was because the Tigers "weren't used to that hurly-burly stuff."[91] In the end, it was the Tigers' size and Barnes's absence that overwhelmed the Friars. The Tigers' win set up a finals-matchup with UCLA.[92] Providence fan Peter Farrelly, who was 16, compared Barnes's injury to that of Roy Hobbs in *The Natural,* except in the movie Hobbs got another chance.[93] For the Providence faithful, it was a painful blow to an anticipated rematch with UCLA.

Following the semifinal win, Tennessee Governor Winfield Dunn, Isaac Hayes, former Memphis State president C.C. Humphreys, and Tigers athletic director Bill Murphy all congratulated the Tigers. Finch let the media know that "black Moses" was their good luck charm. Isaac Hayes, a frequent spectator at Tiger home games, traveled to St. Louis to see the game and was present on the trip when the Tigers played his *Shaft* soundtrack.[94] White Memphis fans indulged Finch's expression of blackness because the Tigers were winning. Finch represented a new construction of blackness in the city. Finch was approachable, charismatic, and humble. Even when Finch wore silk shirts with butterfly collars, a black leather jacket, tight pants, and a captain's hat to ensure that he was "dressed to the nines," he was someone with whom the white student body and fan base felt comfortable. Five years earlier, sanitation workers had carried signs that read: "I Am a Man" on the streets of Memphis. Finch's role as a valorous sports figure enabled him to reconstruct the way that white Memphians viewed the black players on the 1973 roster. Bartow described the moment as "probably the finest hour in Memphis State's athletic history." Finch echoed the jubilation surrounding the moment as he told reporters, "No, I don't care who we play in the championship game. We're there, and that's the most important thing."[95]

In 1973, the NCAA moved the national championship game to prime-time television. That allowed 38 million television viewers to watch Memphis's title quest against vaunted UCLA. By the early 1970s, the NCAA Tournament had become a big business, and UCLA represented a brand of excellence that enhanced the sport's image and the tournament's viability.[96] UCLA coach John Wooden, the Wizard of Westwood, was challenging Adolph Rupp's hold for the title of the greatest coach in college basketball history. His UCLA teams were in the middle of a twelve-year run in which they eventually won ten national championships. UCLA entered the 1973 NCAA tournament riding a 71-game win streak that surpassed the previous record of 60 straight wins set by Bill Russell's University of San Francisco teams in the 1960s.[97] UCLA dispensed Indiana University in its semifinal game with relative ease, 70–59.[98]

The national media believed that Providence had held the best chance to knock off UCLA. The Tigers entered the game as an improbable David attempting to slay a Goliath. Bartow opened by employing a man-to-man defense against the Bruins. Bruins guard Greg Lee kept feeding the ball into the post, where star center Bill Walton was near perfect, going 11–12 from the field in the first half. Halfway through the first half, Bartow abandoned the man-to-man defense and employed a one-two-two half-court zone defense. Lee continued to lob the ball into Walton over the outstretched arms of Larry Kenon.[99] The Tigers caught a break when Walton garnered his third foul with 4:14 left in the first half. Closing the half on an 8–0 run, the Tigers pulled even, 39–39, at the half. Finch's two free throws to start the second half gave the Tigers the lead, 41–39.[100] The Tigers were ready to shock the basketball world. Most of the media outlets outside of Memphis gave the Tigers little chance to defeat UCLA and concluded that they had only reached the finals because of Barnes's injury in the semifinal game. Nevertheless, in that one brief moment, the Tigers looked to be on their way to becoming national champions.

That was the last lead the Tigers held for the remainder of the game. Walton continued his excellence by scoring the next eight points from the 11:42 mark in the second half. The Bruins regained control of the game. During a second half-time out, UCLA guard Greg Lee asked Coach Wooden if someone else besides Walton should shoot. Perplexed, Wooden replied, "Why?"[101] Walton finished with 44 points on 21 of 22 shooting, breaking Gail Goodrich's championship game record of 42 points.[102] Finch's smooth jumpshot, along with the athletic play of Robinson and Kenon, kept the Tigers in the game, but they were no match for Walton and the Bruins. With 2:51 remaining on the clock, Walton sprained his ankle, and Finch helped carry Walton off the floor to the sidelines. Finch showed humility and humanity as the crowd cheered Walton's performance. The Bruins won 87–66. Walton avoided the media after the game, refusing to answer their questions and saying, "I don't want to talk about it, man. I'm really in a hurry to see my friends."[103] Walton's refusal to address the media was central to his own identity as part of the counter-culture movement and its disdain for the mainstream.

In sharp contrast to Walton's adversarial relationship with the media, Finch embraced the opportunity to represent his hometown. He was the face of the program and the entire city. Finch's arrival at the pinnacle of the basketball world signaled to the rest of the country that Memphis was healing. Only five years before, the National Guard had been called in to patrol the city's streets after Dr. King's assassination. In those five years, Finch rose from a local prep star to be the face of the city's marquee basketball program. Finch, a young black star from Orange Mound, became the face of Memphis to the rest of the country. His athletic heroics had revitalized the Memphis State basketball program, landing them in the NCAA finals against UCLA. His image was displayed on national television and became part of the healing image of which Mayor Chandler boasted.

The *Commercial Appeal* applauded Finch's 29 points in his last game with the Tigers as a "fitting tribute to a career which has seen him establish most of the school's scoring records."[104] UCLA guard Larry Hollyfield told reporters, "That Larry Finch is one of the two toughest guards that I have faced in my career." Coach Wooden stated, "I knew about Finch. Memphis State is one of the best teams we've played."[105] Finch relished in the moment of the game. During the game, Finch had talked it up with Hollyfield. According to Finch, Hollyfield told him, "Nice shot." Finch replied that Hollyfield had tried to steal his ball, and he let him know, "you ain't gonna get that ball. I don't play that way."[106] Finch was devastated by the thought that he had let Memphis down against UCLA, but his character and determination only further endeared him to the Tiger fan base. For Finch, his goal had been to lead Memphis State to a national championship. His competitive nature led him to look back on his performance against UCLA as a disappointment because he failed to meet his objective.[107] Finch's character as a man allowed him to help Walton off the floor, but his competitive spirit was so strong that he never got over losing the game.

After UCLA defeated them, the Tigers boarded a plane and returned home to Memphis. The *Press-Scimitar* posted a picture of Finch exiting the plane at the Memphis International Airport with the caption "A Grateful City Greets Its Team."[108] This time, Coach Bartow had the team board a bus and bypass the airport terminal. The team bus made its way through Orange Mound on its way to the Mid-South Coliseum, where 6,000 fans awaited the Tigers. Thirteen-year-old Tiger fan Keith Easterwood jumped on the back of a pickup truck on Southern Avenue to get to the Mid-South Coliseum to welcome the Tigers home.[109] Free to all fans that night, Easterwood and Memphians from all over town made their way to the Coliseum one last time to thank the Tigers. For Easterwood, "the diverse nature of that crowd was something I had never seen."[110] At the Coliseum, the governor and the mayor joined the team for the welcoming party. Fred Davis, a black city councilman, embraced Finch and Robinson. Davis told the crowd gathered at the Coliseum that, "they have been catalysts and done as much to bring this town together as any two people in town."[111] Davis recognized the significance of two black athletes from Orange Mound being able to bring the city together, something that no two politicians on that stage had been able to do. Bartow spoke briefly and turned the program over to Finch. When he did, the crowd exploded with an emotional outburst of support for Finch, which caused Finch to tear up. Finch then emceed the introduction of the rest of the team.[112]

The city continued to revel in the Tigers' success. The *Commercial Appeal* boasted that although UCLA won the game, the Tigers landed two members, Finch and Kenon, on the Final Four all-tournament team while UCLA landed one player. The final blow dealt by the Tigers was when Gene Bartow was named Coach of the Year by the National Basketball Coaches Association over UCLA's Coach Wooden.[113] Although Finch and the Tigers returned with the runners-up trophy, they were champions in the eyes of Memphians.

Finch and Robinson were the catalysts, the hometown players that brought the city together. Finch went against the norm when he signed with Memphis State, a university that many in the black community thought would never accept him as a man. Finch ended his career there holding six career marks in the Tiger record book: the single-game scoring record, most points in a season, most points in two seasons, most points in three seasons, most field goals in a season, and most career assists.[114] Finch never missed a game during his three-year span on the varsity team. His productivity and effort set the standard for excellence in the program. Along the way, the Tigers became a perennial contender for conference champion and drew recognition nationally. These feats came at a time when racial strife divided the community. Bennie Crosnoe, a Tiger fan who traveled to St. Louis for the Final Four, claimed that "About that time the games came along, there was a coming together of the races in this city we hadn't seen before."[115] Clarence Jones, a freshman guard on the 1973 team, summed it up best when he said, "It was basketball that brought the city together. At the time, it was special."[116] Finch's loyalty to the city never waned as a player. The unpopular choice to stay and play for Memphis State, at a time when the school was viewed with justifiable suspicion by the black community, defined Finch.[117] The city rewarded Finch by celebrating his play on the court and celebrating his persona in a way that no previous black athlete from the city had ever experienced. For years the *Commercial Appeal* had enraged black Memphians with a stereotypical black male caricature, Hambone. After the Tigers lost to the UCLA Bruins, the *Commercial Appeal* printed a cartoon with two kids—one white, one black—sitting on a sidewalk, looking slightly dejected. Behind them, a sign read, "Larry, we love you!!!"[118]

Finch's Tigers unified the city in its support of Memphis State basketball, but the city remained divided over desegregation. Three years after busing was first implemented, MCS's director of research and planning Dr. O.Z. Stephens summed up the failure of busing in Memphis: "Consistent evidence does exist in the Memphis City Schools system to support the contention that recent court-ordered desegregation decisions and the subsequent implementation of desegregation plans have contributed to rapidly increasing resegregation of the public school population—thus thwarting efforts to achieve the goal of meaningful integration." The city of Memphis actively supported the Tigers on the court, but it remained as divided as before off the court. Judge McRae's courage in the face of resistance from the white establishment led to a decision with noble intentions. The exodus of white students from public schools to private and county schools, however, spoke clearly to the public's position on integration. But at the same time Finch and his Tiger teammates were cheered on by white Memphians, and herein lies the paradox. African American writer John Edgar Wideman, a former basketball standout at the University of Pennsylvania in the late 1950s, concludes that basketball is an art form that unites the community, celebrates family, and reflects the unique character of the black family. Basketball is also a unique metaphor for the complex attitudes toward race in America.[119] Finch provided white Memphians a glimpse into what family means for black Memphians, and he showed them the unique characteristics found in black Memphians that contradicted the racial stereotypes permeated by cartoons such as *Hambone*. White Memphians celebrated Finch as an iconic figure who united Memphis, but this did not change their attitudes toward black people in general nor alter their political stance on issues like busing. Finch's celebration provides insight into the complex realities that allowed the city to remain divided racially, politically, and socially.

After the Tigers returned from the NCAA championship game in St. Louis, Finch was lauded as a unifier in the city by white and black politicians. For three years, white Memphians claimed Finch as their own and took pride in the fact that "they" had developed Finch into a star. Tim Church, a student reporter for the *Helmsman*, summed up the incongruity of this belief best when he said, "Both of these young men [Finch and Robinson] were ignored, simply because they were black. Both have expressed appreciation for the help they received from various teachers and coaches, but that help came from the ghettos, not East Memphis. Because they were black, Memphis gave these two men the back of their hands twenty years ago and left them in the ghetto where survival was the major issue. Both returned twenty years later to show Memphis a standard of excellence that the city would do well to adopt in other areas."[120] Church's editorial embodies the problems with the narrative that Finch and the 1973 Tigers healed the racial issues in the city. Memphis remained as divided as it had been in 1968. Paula Wooldridge, an African American teacher in Memphis City Schools, called the half-year busing experiment "a waste of time, a waste of gas, and a waste of money."[121] The Mid-South Coliseum was a performance space where white and black people met for a common goal: Tiger glory. White and black politicians latched on to the success of the Tigers, but the racial reality remained in the city away from the Tigers' basketball success. Beyond the Tigers, the city struggled with white flight, political fracture, and a broken school system.

3

Memphis Goes Pro

In the 1970s, collegiate basketball became a focal point for Memphians to rally around. If collegiate basketball could be used to perpetuate the idea that the city's racial issues had healed, then surely professional basketball, which was introduced to the city in 1970, should have been part of the same healing trope. The American Basketball Association's short-lived stay in the city allows us to further analyze the relationship between the city and basketball. The league had a reputation as a "black" league because of its style of play, physicality, and athleticism, and the response of white Memphians to this style provides insight into the racial attitudes that continued to plague the city. The instability of Memphis's ABA franchise mirrors the political instability that was present in the city during this same period. The failure of the ABA to prosper in the city in the 1970s speaks to an underlying racial discord. The ABA franchise's five-year stay in town provides a counter-narrative to the myth that basketball was able to heal the city's racial woes.

The ABA was a league with renegade sports owners who were determined to change the world of professional basketball. They drafted underclassmen, encouraged free agency, held multiple drafts, and challenged the way the game was played. The ABA introduced the three-point shot and a freer style of play that more closely resembled the modern version of the game, as compared to the low scoring defensive battles in the 1970s NBA. The ABA's all-star game festivities introduced us to the dunk contest and to Julius Erving, aka "Dr. J," its most valued commodity. This new league's flashy players made names for themselves with their exuberance and style.

The ABA was the brainchild of Dennis Murphy, who teamed with NBA legend Bill Sharman to propose a new professional basketball league. George Mikan, the league's first commissioner, gave the league legitimacy and the red, white, and blue basketball.[1] The NBA in 1967 was as drab as its brown ball, and Mikan knew a rival league needed an eye-catching gimmick to capture the public's attention. The country was undergoing a cultural revolution and was bogged down in an unpopular war in Vietnam. The red, white, and blue basketball became part of an anti-establishment culture that was becoming predominant throughout the country.[2] The ABA lived on the edge, as did its Memphis franchise. In the summer of 1970, P.L. Blake bought the New Orleans franchise and moved it to Memphis. The team changed names three times over its five years in the city, and its ownership was as schizophrenic as any in the league. Blake first owned the Memphis franchise. When he left, the franchise went to eccentric baseball owner Charlie Finley. After Finley, then ABA commissioner Mike Storen briefly stabilized the franchise in 1975. This instability spelled disaster for the franchise.[3] The league begrudgingly paid the team's bills before selling the franchise to a group in Baltimore. The new Baltimore franchise folded before playing its first game. This foray into professional basketball in Memphis further exemplifies the limited role that basketball performed as a racial unifier in the city. Although playing in the same arena and during the same era as Finch's collegiate career, the ABA's brand of basketball failed to fill the stands and failed to unite the city behind its Memphis franchise.

▲ ▼ ▲

Before moving north up Interstate 55 to Memphis, the New Orleans Buccaneers were one of the ABA's more successful teams. They dominated the ABA's Western Division, with Babe McCarthy at the helm.[4] The team's executives were cognizant of the racial issues facing professional basketball in the Deep South and never kept more than six black players on the twelve-man roster. Memorial Auditorium was their home court for their first two seasons before they moved to the Loyola Fieldhouse for the franchise's third season. According to former Bucs executive Maurice Stern, these venues provided inadequate parking, which led to fan apathy.[5] In their final season in New Orleans, the Bucs started strong but faded after rookie all-star "Skeeter" Swift went down with a knee injury in December. The Bucs finished last in the Western Division that year, with a record under .500. Venues in New Orleans were apathetic toward the Bucs, and so P.L. Blake bought the franchise in the late summer of 1970 and moved them to Memphis. Although the Bucs saw success on the court, they were unable to overcome the challenges faced by professional basketball in the Deep South.

Blake, a native of Greenwood, Mississippi, lettered in football at Mississippi State before making his fortune in real estate.[6] Because college basketball was so popular in Memphis, he believed that this city was better suited to support professional basketball. He also believed that the Mid-South Coliseum in Memphis would be a better venue for home games. Mayor Henry Loeb eagerly welcomed the ABA, saying, "This city grows when something is added, and something big has been added by this basketball team."[7] He purchased the first two season tickets at City Hall from Blake in a ceremony designed to kick start season ticket sales in early September.[8] Jack Dolph, the ABA's commissioner, claimed that the league studied the city's economic growth projections, TV market, and facilities before selecting Memphis. Dolph exalted the Mid-South Coliseum as one of the three best venues in the country to play basketball.[9]

Blake's financial conservatism became immediately apparent to the city's fan base. In a move designed strictly to save the team money, Blake proclaimed that the team's new moniker would be the "Pros." Sportswriters all over the country declared the "Pros" one of the most unimaginative nicknames in all of sports. Blake refused to buy new uniforms. Instead, he had the B-U-C-S removed from the jerseys and replaced with P-R-O-S.[10] Blake's frugal plan to use the same uniforms mirrored Loeb's refusal to offer the city's black sanitation workers a living wage two years earlier. Blake was now mimicking Loeb's paternalism. Blake expected that his players would gladly accept the recycled uniforms in the same way that Loeb expected the sanitation workers to accept his demands.

Two familiar names arrived in Memphis with the new ABA franchise, Mike Butler and Babe McCarthy. Butler was a former Memphis State guard who was often compared to Bob Cousy because of his adroit dribbling and passing skills, which were honed at Kingsbury High School.[11] According to local high school lore, Butler would sneak into the Kingsbury gymnasium at night to shoot jump-shots, with the lights off. Kids around the city remembered his time as a Tiger and mimicked his moves on playgrounds in white neighborhoods throughout the city.[12] Butler's professional stay in his hometown was short-lived: he was traded to the Utah Stars right before training camp opened.[13] Local fans also recalled McCarthy, who had coached at local SEC basketball power Mississippi State. His coaching success brought optimism to the city. McCarthy was best remembered for his role in resurrecting the Mississippi State men's basketball program and for challenging Mississippi's devout adherence to Jim Crow laws. In the 1963 NCAA tournament, his all-white team, the Maroons, faced off against a Loyola University of Chicago team that started four black players. McCarthy had engineered his team's escape from segregationist state politicians in Mississippi who were bent on preventing them from competing against black players.[14] Although McCarthy's team lost, by merely competing against black players, he set the foundation for future racial change in the SEC. McCarthy battled against the "closed society" with the central tenat to the Civil Rights Movement—equality of opportunity.[15] Blake was hopeful that McCarthy could once again manipulate the racial waters of the South with a roster filled with black players.

Problems mounted early for Blake. The league had already announced its schedule when Blake decided to move the team to Memphis. When they arrived, Blake found that the Mid-South Coliseum had previously booked eleven of the dates the ABA league office had assigned for home games. This forced the team to search for other venues. Blake hired Memphis sportswriter Charles Cavagnaro as the team's general manager. Cavagnaro was unable to overcome the scheduling debacle.[16] Out of necessity, Cavagnaro moved these "home games" to other venues in the region. With so many home games played away from the Coliseum and outside of the city, season ticket sales were under the 200 mark when the regular season began.[17] The Pros faced competition from other forms of entertainment in the city and from the NBA pre-season games, which were played in the Pros home arena, the Mid-South Coliseum.

The Pros opened preseason play against the Kentucky Colonels in Paducah, Kentucky, on the same night that the NBA hosted an exhibition game at the Mid-South Coliseum. The game between the Capital [Washington] Bullets and the New York Knicks at the Mid-South Coliseum was an example of the all-out war between the two leagues. The *Press-Scimitar*, Memphis's afternoon paper, gave the NBA the headline in the sports section, which allowed the NBA to top the ABA in its market.[18] Three weeks later, on October 20, 1970, the Pros welcomed the New York Nets to the Mid-South Coliseum in front of 13,000 fans. This time the local media praised the game as Memphis's introduction into the big leagues.[19] If the Pros were going to find success, it would be through the ability of their coach, Babe McCarthy, to put a winner on the floor.

One of McCarthy's favorite roster spots belonged to a former University of Southern Mississippi post player, Wendell Ladner. When McCarthy brought Ladner in for a workout, he told Ladner, "Son, you're just a damn embarrassment to me. When I had you in my summer camps, you were big, but you were cat-quick. And now look at you, you lard-ass. When are you going to get in shape?" Wendell replied, "I'll get in shape when the pro season opens." McCarthy retorted, "None of these damn NBA scouts will have your fat ass. But I'll tell you what—since I've known you all your life, I'll take you and give you a $500 bonus. If you make it, I'll pay your ass."[20] As the Memphis press covered McCarthy's relationship with Ladner, the 6'5" country boy captivated the city's white fans. Ladner was an example of white Southern manhood. Many blue-collar Memphians identified with his hard-nosed, over the edge style of play. Named as the only rookie on the ABA's West All-Star team in 1971, Ladner's play gained him recognition.[21] He also exemplified the rough and tumble image the ABA had around the country. *Los Angeles Times* columnist Jim Murray described the ABA game as "not so much a game as a dock fight with backboards. They recruit their teams from Central Park after dark. If they did on a street corner what they do under the basket, someone would call the cops."[22] Ladner embodied the hooligan nature of ABA post play, yet it was the media's perception that the violence in the league came from its overwhelming blackness.

The image of the powerful and violent black man was permeating American culture during the 1970s. *Shaft* and other blaxploitation films, aimed at black urban audiences, provided strong black characters that enjoyed "sticking it to the man."[23] Black players in the ABA wore afros, dunked the basketball, and ran back on defense with a fist raised high in the air as a salute to the black Power movement.[24] Most of the enforcers in professional basketball were African American, which only reinforced cultural stereotypes of violent Black masculinity. Noted ABA tough guy and black, Muslim Warren Jabali once stomped white guard Jim Jarvis's head into the ground during an altercation.[25] As a Southern white male, Ladner refused to back down, and he continued to challenge these perceptions with his physical play in the post. Guys like Jabali never intimidated Ladner. Pros teammate Steve Jones recalls Ladner squaring off against noted black tough guy John Brisker of the Pittsburgh Condors in his third game as a professional. Ladner started a fight with Brisker during the jump ball of their next matchup with the Condors a week later.[26]

Of the two professional basketball leagues, the ABA was considered "blacker" than the NBA. The Indiana Pacers, an ABA team, opened 1967 with seven black players on their roster while the NBA was still adhering to an unspoken color barrier that kept rosters at least half-white.[27] When the Pros moved to Memphis, the initial roster included seven black players.[28] In the spring of 1971, the Pros signed Ole Miss phenom Johnny Neumann, adding a white star to the roster. As the "white hope," Neumann was signed to help lure more fans to the Mid-South Coliseum after the Pros had struggled at the gate. The 1972 Memphis roster included two prominent black players who had participated in collegiate games that reshaped the racial dynamics of the college game: Les Hunter and David Lattin. Hunter's integrated Loyola of Chicago team played against McCarthy's all-white Mississippi State team in the 1963 "game of change," and Lattin's Texas Western team started five black players on its way to defeating all-white Kentucky in the 1966 NCAA National Championship game.[29] Black players like Hunter and Lattin did not resonate as well with the Memphis fan base. Supporting black professionals who wore afros, goatees, and gold chains meant accepting a black male culture that many Memphians were not ready to accept. As a result, few white Memphians bought tickets, and box office sales for the limited number of home games were low.

Blake lost over $200,000 before December first, which forced him to sell the team by the end of the calendar year. ABA league officers took control of the franchise financially and left Cavagnaro in charge of the team's daily operations. The Pros struggled to win on the court and finished the season 41–43. Although the team was two games under .500, they secured the third seed in the ABA's Western Division playoffs. Matched up with the first-place Indiana Pacers in the first round, they quickly fell behind 0–2 in the best of seven series. When the Pros returned home, fewer than 8,000 fans turned the turnstiles into their two home playoff games; the Coliseum felt like an empty cavernous tomb. Most Memphians learned of the team's two one-point losses in the local newspapers. [30]

When the season ended, the ABA needed to find new ownership if the franchise was going to remain solvent. Local Memphians with the necessary financial wherewithal shied away from the ABA because of its instability. To avoid folding, the team offered a unique solution to its financial problems: public stock. Over 4,000 people paid $5, $10, or $50 for Pros stock certificates.[31] Impressed by the community's support, ABA Commissioner Jack Delph referred to Memphis's bid to take over the franchise as "an impressive display of a community's faith in itself."[32] Memphis Area Sports Inc., the financial group that purchased the Pros through the sale of stock, vowed to keep the team in the city.

Memphis Area Sports Inc. faced division among socio-economic lines during its initial meetings, which mirrored the same divides present in the city. During the first stockholders meeting, dissension arose as a group of stockholders demanded more representation on the board. Fearful of an elitist board, Father Timothy Tighe, a local Catholic priest, asked why there were not more working-class men on the board if the board was meant to resemble all of the city. Herb Kosten, the director of Memphis Area Sports, responded to the community's request by adding twenty board members. Many civic boosters were convinced that if professional basketball failed in the city, then professional football would never come to the city. This led many of them to buy stock in the Pros. Long the major spectacle in the South, football generated interest far beyond college campuses. These boosters believed that professional basketball catered to the black aesthetic and was not as worthy of their entertainment dollars as professional football.

To create a new sense of hope, the Memphis Area Sports Inc. named Buddy Leake chairman of its new board of directors. Leake was a Memphis native who played football at the University of Oklahoma for Bud Wilkinson in the early 1950s. Following a career in the Canadian Football League, he returned to Memphis to work for the Massachusetts Mutual Life Insurance Company. His experience in collegiate and professional football gave the group a semblance of legitimacy. In May 1971, when the ABA and NBA met to discuss a merger, Memphians enthusiastically hoped that the city was about to be rewarded with an NBA franchise. From the creation of the ABA, the league's goal had been to force a merger with the NBA. In fact most cities established an ABA league to attract an NBA franchise. Merger talks only resulted in a series of preseason games between the two leagues, thus dashing the city's hopes for an NBA franchise once again.

As talks with the NBA brought only limited hope of a merger down the road, the ABA continued to think outside of the box to sign players. The Pros signed Ole Miss guard Johnny Neumann with two games remaining in his sophomore season, in the league's renegade style. During his only varsity season, he led the nation in scoring at 40 points per game. Unwilling to wait for the collegiate draft, the Pros signed Neumann in February to a five-year two-million-dollar contract. Neumann immediately joined the team in Memphis. Management hoped that his presence would boost attendance at the Coliseum. Neumann had arguably been the most sought-after high school player in Memphis in 1969 as a senior at all-white Overton High. Neumann's 34 points, with a broken hand, in the 1969 MIAA City Championship against all-black Melrose High solidified his legacy as the city's "great white hope." At Ole Miss, this myth grew when Kentucky's Adolph Rupp claimed that Neumann's talent as a sophomore was on par with Pete Maravich's as a senior at LSU. Neumann's eccentric style and reputation for being self-centered resembled tropes usually associated with the black aesthetic, yet the Pros believed his mythical stature as the city's "great white hope" would place fans in the stands at the Coliseum.

Neumann's arrival met with modest enthusiasm from Pro's coach Babe McCarthy. McCarthy, an old school disciplinarian, did not take well to Neumann's shot selection. Their relationship soured and became public during a February game. McCarthy fined Neumann $100 for lack of discipline following a game when Neumann took another shot after seeing that McCarthy had sent a substitute to the table to check in for him. Neumann told the press that the problem was much deeper than that one shot: "There is a great deal of unrest on this team because of him [McCarthy]." Following this spat with McCarthy, Neumann quit. The next day, to avoid further alienating the fan base and management, McCarthy called Neumann's Ole Miss teammate Steve Farese, the son of Neumann's agent John Farese. McCarthy convinced the younger Farese to get Neumann back to the Coliseum for the game that night. Steve Farese drove the eighty miles from Oxford to Neumann's house in Memphis. Once he arrived, he convinced Neumann that by quitting, he was doing exactly what McCarthy wanted him to do. Convinced he was playing into McCarthy's hands by quitting, Neumann jumped into his 1971 Porsche Pantera and drove to the Coliseum for the game. He led the team in scoring with 38 points.[33] Incidents like these led to the perception that Neumann was a flamboyant superstar who disrupted team chemistry. He became a troubling persona, but white fans still stereotypically attributed this sort of problematic behavior to black players.

The 1971–72 Pros finished with a 25–58 record and missed the playoffs.[34] After their dismal season on the court, the local ownership was eager to find new owners. The Pros operated in the red throughout the season, making the sale of the team a challenge. Ben Kerner, the former owner of the St. Louis Hawks, was approached but declined to offer a bid because of the franchise's outstanding debts.[35] Following another failed bid to sell the team to Joseph and Mamie Gregory of Ft. Lauderdale, Florida, the franchise looked doomed.[36] In an eleventh-hour attempt to save the team, Buddy Leake and local Memphis real estate developer Avron Fogelman signed a tentative deal with Langdon "Zip" Viracola from Dallas to buy the club.[37] After the ABA league offices received the deal, Viracola balked at the league's insistence that he pay the indemnity fee. He withdrew his offer. The ABA made a motion to kill the Memphis franchise, and it was seconded.[38] Professional basketball's end in the city seemed imminent. Fogelman convinced the league to table the final vote for half an hour to give him time for one last attempt to save basketball in the city. He then placed a frantic call to Charles Finley, whom he knew as part of the ownership group of the former Kansas City Athletics.

Charles O. Finley, the owner of baseball's Oakland Athletics, was a ray of hope for the nearly defunct Memphis ABA franchise. Fogelman and Leake gathered the necessary paperwork and traveled to Chicago to secure a deal with the eccentric insurance millionaire. Finley was an intense and complex person. He was a creative innovator, a self-made salesman and businessman, and a megalomaniacal puppet-master.[39] Finley agreed to purchase the franchise, and he assured Fogelman and Leake that the team would remain in Memphis. Fans were hopeful that Finley's determination to win, his desire to outwork his opponents, and his creative marketing ploys would be enough to steady the franchise. The stockholders in Memphis approved the sale, and although they received no money for their stock, they too had a hand in saving professional basketball in their city.[40]

Finley immediately put his mark on the franchise by changing the franchise's beleaguered name and team colors. Finley awarded $2,500 to the local fan who came up with the franchise's new name: Tams, an acronym for Tennessee, Arkansas, and Mississippi (TAMs).[41] The name referenced Scottish poetic hero "Tam O'Shanter," paying homage to the city's Scottish heritage and its geographic location.[42] Finley next made a loud splash by changing the Tams' colors to Kelly green, Fort Knox gold, and wedding gown white—the same colors worn by his Oakland As.[43] He hired Bob Bass as head coach and general manager, whose ABA success in Denver made many fans in the city hopeful. Then, in Finley publicity fashion, he hired Adolph Rupp as the team's president.[44] Finley proclaimed he hired "the man who knows more about basketball than anyone else alive."[45] Rupp had been forced out of the University of Kentucky by the administrators and was looking for a way to prove he was still relevant. Rupp believed that he, with Finley's money, could resurrect the struggling Memphis franchise. Finley paid Rupp over $40,000 a year as president but had no intention of allowing the "colonel" to control the basketball operations. Rupp made appearances at the games and in the Tams offices at the Mid-South Coliseum, but that was it. In June 1974, Rupp quit his role with the Tams and called the

ABA "a bush league." Three months later, he accepted a spot on the board of directors with the ABA's Kentucky Colonels, a jab at Finley.[46]

The 1972–1973 season brought renewed hope to the city that the franchise had stabilized financially and was now better prepared to win on the court. The *Press Scimitar's* George Lapides, a consummate advocate for basketball in the city, urged Memphians to head to the Coliseum to support the team. Lapides lauded Finley for the twenty-five piece band at all home games, the fifteen "attractive usherettes," and the overabundance of Kelly green blazers on Tams employees.[47] Finley initiated a wealth of gimmicks to bring fans to the Coliseum. But these gimmicks, which were a hit in Oakland, fell flat in Memphis.[48] Memphis remained a conservative Southern city where gimmicks like Mustache Night did not sell.

Finley's renegade style suited the approach of the ABA, but it did little to help turn the Tams into a winner. Finley traded away players on whims. Finley brought fan-favorite Wendell Ladner back to the Tams for the 1972–1973 season, but by January Ladner was traded to the Kentucky Colonels for a rookie and an undisclosed amount of cash.[49] By the middle of March, the team faced elimination from the playoffs, and they continued to struggle to fill the Coliseum. At the height of the Memphis State Tigers' 1973 season, the Tams drafted Larry Kenon in a regional draft behind closed doors.[50] As they had done when they secured Johnny Neumann in 1971, the team now placed its hopes on the athletic big man that anchored the Tigers post-game. The *Sporting News* labeled Kenon as, "the best college player to turn pro" in 1973, and the ABA understood his value to the league.[51] New York Nets owner Roy Boe negotiated Kenon's contract for the ABA and his Nets franchise, but the Tams retained his rights from the ABA's January regional draft. Both the Nets and the Tams claimed the rights to Kenon. Robert Carlson, legal counsel for the Nets and league commissioner, handled the dispute that followed between the Tams and Nets over Kenon's draft rights.[52] Carlson's conflict of interest became apparent when he ruled that the Nets possessed Kenon's rights. The Tams lost their draft pick and an opportunity to lure Tiger fans to the Coliseum. Finley was furious.

After losing Kenon to the Nets, the Tams turned to local basketball icon Larry Finch to bring more fans to the Coliseum. His image as a vehicle of racial healing in the city through basketball endeared him to Memphis State basketball fans and, in turn, led the Tams to sign Finch as a free-agent during their 1973 training camp.[53] The Tams' new head coach, Butch Van Breda Kolff, proclaimed the team's excitement for Finch: "Larry has a great deal of talent, and he is a winning player."[54] The *Commercial Appeal* lauded the signing by reminding fans of his success at Memphis State and Melrose High. With local schoolboy heroes Finch and Neumann on their roster for the upcoming season, the team looked to capitalize on its local talent to increase attendance.

Finch was not as well suited to professional basketball with the Tams as he had been to collegiate basketball at Memphis State. Van Breda Kolff's coaching style was a drastic change from Finch's college coach Gene Bartow. His aggressive approach on the sidelines directly conflicted with Finch's reserved demeanor that had flourished under the more restrained Bartow.[55] Finch showed glimpses of his potential as a professional player, but he never lived up to the standard he set during his collegiate career. In late November 1974, the Tams offered a promotional $1 ticket offer to any fan who showed their ticket stub from the World Football League's Memphis Grizzlies game played earlier that day at the Liberty Bowl Stadium. The Liberty Bowl is adjacent to the Coliseum, and the Tams brought in their second-largest crowd of the season with this promotion. Inspired by a crowd the size of those he had seen in the Coliseum during his collegiate playing days, Finch scored 22 points to lead the Tams past the Virginia Squires.[56] But games like these were anomalies in Finch's professional career, and the franchise continued to have poor showings at the turnstiles.

Professional basketball in the city struggled to stay financially solvent, yet professional wrestling drew 12,000 fans to the Coliseum every Monday night.[57] Wrestling (pronounced "wrassling" by most in the city), with its performative exhibitions that reveled in predetermined outcomes, elicited more fan support than the ABA. Scholar Sharon Mazor has claimed that wrestling's appeal lies in three basic premises: "First, the performance is directly catered to the fans and includes them as active participants in the carnival-like atmosphere. Next, the pleasure peculiar to wrestling is the nature in which it engages audiences in affirming and challenging cultural norms. Finally, the myth of wrestling represents an underlying social and moral ethos as a model of lower-class expressions of the desire for a non-ambiguous moral order where virtue does not always prevail."[58] The ABA was rugged and physical, but it did not cater directly to the needs of the fans. The league was challenging the cultural norms found in Memphis with a roster laden with black athletes. Unlike basketball, the chaotic nature of Monday night wrestling, its carnivalesque atmosphere, and the performed brutality gave white fans in Memphis an escape from the shifting racial paradigm outside of the Coliseum. Wrestling provided national exposure; Jimmy "The Mouth of the South" Hart, Austin "The Idol," Ric Flair, and Jerry "the King" Lawler all performed in Memphis regularly, giving the city a major league presence in the wrestling world.[59] Professional wrestling garnered national attention, drew more fans to the Coliseum, and defeated the ABA in ticket sales.

The Tams continued to lose. As the team spiraled downward, Finley let the organization fend for itself. Neumann was traded away in December of 1973 to the Utah Stars in return for Finch's college teammate Ronnie Robinson.[60] Although Finch and Robinson were reunited, the Tams continued to lose on the floor and at the box office. During the ABA's 1974 winter meetings, held during the All-Star break in Norfolk, Virginia, Finley failed to show.[61] Finley refused to appear at this meeting in a stand against the league because it had nullified the team's draft rights to Larry Kenon. His absence was a signal to the league that he intended to sell the club. Back in Memphis, Finley was shopping the team to Al Bell, owner of the locally owned black recording company Stax. Bell, in keeping with his commitment to local black political and economic initiatives, was interested in the club. [62] Shortly after the ABA's winter meetings, Stax vice president Larry Shaw announced the impending purchase of the team.[63] By the late spring of 1974, however, Stax Studios was under investigation for payola—the illegal practice of paying radio stations to play and promote recordings. Such investigations had crushed smaller recording studios. The FBI's investigation exposed Stax's financial books. Union Planters Bank, Stax's local lender, discovered that the company could not repay its more than $10 million debt.[64] Had Stax completed the deal to purchase the Tams from Finley, it would have become the first black-owned professional sports franchise in America outside of Negro leagues baseball.[65] After the Stax deal fell through, Finley cleaned house. He placed all of his professional sports franchises up for sale: the Tams, the A's, and the California Seals of the World Hockey Association.[66] The Tams' 21–64 record only added to the dismal atmosphere surrounding the franchise.[67]

In an unprecedented move, ABA commissioner Mike Storen resigned and purchased the team in June 1974.[68] Storen was a former Marine, a man with NBA front office experience, and someone who brought toughness and basketball acumen to Memphis. Those traits were desperately needed to rectify the city's franchise.[69] Before he became the ABA's commissioner, he had acted as president and general manager of the Indiana Pacers. His Pacers led the ABA in attendance and developed the league's most intense rivalry, with the Kentucky Colonels.[70] Storen was a breath of fresh air for the city and immediately endeared himself by renaming the franchise the Sounds. This moniker embodied the musical heritage of the city, from Elvis to Isaac Hayes.[71]

Storen immediately set out to include Isaac Hayes in his ownership group. At the height of his musical career, Hayes had just won a $5.3 million lawsuit with Stax over the rights to his music.[72] Although Hayes was committed to keeping the Sounds in Memphis, he found himself stretched thin between community outreach and his fast money lifestyle. Hayes had recorded the theme song to the blaxploitation film *Shaft*, and his lifestyle outside of the studio embodied its leading character, John Shaft. Hayes's payments became inconsistent, and one of his payments, of $100,000, was delivered to Storen in cash in a brown sack. Storen quickly returned the bag to Hayes and ended their partnership.[73] Storen felt that it was essential to include prominent black investors in his bid to stabilize the franchise, but not at the expense of doing business in this fashion

On the court, Storen sought to recreate the success he had achieved with the Indiana Pacers. He hired Jim Mullaney as head coach. Mullaney, a tough, blue-collar coach with experience at both the professional and collegiate levels, immediately gave the club credibility.[74] Storen also signed Mel Daniels, Freddie Lewis, and Roger Brown from the Pacers in an attempt to recreate the Pacer roster success in Memphis. Most thought that Storen had paid too much for these players as they were past their primes.[75] Storen then negotiated forty-two-weekend dates for home games at the Coliseum.[76] The city's political fathers joined the push to stabilize the franchise by allowing city employees to use payroll deduction to purchase season tickets.[77] Heading into the season, fans in Memphis once again had hope that their ABA team would prosper on the court.

Under Storen's leadership, the number of fans coming through the turnstiles did increase but not enough to financially sustain the club. Another sub-par performance by the team on the court, thirty games under .500, spelled the end for the ABA in the city. Sports columnists George Lapides chastised "the local wealth for not assuming more of a leadership role."[78] Since 1972, Lapides columns had helped to bridge the gap between the white and black communities in the city by highlighting how basketball could heal the city's racial scars. The *Press-Scimitar*, Lapides's newpaper, historically defended issues of social justice for the black community. Through this narrative, Lapides created an opportunity for basketball fans, politicians, and others to mend the city's racial wounds through sport. Now he was lamenting the city's lost opportunity to heal even further through professional basketball. The league offices issued a statement that, in essence, killed the Memphis franchise.[79]

While the city was reeling from the failure of the ABA, it also rejoiced that the World Football League had decided to play a second season in Memphis in the fall of 1975.[80] The Memphis Grizzlies pulled off one of the biggest coups in professional sports when they signed Larry Csonka, Jim Kick, and Paul Warfield. The Miami Dolphins' "Big 3" left the NFL to play for the Memphis Grizzlies in the WFL.[81] The white establishment in the city put its support behind the new professional football league. Memphis chose football over basketball at a time when the racial dynamics dictated that a safer mode of blackness was preferable. In another attempt to save the ABA, Avron Fogelman reached a verbal agreement with the Grizzlie's owner John Bassett to solidify the Sounds financially. Bassett hired Storen as executive vice-president for the Grizzlies to consolidate the two operations.[82] The ABA scoffed at this final attempt and announced on August 28, 1975, that the Memphis franchise was moving to Baltimore.[83]

George Lapides eulogized the team's five-year stay in the city, "Here Lies the Memphis Pros-Tams-Sounds. Born August 1970, Died August 1975. Victim of Poverty, Mismanagement, and Terrible Teams."[84] Lapides's eulogy was an apropos synopsis of the ABA's time in Memphis. As an attraction, the ABA had limited potential in the city during the 1970s for several reasons: the final Memphis Sounds roster was predominately black at a time when the city was still struggling with a shifting racial paradigm; ignited by court-ordered busing in the city's public schools, white flight was draining the city's tax base; the team never won enough games to be considered a contender; continually changing ownership created economic instability; the team brought the city's "great white hope" and the city's black mythical unifier together, yet neither brought enough fans to sustain the franchise; Avron Fogelman saved the franchise once but was unable in the end to save professional basketball in Memphis; white working-class Memphians embraced professional wrestling and professional football instead of the ABA; and despite Lapides's journalistic passion for Memphis basketball, he could not get the city's residents to engage with professional basketball the way they did with college basketball. Professional basketball left the city and did not return until the NBA's Vancouver Grizzlies relocated to Memphis in 2001. During the ABA's stay in the city, professional basketball exaggerated race. Although the city seemed to accept black collegiate players, they did not accept black professional players to the same degree. College basketball had a deep legacy in Memphis, while professional basketball did not. And Memphis college basketball had a history of supporting and recruiting players from the city's high schools. As a Memphis native and high school basketball star, Finch could unify the city's white and black college basketball fans. Most of the professional players did not have this connection with the city and so were not admired in the same way. The racial animus surrounding black players was exposed more vividly on the professional level. Memphis, a city in the Mid-South, was at odds with its own racial identity in the 1970s.

Champions Behind the Wall

The 1974–75 LeMoyne-Owen Magicians

The story of the 1975 LeMoyne-Owen national championship season provides a unique perspective into the myth that college basketball could heal racial tensions in Memphis. If basketball could heal Memphis the way the city's fathers proclaimed that it did, then why was the LeMoyne-Owen's championship season hidden behind the veil of segregation in the annals of the city's basketball history? This chapter seeks to shed light on the city's only men's collegiate basketball championship season. The accomplishments of Jerry Johnson, LeMoyne-Owen College's basketball coach, arguably belong in the same conversations as those of Gene Bartow, Dana Kirk, and Larry Finch. Johnson's coaching tree extends back to James Naismith and forward to Verties Sails, Larry Finch, and Afernee Hardaway, placing him among the city's and country's best basketball minds. LeMoyne-Owen Magicians' players Robert Newman and Clint Jackson, who were also homegrown Memphis talent, deserve the same recognition accorded Ronnie Robinson and Larry Finch. Alabama native Willie Parr led the 1975 Magicians as favorably as Alabama native Larry Kenon had led the 1973 Tigers; both played the kind of game coveted by professional teams. Herein lies the duality of race in the city's basketball history: Memphis State's 1973 team received the accolades and glory as they played for the city's predominately white university. On the other side of the tracks, however, LeMoyne-Owen's equally good, all-black 1975 team went unrecognized.

In the fifteen years leading up to the 1974–1975 season, Coach Jerry Johnson toiled in obscurity on the corner of Walker Avenue and Neptune Street as the head basketball coach of the small HBCU, LeMoyne-Owen College. Bruce

Hall, the home to the Magicians, was located directly across the street from the federally funded housing project LeMoyne Gardens. For most white Memphians, LeMoyne-Owen College was part of a separate community, one meant to stay hidden and silent behind the wall of segregation. Even as Larry Finch and Ronnie Robinson began a new relationship with the city, there remained a divide in the city that basketball could not bridge. While black basketball players at Memphis State faced unique challenges on MSU's predominately white campus, LeMoyne-Owen players faced another set of hardships. As integration moved forward, the role of HBCUs like LeMoyne-Owen was questioned by many in the white and black communities. These people believed that HBCUs would be outdated once white colleges were integrated.

Jim Crow laws kept black players from competing against white players in the South. Under these laws, black athletes in the South could only play collegiate sports at HBCUs, and they could only play against other black athletes. Unofficial gentlemen's agreements dating back to the beginning of the twentieth century kept black players on college teams in the North from playing against schools in the South.[1] Sports on historically black college campuses became a response to the prevailing notion of African American inferiority. Set against the backdrop of contrasting educational ideals, sports at HBCUs highlighted the vitality of student culture on black campuses. Collegiate athletics offered a limited means through which historically black schools could be assimilated, on their terms, into a national collegiate culture.[2] Sports at HBCUs were crucial for building a much-desired sense of institutional pride and national reputation. They engendered school spirit by bringing students, faculty, and alumni together to share in the thrill and excitement of shared pursuits.[3]

As a smaller HBCU, LeMoyne-Owen College (LOC) focused on the success of its basketball program to create this sense of pride. Before integration, many Southern-born African American athletes attended HBCUs that were close to their homes. HBCUs were as much a part of the community as were the families themselves. Student's family networks remained stable because their family members were close-by.[4] Post-World War II HBCUs like LeMoyne-Owen College created prosperous sporting congregations behind the veil of segregation. This network of athletes, administrators, coaches, sportswriters, and fans had a certain degree of autonomy and, by extension, power, according to historian Derrick White.[5] LeMoyne-Owen, like so many other HBCUs, was much more than an institution of higher learning; it was a source of pride for African Americans in Memphis. According to graduate Charles Diggs, "the hardworking families, poor, middle class, and a few upper-class supported the students at LeMoyne."[6] LeMoyne-Owen provided a separate space for the black community in Memphis. LeMoyne-Owen also brought the city of Memphis a collegiate men's basketball national championship, something that Memphis State failed to do.

When Coach Johnson decided to leave the all-black Southern Intercollegiate Athletic Conference to become the lone all-black school in the Volunteer State Athletic Conference (VSAC), he brought LeMoyne-Owen to the forefront of athletic integration in the South. LOC's inclusion in the VSAC provided hope for racial reconciliation throughout the region. Even as LeMoyne-Owen broke through previous barriers of racial discrimination, the team received limited media coverage outside of Memphis's black weekly newspaper, the *Tri-State Defender.* Despite the team's national success, the white political and social establishment in the city largely ignored them. Local sports reporter George Lapides referred to the 1975 Magicians' NCAA Division III title as the "coup de grace" for Memphis sports.[7] Lapides understood the importance of this team's victory to the historical narrative of basketball in the city. Unlike the white politicians who catered only to the whims of their white constituents and so ignored the accomplishments of this black college, Lapides offered an authentic understanding of LeMoyne-Owen's accomplishment. A sportswriter for the progressive *Press-Scimitar*, Lapides's opinions on LOC fell on deaf ears within the white community at large. Those deaf ears testify to how little value most white Memphians placed on black success at LeMoyne-Owen. Yet, to Memphis's black community, the 1975 NCAA Division III national title provided a moment of racial pride.

△ ▽ △

In 1968, LeMoyne College, founded by the American Missionary Association of Congregational Church in 1870, merged with Owen College. Owen College was a two-year college founded in 1954 by the Tennessee Baptist Missionary and Education Convention. The merger created LeMoyne-Owen College. By 1975 the school's population remained small, with approximately 900 students enrolled.[8] LeMoyne was known for its work educating the black community and held the honor of being the oldest continually running college in the city. As a symbol of stability and pride in the black community, LeMoyne held a special place within the hearts of Memphis's black community. In the years before Coach Johnson took over the basketball program, LeMoyne struggled to field competitive teams. When he arrived on campus in 1959, he changed the fortunes of the Magician basketball program.

As white universities in the South integrated in the late 1960s through the mid-1970s, they drew many black students away from the HBCUs. Athletic programs at southern universities did not stray very far from their state's mainstream social and racial norms. Even after African Americans won admission into undergraduate classrooms, a retreating color line still encircled the basketball court and preserved the whiteness of that particular space.[9] Vanderbilt University began to integrate the SEC when it signed Perry Wallace and Dillard Godfrey in 1966. Wallace was a member of the 1966 Nashville Pearl High basketball team that defeated Memphis's Treadwell High in the first integrated TSSAA State Championship game. By signing Wallace, Vanderbilt was, in effect, opening the door for coaches at other universities in the SEC and in the state of Tennessee to recruit players from predominately black high schools. Over the next five years, other SEC schools began to add one or two black players to their rosters. Many of the best black athletes were now signing with white universities because they had larger athletic budgets, better facilities, and more exposure, while HBCUs had limited budgets and facilities.

In an attempt to adapt to the changing social atmosphere, the conservative, black, middle-class board at LeMoyne-Owen College decided to leave the Southeastern Intercollegiate Athletic Conference in 1968. LeMoyne College had been a member of the SIAC since 1932. Founded in 1913, the SIAC was the second oldest HBCU athletic conference.[10] In the SIAC, LeMoyne College competed against many of the best black schools in the nation. As integration became part of the changing social structure in college athletics nationwide, Johnson decided to be proactive. The process began in 1964 when Al McGuire, who was coaching at Belmont Abbey College in North Carolina, contacted Johnson and suggested that LOC join the Volunteer State Athletic Conference. McGuire left Belmont Abbey in 1964 to take a job at Marquette University, but not before he had convinced Johnson to seek membership in the VSAC. LeMoyne's board of trustees was intrigued by the possibility of joining a league outside of the all-black SIAC, but only if Johnson could find other HBCUs to join the VSAC with LeMoyne College. As athletic director, Johnson contacted Fisk College, Knoxville College, and Lane College and convinced them to join LeMoyne in moving to the VSAC.[11]

Just as the VSAC was nearing an agreement to accept the four HBCUs into the conference, an incident on the campus of Knoxville College in March of 1968 dissuaded Lane, Fisk, and Knoxville College from moving forward. Arrested for allegedly transporting Molotov cocktails to campus, three black Knoxville College students became the focus of racial tensions in Knoxville. To protect the rights of the three students, the Knoxville College, President Dr. Robert L. Owens III, and the leader of the Student Social Action Committee, Curtis Johnson, went to the police precinct. While they were at the precinct, crowds gathered on campus in support of the students. According to Knoxville Police reports, A.J. Boruff, a white taxi driver for Checker Cab Company, drove onto campus in the early hours of the morning. Police alleged that a mob of black student protesters overturned Boruff's cab, and then one of the students shot him with a .22 caliber shotgun. Knoxville College students claimed that the group of students had chased Boruff off-campus, and so he must have been killed off-campus by someone else. Tennessee governor Buford Ellington offered a $5,000 reward for any information leading to the arrest of the perpetrator. The Knoxville chief of police believed that there was a conspiracy among the students at Knoxville College to conceal information concerning the murder.[12] The tension between Knoxville College's student body and the city's white establishment illustrates the impact of the Black Power Movement on HBCU campuses, and its burgeoning impact on civil rights nationally. After this incident, Knoxville College's moderate administration decided that it was in the school's best interest to remain in an all-black conference and not join the VSAC. Once Knoxville College decided not to join the VSAC, Lane College and Fisk College also removed their requests to join.[13] LeMoyne-Owen, as it now was called, was on its own and became the lone HBCU member of the VSAC in the fall of 1968. By the 1970s, historically black colleges were gaining admission into integrated leagues in both the National Association of Intercollegiate Athletics (NAIA) and the NCAA. LeMoyne-Owen's membership in the VSAC was an example of both the progressive possibilities and the controversial impact of college sports on race relations in the South.

After Dr. King's 1968 assassination, many people and groups involved in the struggle for black freedom shifted their approach. Rather than trying to appeal to the moral consciousness of white Americans, they instead focused on developing the moral, cultural, and political consciousness of African Americans in order to create a sense of black unity, power, and agency.[14] While the earlier approach had focused on off-campus resistance and activism, proponents of this late 1960s movement carved a unique space on college campuses.[15] On November 25, 1968, a handful of LeMoyne-Owen students, along with local Black Power movement leaders, occupied Brownlee Hall.[16] These students, in keeping with the goals of the Black Power movement, were protesting the closed-mindedness of their professors, the Euro-centric bias that remained in their classes, and the lack of scientific evidence to support these biases. This type of thinking by academics, politicians, and benefactors made whiteness—white ideas, people, and scholarship—the standard for society.[17] A handwritten manifesto by an unnamed senior entitled "Force and Power" circulated on campus. The manifesto outlined the students' demands, which included creation of a black studies curriculum, use of a student lounge, publication of the President's qualifications, lower tuition, and improved dormitory facilities for athletes. The twenty-hour take-over of Brownlee Hall ended when the administration agreed to their demands, except for lower tuition, and the students released control of the building.[18] The Black Power movement forced schools like LeMoyne-Owen to look introspectively at their mission and to move away from an approach that could be called education for the Negro to education for black students.

In contrast to the tensions found in many classrooms at HBCUs, sports programs at schools like LeMoyne-Owen escaped elevated racial tensions because of their monolithic racial construction. The turmoil found in the athletic departments of predominately white universities in the late 1960s and 1970s was absent from the athletic departments of historically black colleges and universities. Although students at HBCUs protested the curriculum and the academic administration, athletes at HBCUs did not protest or try to change the sports departments. Three distinct social structures that prevented dissension guided black athletes at schools like LeMoyne-Owen, according to sociologist Harry Edwards. Firstly, black athletes at HBCUs found new social contacts when groups of black students made demands on them that were not consistent with their role as athletes. Next, black athletes at HBCUs could not be true to the essential values of the black student movement if they treated the black coach as a scapegoat and charged the coach with discrimination. Finally, attacking black coaches at HBCUs was out of the question because it was inconsistent with the Black Power movement's demand for more black coaches in organized sport.[19] LeMoyne-Owen's players lived on a campus that embraced their culture. While their Memphis State counterparts, many of whom were from the same Memphis neighborhoods, faced a different set of racial challenges.

As college basketball grew nationally, black athletes in the Jim Crow South had to attend predominately black colleges in order to play. These black colleges played in segregated leagues; they did not compete against predominately white schools. Black college basketball and black players, therefore, were hidden behind the wall of segregation. Black coaches at these schools were also obscure. In the South, as schools began to integrate in the mid-1960s, black players who had once opted for HBCUs began signing with predominately white universities that offered better facilities and more exposure. As racial barriers eroded and white colleges recognized how much black talent they had ignored, they cherry-picked black players until nearly all of the most talented black players were playing for predominately white colleges.[20] Desegregation of schools in the South in the late 1960s and early 1970s took jobs away from black high school coaches. Newly integrated high schools hired white coaches. These coaches had no connection to HBCUs and were less likely to encourage their black players to attend an HBCU, weakening the ties between black athletes and HBCUs. Previously, black head coaches at segregated schools, who were usually graduates of HBCUs, had maintained a powerful connection to the HBCU sporting congregation.[21] When predominately white institutions, with the help of prominent black voices in the community, began to recruit black athletes, the pool of black talent in Memphis, from which LeMoyne-Owen or other HBCUs had historically recruited players, eroded.

▲ ▽ ▲

Jerry Johnson's youth was emblematic of early twentieth-century black life in the Southwest. Johnson's father's family was part of the post-emancipation migration of black families to East Texas. His father took a job repairing asbestos bricks in an oil refinery after that same oil company forced his family to sell their oil-rich land. His father passed away while Johnson was still in high school.[22] His mother raised the family in Tulsa, Oklahoma, and sent Jerry to Booker T. Washington High, where he became an all-state football player. Tragedy struck Johnson again when his mother passed away during his senior year. He enrolled at Wiley College to play football after graduation to be closer to his father's family in Longview, Texas.[23] Wiley College introduced football to black colleges in the region and was a leader in forming the Southwestern Athletic Conference, although their debate team was even more successful.[24] Johnson earned All-American status twice in the *Pittsburgh Courier* for his accomplishments on the gridiron at Wiley. When his battering mate at fullback on the Wiley team decided to transfer to Fayetteville State Teacher's College in North Carolina, Johnson joined him.[25]

Johnson's time at Fayetteville State was a significant turning point in his life. He started at running back on the 1939 football team, which finished at 8–1.[26] He also joined the basketball team, where the Broncos competed in the Colored Intercollegiate Athletic Association against John B. McLendon's North Carolina Central teams. McLendon's fast-break style and pressure defense revolutionized college basketball during the 1940s. As a member of the Broncos, Johnson experienced the up-tempo brand of basketball that McLendon taught at North Carolina Central. North Carolina Central's opponents were usually worn out physically by the fast pace of their games. In many games, referees were forced to stop the game because the players were exhausted.[27] Playing against McLendon's teams convinced Johnson that coaching basketball was the path for him.

Following his two years at Fayetteville State, Johnson accepted a position as the head coach for football, boys basketball, and girls basketball at Longview High in Hickory, North Carolina. Over his eighteen-year tenure at Longview, his boys' basketball teams won five state championships and his football team won one state championship. McLendon recruited many of Johnson's players and mentored Johnson as a coach. McLendon imparted various elements of his fast-break style and pressure defense to Johnson. When McLendon took the head coaching position at Tennessee A&I (now Tennessee State University) in 1954, Johnson tried to join McLendon's staff in Nashville. He was unsuccessful. In 1959, however, McLendon suggested that Johnson accept the men's basketball position at a small HBCU in Memphis, LeMoyne College. McLendon made a phone call on Johnson's behalf, which helped him land the job. McLendon gave Johnson an important recruiting lesson: "be careful not to recruit too many boys from the same town. Get good kids from as many places as possible."[28] One of the keys to Johnson's success was his ability to mold teams together with this advice. This contradicted a common belief in Memphis that a coach can create a championship team by recruiting only from within the city's limits.

Johnson applied the lessons he learned while playing and coaching in the Jim Crow South to build the program at LeMoyne-Owen. He continued to sign players from various cities and did his best not to sign too many players from the same high school. One of the keys to his success was his recruitment of players through local community and recreational centers. Major white colleges relied solely upon high schools to locate their players. Black coaches learned that the best players congregated and competed at community centers. With limited budgets, black coaches spent their own money on recruiting trips. By learning who the directors were at the recreation centers in each city, they were able to see the best players in town without having to visit every high school. Johnson's 1975 championship season proved the success of these methods.

The NAIA's VSAC, created in the 1940s, was a prominent fixture in college basketball in Tennessee through the 1980s.[29] The VSAC opened its doors to LeMoyne-Owen in 1968. The conference had begun to integrate in 1954 when the NAIA invited Tennessee A&I to participate in its pre-season tipoff classic in Kansas City.[30] By the beginning of the 1974–1975 season, the other members of the conference all had at least one black player on their rosters. After six years in the VSAC, LeMoyne-Owen still faced racially charged crowds who were less than welcoming to the Magicians. Forward Milton Stephens described going into some of the gyms in the VSAC: "There were a couple of black [people] (on the other team), and the rest were white boys. Some of the places you could feel the tension and hear the things being said in the stands. It was racial."[31] As black players playing on an all-black team in the VSAC, Stephens and his teammates understood that the racial tension in opposing gyms was symbolic of the times. The obstacles they faced were not only on the court but also in the stands.

The Magicians opened the 1974–75 season as the defending regular and post-season VSAC champions. In the 1974 NAIA District 24 semifinals, the Magicians defeated Cumberland University by eight before falling to Kentucky State 75–65 in the district finals.[32] Falling one game short of the NAIA national tournament left a bitter taste in the teams' mouths. Kentucky State's enrollment was much larger than LeMoyne-Owen's, and the university was a national power in the early 1970s, winning NAIA national tournaments in 1970, 1971, 1972, and 1973.[33] Johnson was intrigued when the NCAA introduced a small school tournament in 1975, the NCAA Division III Tournament. This new tournament meant that LeMoyne-Owen would not have to play Kentucky State in order to compete for a national championship.

A trio of players led the 1974–1975 LeMoyne-Owen Magicians. The *Tri-State Defender* labeled them the "Three Man Wrecking Crew."[34] Robert Newman, 6'1", and Clint Jackson, 6'4", were both highly touted local recruits from Hamilton High. As local Memphis kids, they had hoped to follow in the footsteps of Finch and Robinson and sign with Memphis State.[35] Both played in many pickup games at the Elma Roane Fieldhouse on Memphis State's campus before their senior year. They were surprised when Coach Gene Bartow did not offer either a scholarship out of high school.[36] Word leaked out that Bartow did not think that Memphis had any significant prospects in its 1972 class. After this public sign of disrespect, Hamilton Coach Lloyd Wright vowed never to send a Hamilton High graduate to Memphis State.[37] The black community remained leery of Finch's signing, and after Bartow's statement that the city lacked talent alienated its black coaches. Overlooked by Memphis State, Newman and Jackson signed with John B. McLendon's Tennessee State program. Both saw limited playing time during their freshman year at TSU and decided to return home to LeMoyne-Owen.

Completing the "Three Man Wrecking Crew" was 6'7" Willie Parr from Tuscaloosa, Alabama. Parr possessed a rare combination of skills and athleticism, and his ability to handle the ball like a guard complemented his shooting ability from inside and out.[38] Parr's roommate, point guard Jerry McNeal, claimed that Parr, "as a 6'7" southpaw, could step out and make shots from the deep corner that looked as if he was shooting over the backboard."[39] Parr was an accomplished player and had received multiple offers to play college basketball. As an all-state player at Druid High he averaged over 35 points a game.[40] After his senior year at Druid, Parr remained in Tuscaloosa because he was not academically qualified for any of the schools that recruited him. During the winter of 1972, when LeMoyne-Owen traveled to Stillman College for a game, Coach Martin of Druid High sought out Coach Johnson and suggested Parr to him. Johnson offered Parr the opportunity to visit Memphis the following summer. Once Parr arrived in Memphis, he never went back to Tuscaloosa. Parr remembers that Johnson placed him in a house just off campus, called the "Big House," where he roomed with the rest of the out of town players. Parr found a father figure in Johnson. He took care of Parr and made playing basketball fun.[41]

Jerry McNeal from Decatur, Georgia, joined Willie Parr in the "Big House." McNeal grew up in the Decatur Housing Authority projects in a community just northeast of Atlanta. The Decatur Housing Authority projects, part of the black Beacon Hill community, fed into all-black Trinity High.[42] In 1968, during McNeal's junior year, the Decatur schools integrated by closing Trinity High and sending all its students to Decatur High. McNeal described those first few years of integration as tense: "We didn't go through as much as other schools around the country, but you could feel the tension."[43] Although many of the black players felt isolated in their new surroundings, they found friends through basketball as they won the school's first regional championship in basketball.[44] The following year, basketball was once again bringing a community together. The team won Coach Bob Reinhart's first of three state basketball championships at the school.[45] McNeal credits his years at Decatur High, during the early years of integration in Georgia, with preparing him for what he would face at LeMoyne-Owen in the VSAC. McNeal began his college career at Tyler Community College in Texas. After a successful freshman campaign at Tyler, however, the coach informed McNeal and his black teammates that Tyler's experiment in integration was over. They would not be offered scholarships for the following season. McNeal's older brother, Bob Welch, worked in the business office at LeMoyne-Owen and convinced Johnson to bring McNeal to Memphis.[46] Johnson told McNeal that if things did not work out at Tyler, he was welcome to come to LeMoyne-Owen.[47] McNeal valued the commitment Johnson made to him as a player. Johnson's own story of perseverance allowed him to understand the journey each of his players had to make to reach LeMoyne-Owen.

Milton Stephens, from Cleveland, Ohio, rounded out Johnson's starting five and was another resident of the "Big House." Stephens grew up on the east side of Cleveland, which had been transformed by the Second Great Migration into a predominately black neighborhood. By the late 1960s, his high school, East High, was predominately black.[48] The Bombers only played other black schools in Cleveland during the regular season. They did not see any integrated or all-white teams until the regional level of the state playoffs.[49] After a two-year stint at Cuyahoga Community College Tri-Cities, Stephens's college coach, David Green, contacted Coach Johnson to tell him about Stephens. On his recruiting visit to Memphis, Stephens met Jerry Dover, Willie Parr, and Robert Newman and knew right away that he had found a home. When Stephens met Parr, who was about an inch taller than him, he remembers thinking, "he was pretty good and I want to play with him. With me, Newman and Dover, I knew we'd have a pretty good team."[50] Stephens received other offers from predominately white schools in Ohio, but claimed, "I was more comfortable at LeMoyne-Owen."[51] He felt more comfortable at an HBCU like LOC because of his experience in segregated Cleveland. Stephens faced racial tension during his prep school days. He looked to Coach Johnson and LOC to provide a sense of comfort and insulation from racial tensions he would have found at a predominately white school.

In an early-season matchup with crosstown VSAC rival Christian Brothers

College (CBC), the Magicians confronted the prototypical white collegiate team. CBC employed a methodical offense that screened continually and employed numerous back door cuts. CBC's style exemplified typical collegiate basketball in white America. Former UCLA star Kareem Abdul Jabbar described the clash in cultural styles taking place in American basketball at this time: "White college basketball was patterned and regimented like the lives awaiting its players. The black schoolyard game demanded the flash, guile, and individual reckless brilliance each man would need in the world facing him."[52] The black aesthetic began to permeate collegiate basketball after two national events: the 1963 NCAA Finals, in which Loyola University started four black players, and the 1966 NCAA Finals, in which Texas Southwestern started five black players.[53] The NAIA had already started to accept the black aesthetic after McLendon began coaching Tennessee A&I in 1954. Johnson considered himself part of McLendon's coaching tree and employed McLendon's up-tempo style of play, familiar in HBCUs throughout the South. LeMoyne-Owen's 54–52 defeat of CBC confirmed that basketball as played by all-black schools merited the same level of respect as the white, regimented-classroom style of play. Their success against CBC also foreshadowed the success LOC found later in the NCAA Division III tournament against teams who played a style similar to CBC's.

Although the move to the VSAC was a progressive step forward, Johnson continued to schedule games against other predominately black schools. Before the NCAA introduced Division II to lure HBCUs away from the NAIA, schools like LeMoyne-Owen played challenging schedules against the best all-black schools in the South. Although the future of college basketball was moving toward complete integration nationally, LOC's schedule still echoed the segregated past. Johnson scheduled former SIAC foes Tuskegee University, Florida A&M, Xavier University of New Orleans, and smaller HBCUs like Lane College and Dillard University. Guard Clint Jackson earned his nickname "Radar" in a game against Tuskegee. After his 20-point second-half performance against Tuskegee, Coach Johnson told Jackson, "you don't even look at the goal and the ball goes in."[54] Jackson looked back at his teammates on the bench, known as the "Wrecking Crew," and told them, "I won't be back."[55] The nicknames and the flare of the basketball played at HBCUs remained a part of LOC's program even as the team moved into the VSAC. However, playing in small gyms on the campuses of HBCUs often created problems. During a game in New Orleans against Dillard University, the Magicians fell victim to foul play. While they were shooting around, someone went into the locker room and made off with most of its contents; the team lost most of their clothes.[56] As college basketball began to integrate, HBCUs began competing against larger, historically white colleges who played in modern facilities. HBCUs such as LeMoyne-Owen and Dillard University played in much smaller venues. Their athletic budgets limited not only the size of their facilities but also the security of their locker rooms before and during games.

Although road trips further exposed the financial limitations that restricted small HBCUs, they also created a sense of family. When the team went on the road, Coach Johnson allowed Jerry McNeal to drive his Cadillac Eldorado. The rest of the team would fit into two Mercury station wagons that followed behind.[57] As Milton Stephens remembers, these road trips gave the teammates the opportunity to bond. Five guys, all over six feet tall, packed into one of two station wagons, singing to songs of the times that were recorded around the corner from Bruce Hall at Stax Studios on McLemore Avenue. Whether it was David Porter, Isaac Hayes, or Otis Redding, the soulful sounds of Stax's music provided the background for laughter and conversations that built life-long friendships.[58] These trips brought the players closer together as they maneuvered through the remnants of the Jim Crow South. The student body at LeMoyne-Owen often drove the ninety miles to Jackson, Tennessee, to see the team play Union or Lambuth. They, too, packed into cars to support the team on the road.[59]

Over winter break, Coach Johnson took the team north to test their mettle against larger HBCUs in the Chicago Classic. The Chicago Classic at Kennedy-King College sheds light on the potential of HBCU basketball during this era, but also reveals the difficulties that black players faced in this time of increased integration in college basketball. In December of 1973, LeMoyne-Owen won national attention when it upset highly-touted Morgan State University in the opening round of the Chicago Classic. To do this, LeMoyne-Owen's players had to overcome Morgan State's seven-foot-tall Marvin "The Human Eraser" Webster. Webster was the MEAC's two-time player of the year and the third overall pick in the 1975 NBA draft.[60] The Morgan State Bears reflected the strength of HBCUs during this period. As an HBCU and member of the NCAA's Division II, Morgan State's 1973–1974 team won the Division II national championship. Although relegated to Division II because they were an HBCU, they continued to produce players with NBA talent.[61] After the Magicians' second-round victory over former SIAC foe Xavier, the *Chicago Tribune* labeled LOC the Cinderella of the tournament.[62] In the finals, the glass slipper fell off when the Magicians lost to MEAC power Maryland Eastern Shore, which played three future NBA draft picks.[63]

While the 1973 Chicago Classic demonstrates the strength of HBCU basketball, the following year's tournament reveals the weaknesses. The 1974 Chicago Classic could not cover the teams' travel expenses. Only three teams arrived in Chicago to play, and the hotel the tournament provided was worse than the Chicago weather. Nicknamed the "Surprise Hotel" by some of the Magicians, hotel room doors all faced the street and did not lock.[64] Robert Newman told his teammates, "I don't think UCLA travels like this."[65] In their first and only game, at the tournament the Magicians defeated Shaw College. Mississippi Valley State refused to play because it had not gotten the money it was guaranteed, and they returned home. As a school with a minuscule budget, the need to be paid outweighed the benefits of national exposure. The 1974 Chicago Classic exposes the financial struggles faced by black college basketball programs in this era. Historically white colleges and universities had begun to drain more black players from predominately black leagues, further limiting revenue these programs could generate. Predominately white institutions, with their larger athletic budgets, enticed black athletes to attend their colleges. They argued that at their schools, black athletes would receive more national attention and increase the likelihood of having a professional career. While predominately white institutions (PWIs) profited from the labor of black athletes, HBCUs lost out financially as their talent level diminished. Tournaments, like the Chicago Classic, were no longer financially feasible. For HBCUs that depended on these large tournaments to supplement their traveling budgets, this was another financial loss.

Nestled in the northeast corner of campus, on the corner of Walker Avenue and Neptune Street sits Bruce Hall, the intimidating center of athletics for LeMoyne-Owen. Upon their arrival at Walker Avenue, many VSAC teams felt trepidation. LeMoyne-Owen had a considerable home-court advantage in this arena. The bleachers are seven rows high and sit below a series of twelve-foot windows that run the length of the gymnasium. The student body of LeMoyne-Owen and the community from the LeMoyne-Gardens housing projects regularly filled these bleachers from top to bottom as well as the bleachers on the stage in the 1970s. Fans stomped on the benches and created an intense environment that elicited fear in opponents. Some white players on VSAC teams refused to make the trip to Memphis to play at Bruce Hall.[66] LeMoyne-Owen players fed off the energy from the fans during home games. When describing this atmosphere, former LOC student Stevenson Bratcher said, "Ain't nothing like it. A packed gym was a pivotal part of LeMoyne-Owen's homecourt advantage. Most of the kids were inner-city kids, and each sport supported the others because everybody knew everybody."[67] Point guard Jerry McNeal recalls, "Bruce Hall was standing room only, especially my senior year [1974–1975], and that really gave me some motivation. The fans had us so pumped up."[68] Milton Stephens echoed McNeal's sentiment, "the stands were full, and the fans filled up the stage. There was a lot of excitement."[69] Robert Newman remembers, "the excitement of playing at home. We felt obligated not to lose."[70] The Magicians held up their end of the bargain—they lost only one home game during the 1974–1975 season.

Bruce Hall served as the home-court for basketball games, but it also was a multi-purpose facility that met other needs for the school. Locker rooms, classrooms, and athletic department offices are on the level below the gym floor. At the west end of the gym is a stage, giving the small school an auditorium. The cozy confines of Bruce Hall reflect LeMoyne-Owen's status as a small school with a limited budget. During the 1974–75 season, most home games surpassed Bruce Hall's 2,000-seat capacity, and these fans created an ideal atmosphere for winning.[71]

LeMoyne-Owen remained a safe space for black college students in the city, even as Memphis State desegregated. Although the city's athletics teams began to play each other across racial lines, the neighborhoods remained segregated. As the historically black college in Memphis, the student body at LOC was made up primarily of students from the city's black high schools. Rivals during their high school years at Melrose, Hamilton, Manassas, Carver, Northside, Douglass, or BTW, students now came together as one at LeMoyne-Owen. It was a community that thrived inside a divided city and nourished the social, economic, and academic needs of the black students entrusted to its care. Classes were smaller, which allowed students to develop personal relationships not only with each other but also with their professors. Before and after classes, students would meet at the Four Way Grill on Walker Avenue and Mississippi Boulevard for soul food.[72] One of Boss Crump's chauffeurs opened the Four Way Grill in 1946, and the restaurant has been an institution in the LeMoyne-Owen neighborhood ever since.[73] Jerry McNeal remembered the Four Way fondly, "they put their feeling in the food. It was good. It tastes like my mom's, cookin'."[74] Stephens echoed McNeal's sentiments, "they had some good soul food."[75] Attending Memphis State meant leaving the security and comfort of the black community to break ground in a world foreign to most black students from Memphis in the 1970s. LeMoyne-Owen, on the other hand, was part of the black community. HBCUs like LeMOyne-Owen crafted an active, communal congregation for their students and alumni. Nevertheless, these schools played into segregation, a system designed by white people to minimize black people.[76] Many black students in Memphis chose to attend LeMoyne-Owen rather than enroll in larger schools like Memphis State where they might get lost in the shuffle.

In the late 1960s, the NAIA maintained its grip on HBCUs despite the NCAA's creation of Division II. The NCAA and the NAIA were in a war for control of college athletics, and basketball was a major pawn in the chess match between the two associations. The NCAA offered the Magicians the opportunity to play in its inaugural Division III tournament in an attempt to lure another HBCU away from the NAIA. LeMoyne-Owen would not have to rescind their membership in the VSAC or the NAIA. It would only have to announce by mid-January if it would accept the NCAA's offer to compete in its tournament.

By the 1970s, determining a consensus college basketball champion remained as challenging as it had been before World War II. Before World War II, the National Intercollegiate Championship in Kansas City and the National Invitational Tournament in New York City were the most promising competitions from which to chose an overall champion. Emil Liston and the National Association of Intercollegiate Basketball (NAIB) organized the National Intercollegiate tournament in 1937. As a regional tournament, this competition opened the door to smaller schools. In New York City, promoter Ned Irish worked in conjunction with the Metropolitan Basketball Writers' Association in 1938 to create the National Invitational Tournament (NIT) at the Madison Square Garden. That same year, Harold Olsen helped the NCAA create their own version of a collegiate basketball national championship, which he designed to rival the NIT.[77] In 1942, *New York Times* sports editor John Kieran described the divide between the NIT and the NCAA championships as "class warfare."[78] During World War II, the country adjusted to the changing nature of collegiate sports. The NCAA moved its Eastern Regional and tournament finals to the Madison Square Garden to increase ticket sales, revenue, and tournament payouts in an effort to challenge the NIT. Once the war was over, and the NCAA had established itself on equal footing financially with the NIT, the NCAA began rotating the location of their national championship.[79]

Having raised the NCAA's prestige to equal that of the NIT, the organization set out to selfishly dominate all of college basketball. The NCAA wanted complete control of college basketball. They viewed the NIT's organizers as exploitative businessmen from New York City, and the NAIB as a small-scale operation that would not be able to accommodate the growing game.[80] The National Collegiate Basketball Association held its championship tournament in Cincinnati in 1941, which pitted the best African American college teams against each other. Racial animus against the tournament forced the players to sleep overnight in gymnasiums and eat wherever their limited budgets allowed because they feared that the white residents of the city would react violently if they ventured into the city at large. Additionally, the tournament lost money because few people bought tickets. Thus, the tournament was unable to create a second annual tournament the following year. This left black collegiate basketball without a tournament. Before 1948, the NIT in New York City—a tournament with slightly more progressive racial views—was the only tournament, of the three major tournaments, that allowed black players to participate in its championship. The NAIB, as the smallest of the three tournaments, lifted its racial ban that year in order to keep John Wooden's Indiana State team from spurning the NAIB in favor of the NIT.[81] The race to dominate college basketball and college sports, in general, required leagues to increase their number of member schools. By 1952, the NCAA's membership included over 380 schools, and it attempted to wrestle control over college athletics. That same year, however, the number of NAIB member schools grew to over 400, and they incorporated track, golf, and tennis into their association.[82] The NAIB rebranded itself as the NAIA, and the war for control of college athletics continued in earnest for the next twenty years.

The NCAA understood that schools like LeMoyne-Owen were at a disadvantage compared to larger schools like Kentucky State, which had larger student populations and athletic budgets. Kentucky State's resources gave them a huge advantage over LeMoyne-Owen in NAIA District 26. When the NCAA asked Coach Johnson to compete in its new Division III tournament, it was a unique opportunity for LeMoyne-Owen to compete against teams with resources similar to their own. Johnson had already decided to compete in the tournament, but he allowed the players to vote on the decision. The team listened to the persuasive argument Coach Johnson made for the new tournament.[83] LeMoyne-Owen was now directly in the middle of the chess match between the NCAA and the NAIA. Its decision to join the NCAA Division III tournament became one more victory for the NCAA in its march to dominate March Madness. The

NCAA rewarded the Magicians by making them the host site for the South Region in its inaugural Division III basketball tournament.[84]

The Magicians entered the VSAC tournament as regular-season champs and were committed to playing in the NCAA Division III tournament. The VSAC tournament was at Carson-Newman University in Jefferson City—where the Magicians had previously been chased out of town by the KKK. During the game with Carson-Newman earlier in the year, one of the Carson-Newman players shouted a racial slur at one of the Magicians, and a scuffle broke out between the teams. After LeMoyne-Owen won the game, they had to be escorted off campus through the cafeteria for their own safety. When the team returned to their hotel, Coach Johnson discovered imminent danger from the local klavern. A rumor surfaced among the players that the klan was burning a cross outside of town. Johnson gathered the team and immediately began the return trip to Memphis.[85] Jerry McNeal claimed, "It didn't phase me. It motivated me."[86] When the team returned in late February, they put aside those memories and were able to capture the 1975 VSAC tournament.[87] Faced with the unknown, the team prepared for the NCAA Division III tournament. The Magicians were awarded the highest seed in the South Regional and would host the first two rounds in this thirty team, eight regions bracket.

As the NCAA Division III tournament opened in Memphis, the Magicians had to jump through another hoop: because of his small coaching staff and limited budget, Coach Johnson was unable to scout any of the three opponents the NCAA would send to Memphis for the opening rounds. LeMoyne-Owen opened with Transylvania University from Lexington, Kentucky, in the first round. The Pioneers of Kentucky arrived at Bruce Hall with a 19–6 record and riding a seven-game win streak.[88] The *Press-Scimitar* provided the only preview of Transylvania University, and that was only a list of the team stats that it had received from the wire service. Just as Coach Johnson had done when he steered his team through the King College Classic in Chicago, he focused solely on what he could control: his team. The Magicians' aggressive man-to-man defensive pressure allowed them to pull away in the second half.[89] One of the keys to their victory was the strong defensive play of guard Robert Newman. The Magicians' defense, keyed by Newman's quick hands, turned steals into fast-break points. Newman described his thought process behind his steals: "Between his hand and the floor, the ball handler has no control. And, from the floor to his hand, he has no control. That's a lot of space for me."[90] Newman's ball stealing skills led to easy baskets for the Magicians throughout the season and their tournament run. After Transylvania University, the Magicians defeated Miles College in the South Regional Finals with that same defensive mentality.

Johnson's ability to recruit players from other universities and successfully integrate them into his existing team was one of the keys to his success. Newman and Jackson transferred to LeMoyne-Owen from Tennessee A&I. Six-foot-four shooting guard Terry Gray, a Memphis-Manassas High graduate, joined the Magicians after one season at Texas Southern University. Gray's performance against Miles helped catapult LOC past Miles College. Assistant Coach Powell praised Gray in his postgame interview, saying: "We teach our kids here to play as a team, and the job Gray did proves we have a strong bench."[91] Johnson never sugarcoated his assessment of players who transferred into the program. Many of the transfers were forced to sit out a year, not because of NCAA or NAIA rules, but because Johnson felt they were not yet ready to play for him. He challenged his transfers to become better. These clear appraisals not only offered a second chance but also reinvigorated the drive and passion that so many of these young men had lost. Transfers knew that he gave them the attention they needed as individuals and that he cared more about them as young men than as basketball players.[92]

As the Magicians continued their path through the NCAA Division III tournament, the city of Memphis began to take notice. Before the game against Wittenberg University, Mayor Wyeth Chandler gave Robert Newman and Wille Parr "keys to the city."[93] Unlike the fanfare at the airport that the Memphis State Tigers had received when they returned home after their Elite 8 victory over Kansas State in Houston, the Magicians were given their honors in a quiet ceremony on the LeMoyne-Owen campus. No one claimed that the LeMoyne-Owen team brought the city together. White Memphis remained in the dark about the success of the Magicians. Chandler merely completed his civic duty by offering two of the Magicians a token of the city's appreciation. LOC's status as a small college relegated any news surrounding the program to the back pages of the local media.

As the Magicians continued to advance through the tournament, the *Commercial Appeal* and the *Press-Scimitar* increased their coverage of the team. Over 2,000 fans crowded into Bruce Hall to watch the Wittenberg Tigers and Magicians do battle. Coach Johnson and the Magicians were caught by surprise as Wittenberg led 36–35 at the half.[94] The Magicians regained control of the game for good when Willie Parr scored twenty-one points, a team-high.[95] After their victory over Wittenberg, the Magicians set their sights on the Final Four in Reading, Pennsylvania.

When the Magicians arrived in Reading for the inaugural NCAA Division III Final Four, they were the only HBCU school in attendance. Like McLendon's teams in the 1950s, LeMoyne-Owen was blazing a trail for other black schools to follow, but there was a price to pay. LeMoyne-Owen's hectic, up-tempo style of play was still considered "blackball." White basketball traditionalists downgraded Johnson's merit as a coach and as a strategist because he did not coach a more traditional style of play. Twenty years earlier, Crispus Attucks High in Indiana won its first state championship when Oscar Robertson's all-black team defeated Dick Barnett's all-black team from Roosevelt High. Both of these coaches were black men. That Indiana championship game undermined the myth that black players needed the guidance of the white man to accomplish anything significant.[96] But, according to the white establishment, black head coaches were still inherently less capable than white coaches because they coached "blackball." College basketball was evolving, but these prevailing stereotypes followed the Magicians north as they prepared to compete for their first national championship.

On a cold March night in Reading, Pennsylvania, 1,500 brave fans weathered the icy roads to pack the George C. Bollman Physical Education Building on the campus of Albright College. LOC opened the Final Four against Augustana College from Rockford, Illinois. Some of the players recalled hearing boos from the stands before the opening tip, and they assumed it was because they were the only all-black team.[97] Having been the lone HBCU in the VSAC, the Magicians were used to racial animosity from the stands. Clint Jackson claimed that "with our experience playing CBC, Bethel, and Belmont, in the VSAC, we were ready for the other teams in the field."[98] According to Robert Newman, not only did playing those schools prepare LOC defensively but "it also taught [them] not to take quick 25-foot jump shots on offense."[99] When the game began, LOC went on a ten-point run in the first half, using their speed and outside shooting ability to gain control of the game. They never looked back. Augustana Vikings head coach Jim Borcherding commended the Magician players for their play in the semifinals: "Simply unbelievable shooters. It deflates the confidence of a defensive player to be all over a shooter from 25 feet from the basket and still have him make it."[100] Newman led all scorers in the game with 32 points. Coach Johnson praised his team's efforts in their semifinal victory.[101] The Magicians were confident. Robert Newman proclaimed, "It's in the bag." Clint Jackson said, "I can smell it." Willie Parr told the world, "We're going after it."[102] The eyes of Memphis were on the Magicians as the *Commercial Appeal* and *Press-Scimitar* reported their victory in the semifinal game and their quest for a national championship.

Although the team had heard boos from the stands on their first night, the fans greeted the Magicians with cheers during player introductions in the championship game the next day. Their play the night before had earned the respect of the crowd at Albright College.[103] LeMoyne-Owen played Glassboro State College in this second game. The Glassboro State Profs had won sixteen of their last twenty games without being challenged on their way to the Finals.[104] Early in the first half, Greg Ackles, the Profs' shooting guard, made a series of short jumpers that pushed Glassboro State out to an early 23–16 advantage.[105] As the first half was winding down, the Magicians caught a break from the officials. The referee whistled Profs guard Denny Flaherty for a foul, but when the referee reported the foul to the table it was mistakenly assessed to Profs leading scorer Greg Ackles. With four minutes remaining in the half, Ackles sat out to avoid picking up his fourth foul. LeMoyne-Owen countered with a 10–4 run to claim a 30–27 halftime lead. According to John Smith, who was on press row, the official scorekeeper gave Ackles the foul in error. However, both the press and the official NCAA statistician had Ackles with two fouls. The officials refused to talk to the press or the NCAA statistician. The error at the score table gave the Magicians a lead, and they refused to relinquish it for the rest of the game. LeMoyne-Owen never led by more than seven points in the second half, and Glassboro cut the lead to three with 2:07 left in regulation. The Profs had several chances to pull within one, but the Magicians secured the win when Jerry McNeal made three of four foul shots in the final fifteen seconds. The Magicians won 57–54 and became the first NCAA Division III champions. Earlier that year, during the preseason, McNeal had asked Coach Johnson for the opportunity to lead the team as its point guard. He told Johnson, "if you let me run this team on the floor like I'm capable of doing. We'll win everything."[106] McNeal's prediction came to fruition. Johnson allowed his players to display their talents as a team, and they brought home a national championship, Memphis's first NCAA men's basketball championship. Robert Newman was named the tournament's most outstanding player for his performance in the Final Four.[107]

The LeMoyne-Owen players understood most people in Memphis did not value their national championship as much as they would have valued a Memphis State national championship, had the Tigers won. Robert Newman and his teammates wanted to play the Tigers. "It was personal," he said.[108] The Tigers' players understood that they had nothing to gain and everything to lose by playing or scrimmaging the Magicians, especially after they lost in the first round of the NIT tournament. The Magicians settled for pick-up games against the Tigers players at the Elma Roane Fieldhouse.

Herein lies the key to understanding the peculiarity of the LeMoyne-Owen championship. When the team landed at the Memphis Airport, there was very little fanfare. The 1973 narrative contended that the Memphis State basketball team brought the black and white residents of the city together. According to this narrative, the city unified during one of the most tumultuous periods in its history when two local, black basketball stars played at the predominately white university. The story of the 1975 LeMoyne-Owen national championship, however, is the story of two cities: one white and the other black. It shows that the city still suffered from the segregated past that it never openly acknowledged. Black colleges, like LeMoyne-Owen, were vital institutions. The 1975 LeMoyne-Owen championship was meaningful to the black community. The players felt slighted because the city at large did not recognize their success. Guard Jerry McNeal summed it up best: "The press wasn't there. Its something I'll never forget."[109] To white Memphians, the Magicians' accomplishments existed only in a parallel community that they knew little about and cared about even less.

Johnny Neumann at Overton High School. Benjamin L. Hooks
Central Library, Memphis Public Libraries.

Clint Jackson Shooting at Bruce Hall, LeMoyne-Owen College.
Jackson Family Collection.

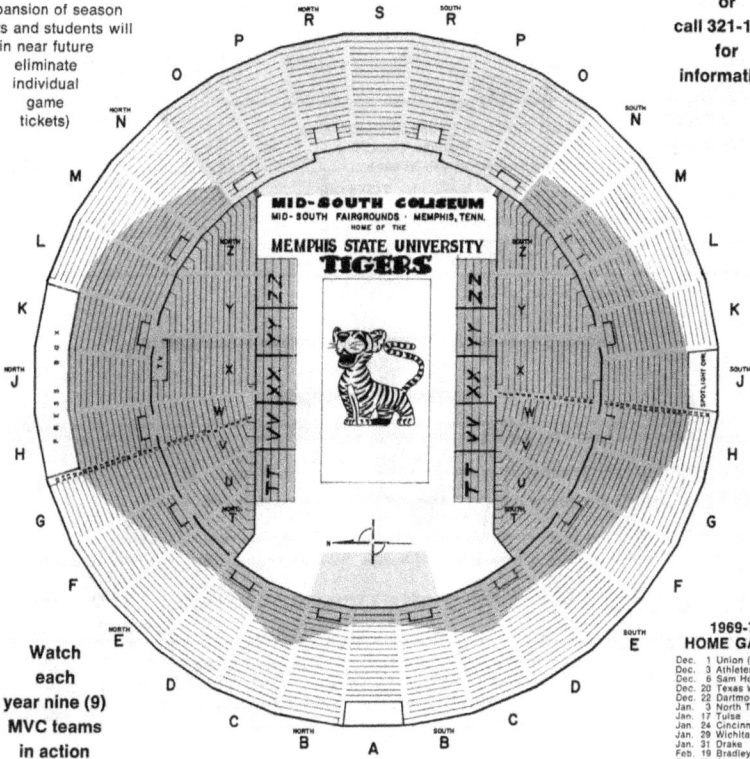

The 1969–70 Memphis State Season Ticket Order Form. University of Memphis.

Upper Deck View of MidSouth Coliseum, 1970. University of Memphis.

MidSouth Coliseum Postcard. Benjamin L. Hooks Central Library,
Memphis Public Libraries.

Hubie Smith, Larry Finch, Dana Kirk, and Lee Fowler. University of Memphis.

1971 Memphis State Basketball Team Photo. University of Memphis.

Bill Spook Murphy.
University of Memphis.

Larry Finch, Gene Bartow, and Ronnie Robinson, 1972.
University of Memphis.

Larry Finch. University of Memphis.

Ronnie Robinson Shooting. University of Memphis.

Melrose High School's Undefeated Team, 1974. Sails Family Collection.

New York Nets' Larry Kenon versus the Memphis Sounds. Benjamin L. Hooks Central Library, Memphis Public Libraries.

Memphis's Black, Basketball-Coaching Moses

Verties Sails

While playing basketball at Melrose High, Larry Finch developed a life long friendship with assistant coach Verties Sails. Sails became Finch's mentor and stood by him throughout his playing and coaching career. After Finch signed with Memphis State, Sails became the next head boys' basketball coach at Melrose High. In 1975, Memphis State decided to hire their first full-time, African American assistant coach. Sails's success at Melrose High put him at the top of the list for this position. At the time, schools throughout the South only used black recruiters to bring black players to their universities. These recruiters were given part-time positions as secondary members of the coaching staff. Sails became the first full-time, African American assistant coach in the South. His responsibilities included not only recruiting, but also coaching the freshman team, scouting opponents, and aiding in in-game decisions. Sails disproved the racist assumption that only white men were capable of coaching basketball at predominately white colleges and universities throughout the South. Like many other racial pioneers in the sport, Sails faced numerous obstacles and racial animus throughout his four-year tenure as an assistant coach at Memphis State.

Sails and Finch are part of the same coaching tree that stretches back through the city's basketball tradition. Sails's commitment to Finch as a player at Melrose High helped Finch defy the will of many in the Orange Mound community in order to sign with Memphis State. Throughout Finch's playing days at Memphis State, he returned to the Orange Mound community because of men like Sails. Sails's role in the history of Memphis basketball is hidden under Finch's shadow.

Sails never openly complained about the racism that prevented him from advancing at Memphis State. Instead, he moved to Shelby State, the local community college, to be the head basketball coach and remained an integral part of the basketball fabric in the city. Sails never became a Division I head men's basketball coach, but he laid the foundation for Finch to become the first African American head basketball coach at Memphis State.

Finch's success as a player for Memphis State was used to create the narrative that basketball had unified the city. This chapter investigates how Sails's story has become a footnote in this same narrative. By examining Sails's coaching career, we can better understand the racial dynamics driving the city during this era. Sails, Memphis State's first black assistant coach, was passed over for the head coaching job in 1979. The racist implications of this further complicate the story that basketball had healed the city's racial divides.

▲▼▲

On March 28, 1942, Verties Sails Jr. was born into a world framed by Jim Crow laws. He grew up in Rosemark, Tennessee, a small community in Tipton County just north of the Shelby County line. As a young boy, he was unable to attend white schools. He attended E.A. Harold School in Millington. When the county recast E.A. Harold as an elementary school as part of their desegregation plans, his parents sent him to Woodstock High School just south of Millington. Woodstock High School offered black high school students a chance to work to earn their way through school. The students worked in agricultural, vocational, and other odd jobs to help pay for housing.[1] Woodstock's mission correlated with Booker T. Washington's concept of racial uplift through education and economic opportunities. Principal R.J. Roddy governed Woodstock for over thirty years and believed that his students needed the best teachers. He brought in teachers from all over Tennessee, following the model set by Tennessee's Normal Institute (Tennessee State University).[2] Roddy's no-nonsense administrative style instilled discipline in his young charges, including Sails.

As a young boy growing up in Rosemark, baseball was Sails's first love. Soon after arriving at Woodstock, however, he developed a passion for basketball. Woodstock competed in competitive African American leagues in Memphis. Like other segregated schools, they were not allowed to play white schools. Articles on the African American prep league battles in Memphis and Shelby County filled the sports pages of the *Memphis World* and the *Tri-State Defender* every week. Woodstock was a local power in the 1950s and claimed the Tennessee High School Athletic Association (black) state championship in 1951.[3] In the fall of 1959, Sails's senior year, a new assistant coach arrived on campus and left an indelible mark upon Sails. Sam Montgomery had played under Tennessee State University's legendary Coach John McLendon. Montgomery opened fall workouts with the players playing three on three games. The Woodstock players were accustomed to playing conditioning games in the half-court, but Montgomery insisted they use the entire ninety-four feet of the court.[4] To Sails and his teammates, this seemed preposterous—it was a change from their accustomed conservative style. Montgomery became Woodstock's head coach the following year. His lessons on how the speed of play impacted the game stuck with Sails throughout his own coaching career.

John B. McLendon's influence stretches throughout college basketball. The fast-paced offense style that Sails learned under Montgomery came from McLendon. McLendon's basketball lineage can be traced directly back to James Naismith, who was head coach at the University of Kansas when McLendon was a student there. Unable to play on Kansas's all-white varsity basketball team, McLendon became a student of the game and learned as much as he could from Naismith. When McLendon became head coach at Tennessee A&I, his motion offense and up-tempo style took his team to three NAIA championships. Sails was a student at Woodstock at the same time that McLendon was coaching Tennessee A&I.[5] Under Sam Montgomery, Sails learned McLendon's up-tempo game style, a style that showcased the abilities and talents of its players.

After high school, Sails was offered a scholarship to attend LeMoyne College and play for Coach Jerry Johnson, another disciple of McLendon. LeMoyne was an SIAC member, and their talent and schedule were as competitive as Memphis State's. Yet SIAC relegated LeMoyne to second class status because of Jim Crow laws. Sails was a seldom-used reserve at LeMoyne described as, "one of the most dependable substitutes on LeMoyne's varsity basketball team. He is an accurate scorer and a good playmaker."[6] Although he was never the star at LeMoyne, Sails studied Coach Johnson's system and recruiting style. His ability to bring players from across the country to LeMoyne's small campus in South Memphis stuck with Sails. As a reserve, Sails was able to watch his coach and team and see how a team works from the ground up. Sails watched how players in front of him succeeded and failed. His four years at LeMoyne under Johnson provided a foundation that served him well throughout his coaching career.

Sails first became an assistant coach at Melrose High under William Collins. Collins's Melrose program was one of the most successful high school programs in the city and produced several collegiate stars. Following Melrose's 1968–1969 season, which included an MIAA City Championship, Collins left Melrose to take over the reins at Tech High. When Collins departed, Sails inherited a team that graduated most of its offensive talent. Undeterred, Sails led a solid group of young players to Melrose's second consecutive MIAA city championship over Manassas High. Melrose advanced to the state championship game where they lost to Nashville Cameron, 62–52.[7]

Sails continued his ascent through the Memphis prep ranks. In 1971, Melrose returned to the MIAA City Championship game for the third straight year. After missing the 1972 MIAA championship game, Melrose returned to the top of Memphis prep basketball with a lineup that included John Gunn, Alvin Wright, and James Bradley. Melrose reclaimed the MIAA City Championship in 1973. In 1974, Melrose secured its place as arguably the best team in the city's celebrated basketball history by completing the 1973–1974 season undefeated. That season included an MIAA City Championship over rival Northside and a 76–30 dismantling of Brownsville Haywood in the state championship game.[8] Sails returned Melrose High to the top of prep basketball and forged Melrose's legacy as a state basketball power. In doing so he drew Memphis State's interest.

When Gene Bartow moved to the University of Illinois in March of 1974, the Tigers announced that Wayne Yates would take over as their new head coach. After a successful career as a Tiger, Yates had played one season with the Los Angeles Lakers and another with the ABA's Oakland Oaks before he returned to college basketball as an assistant under Gene Bartow.[9] Soon after he was elevated to the head coaching position, Yates hired Sails and M.K. Turk as assistants. Yates's primary objective in hiring Sails was to secure a commitment from Melrose's All-American center John Gunn. Yet it was Sails who gave Yates an ultimatum: if he wanted Sails as an assistant, he would have to sign John Gunn and Alvin Wright. Sails's primary concern as a coach was always to place the best interest of his players ahead of his personal goals. Sails told Yates, "if you want me, then you are going to have to sign Alvin Wright to a scholarship along with Gunn."

Yates doubted Wright's ability to play Division I basketball. However, he needed Gunn's athletic abilities, and he needed Sails to communicate with the black players he was recruiting. Wright's older brother Herb was the first black basketball player at Shelby State C.C. Herb had not played basketball at

Melrose High because he needed to help support his family financially. Sails knew the family and understood that if Alvin was going to have a chance to play for Melrose High, then he needed to help support his family financially. Sails allowed him to work the concession stand when Alvin was not at practice or playing in a game.[10] Coach Sails believed Alvin Wright deserved the opportunity to compete at the Division I level. Sails's perseverance and commitment to his players as young men forced Yates's hand, and Wright signed with the Tigers.

Verties Sails Jr. became the first African American, full-time men's assistant basketball coach in the South in the fall of 1974. When Sails joined the Tigers coaching staff, the university gained a man who could recruit the city's best high school talent and was more than competent enough to coach on the Division I level. Yates's was being pragmatic when he hired Sails. Sails had won four city championships and one state championship, and he had a .790 winning percentage.[11] When Memphis State president Bill Jones and athletic director Bill "Spook" Murphy agreed to hire Sails, they valued his image in the community. Sails projected himself in a way that garnered the respect of white Memphians. Sails did not belittle referees during games. He was a stern taskmaster yet did not explode at his players during games. He was viewed as a gentleman by his peers. His respectability shown through in a game against Frayser High. Only one white referee showed up for the contest. He turned to his team and told them, "say nothing to the referee. You are not to question a single call."[12] Sails understood the racial implications of his team disputing any decision by the lone white referee.

Sails's ability to gain the respect of the white community in Memphis while simultaneously maintaining that of his black peers is critical to understanding his character. Melrose's biggest rival in the early 1970s was Hamilton High, coached by Sails's longtime friend Lloyd Williams. During practices and games, Sails used Williams's press clippings in the local papers as motivation for his team. However, after the intense rivalry played out on the floor, Sails and Williams could be found at a local restaurant, renewing their friendship.[13] Black coaches across the city respected his acumen, and Orange Mound community appreciated his hard work in elevating the program to elite status during his tenure as head coach. His commitment to his players in the Orange Mound began with his days at the local community center. His team's success also gave the residents of Orange Mound and the rest of the city's black community a sense of pride. His ability to negotiate successfully between the white and black communities was a sign that he could help Memphis State build racial bridges across the city.

Early in the fall of 1974, Sails was summoned to the athletic director's office to learn the boundaries for the school's first African American men's basketball coach. Memphis State University's athletic director Spook Murphy made it clear to Sails that respectability was a vital factor in his hiring. Murphy was an iconic figure in the Memphis State community who spent fourteen years as the head football coach before becoming the school's athletic director in 1972. His decision to move the Tigers into the Missouri Valley Conference helped to improve the school's position nationally in both basketball and football.[14] In his directions to Sails, Murphy's concern was protecting the national reputation of the school in an era of volatile race relations on campus and around the country. Murphy told Sails, "if you have any trouble out here, don't go running to Maxine Smith or the newspapers. You come to see me, and I'll take care of it."[15] Murphy wanted to avoid racial strife and the publicity that would come with it as much as possible. Murphy's fear was grounded in his experiences with Maxine Smith, who had made a career of fighting segregation at Memphis State University after she was denied admission in 1957.[16] Smith's vocal disapprobation made the school's administration leery of hiring someone who might be a racial protester. Murphy believed that Sails's quiet, nonaggressive style was necessary to achieve racial harmony. From the point of view of many in the black community, however, Smith's style of resistance made progress toward equality in the city possible. Sails walked a thin line between the two approaches during his time at Memphis State.

As a coach, Sails gained the respect of his players because he rewarded talent and hard work. He displayed an authenticity that players could sense. Sails's ability to empathize with his players and understand them as people first and basketball players second aided his success on and off the court. He believed that if players were allowed to compete against each other, then the best players would rise to the occasion and earn their positions. Off the court, Sails believed in the same principle. He treated people with respect, and he expected the same in return. During his five years at Memphis State, this principle was tested repeatedly on and off the court by the prevailing racial climate in the city. As Sails broke racial boundaries at the university, he met resistance from several white people in the city who were not yet ready for change.

When Murphy called Sails into his office in the fall of 1974, he was setting boundaries for Sails on campus. As Memphis State's athletic director, Murphy was asserting his position as the preeminent voice on racial issues in the department. Under the cultural norms of the period, Sails had to adhere to Murphy's decrees. Over the next five years at MSU, Sails encountered racism. Sails was not alone in these trials. His family was also insulted because of their race, which drew more ire from Sails then did the personal slights he faced. Sails treated his players fairly, and he expected the Memphis State community to treat him the same way. As a product of a Jim Crow society, however, he understood that the white establishment was not going to give him the same egalitarian treatment that his players received on the court. These slights were part of the price that Sails paid to be the first African American assistant coach at MSU.

A series of incidents from Sails's first season at Memphis State demonstrate these racial dynamics. Early in his first season, Sails's wife Francine, who was pregnant at the time, drove to a game at the Mid-South Coliseum. When she tried to park in the gated parking lot next to the Coliseum—the same lot used by the other coaches wives—the parking attendant refused to let her park there because she did not have a pass and she was African American. The other coaches' wives had parking passes, but Francine had not been given one. Sails understood the implications of this incident. The next day, Sails tracked down the athletic ticket manager on campus and questioned him directly. The manager told Sails there had been a clerical mistake. Coach Sails refused to accept that excuse. He bluntly berated the ticket manager: "Of all the coaches on the staff, wouldn't you figure that my wife would be first to get a pass to avoid this very situation?"[17] Sails did not report the incident to the NAACP, the *Commercial Appeal*, or the *Tri-State Defender.* Instead, he went directly to the person in charge of parking passes in the athletic department and handled it respectably.

In another incident at the Coliseum, a thirsty Francine tried to enter the Rebounders Room, where boosters met before games to socialize, to get a drink. Denied again, she kept the slight to herself this time. Francine was afraid that her husband would lose his job if he came to her defense. When she finally shared the incident with Sails, he was furious. At the next home game, Sails sent his wife back to the Rebounders Room. He followed her, staying far enough behind that he could not be seen around the corner in the circular shaped Coliseum. When she attempted to enter the Rebounders Room, she was rebuffed at the entrance once again. From his position, Sails could see that Murphy was close enough to the door to recognize Francine. Sails made his way around the corner and confronted Murphy. Murphy's quick cover-up and apology did not sit well with Sails.[18] Through these racist slights, Sails maintained his composure. He understood the expectations of the prevalent social norms, yet he demanded that Murphy and the athletic department treat him and his family the same way they treated white staff members.

▲▼▲

In 1975, racial discord reached the Tiger basketball program. In this era, socially conscious student bodies and faculties became increasingly outspoken on administrative policies and involved themselves in hotly debated issues on campuses across the country. Most alarming to administrators on predominately white campuses were the demands being placed on them by black students, including athletes. Black athletes spearheaded the "athletic revolution" by challenging the racial discrimination in athletic departments at universities across the country.[19] In February, Yates was at odds with some of the black players on the Memphis State team over the dress code he insisted on during the taping of his weekly television program. Yates required the players who appeared on his show to follow a specific dress code, but the black players wanted to wear new black leather jackets. Yates assumed these jackets were symbols of the Black Power movement, which was present on college campuses across the country. He forbade the players from wearing them. Frustrated by Yates's decision, the black players sought Coach Sails's advice. He suggested they follow Yates's dress code and go on the show without their leather jackets.[20] While Sails was in Chicago scouting DePaul, the black players decided to boycott the taping of the Wayne Yates Show.

Yates was furious and dismissed those players.[21] Coaches in this era were bewildered, angry, disillusioned, and no longer confident of their mission, or in some cases, their relevance.[22] When this group of black players confronted Yates, he felt disillusioned enough to dismiss them from the team for their actions. While Sails was in Chicago scouting DePaul University, the black players decided to boycott the show. Yates reacted as a man desperate to maintain control of his black players. However, he understood that his rash decision might have far-reaching implications for his program. He began to frantically leave messages at Sails's hotel in Chicago and his Memphis home.

Except for their black teammates, black athletes found themselves alone on predominately white campuses. Memphis State's campus had a small black population in the 1970s. If one of these black players had decided not to boycott the show, he would likely have become a social outcast. Tigers point guard Alvin Wright initially intended not to boycott the show. Since his high school days at Melrose, Wright had trusted Sails to guide him. Sails was out of town at the time, however, and the peer pressure to join his black teammates was too tenacious. Wright was in a precarious situation. He did not want to become an outcast among the few black friends he had on campus, his black teammates. So Wright went against Sails's advice and joined his teammates in the boycott. Wright and his black teammates were now in an uncertain situation.

The *Tri-State Defender*, the city's black newspaper, reported that Murphy held an emergency meeting with the players involved and Yates. The dissident players were allowed back on the team, but they were required to attend a "special practice" with Yates.[23] Behind the scenes, Sails was key to this compromise. He flew back into town on Saturday morning. When he walked in the front door of his house, his wife Francine handed him the phone and told him that Yates had left dozens of urgent messages. Yates demanded that Sails report to campus immediately to meet with the black players who had boycotted his show. Unable to communicate with his black players, Yates needed Sails to bridge the racial gap and remedy the situation.

The meetings between the coaching staff and the black players lasted most of that Saturday. They ended just in time for the players to get on the bus to go to the Coliseum for their game against the University of Milwaukee. After the meetings, Sails drove home to shower and shave and had just enough time to make it back to the Coliseum for the tip-off.[24] The press release credited athletic director Murphy for the reconciliation between Yates and his players. Sails had truly solved the crisis, however, by bridging the racial divide between Yates and the black players. Yates, still venting from the attack on his authority, suspended Bill Cook and Marion Hilliard for a bed check violation the week after the television show boycott.[25] Reconciling the counterculture and civil rights resistance with a coach's authoritarian power was a problem for sports departments in colleges around the country, including Memphis State.

As the Tigers completed their first season under Coach Yates, they traveled to New York City to play in the 1975 National Invitational Tournament against Oral Roberts. When the team arrived at Madison Square Garden, Georgetown University's basketball team caught the eyes of Alvin Wright and James Bradley. This all-black basketball team, from a predominately white, private university on the east coast, was coached by a black man, John Thompson. "Big John" Thompson loomed large as he walked through the halls with his team. Seeing Thompson made the Tigers' black players wonder when their school would hire a black man as head coach. Both Bradley and Wright asked Sails, "Who was that man?" Coach Sails responded, "That's Coach Thompson from Georgetown."[26]

Thompson's storied career as head coach at Georgetown University began in the fall of 1973. (Finch and the Tigers had advanced to the NCAA finals against UCLA in the spring of that same year.) Thompson—a Washington, D.C. native, a graduate of Providence College, and a former Boston Celtic—became the first black head basketball coach at Georgetown. The *Washington Post* celebrated Thompson's hiring; he was only the sixth black head coach to be hired at a predominately white college in the country.[27] Thompson had a reputation for discipline and for placing studies before basketball. His success at St. Anthony's, a small Catholic high school in Northeastern Washington, D.C., positioned him well for the opportunity at Georgetown. Thompson was selected for the job at Georgetown over the white head coach from Demetha High, Morgan Wooten. This choice signaled a direct shift in Georgetown athletic department's intentions. Demetha High School, a Catholic school in the neighboring white suburban enclave of Hyattsville, Maryland, was a national basketball power. Wooten was assumed to be the logical choice by many in the D.C. community to become the next head coach at Georgetown. Racism complicated the rivalry between these two high school teams and their coaches. Wooten avoided playing Thompson's St Anthony's team in local tournaments. He refused to play Thompson in black neighborhoods because, "he didn't think (white) followers of Demetha, would feel comfortable in (black) neighborhoods like Howard."[28]

After a year of racial tumult in the city, Georgetown named Father Henle president of the university in 1969. Henle initiated a series of programs that brought more inner-city youth to Georgetown as a response to the 1968 race riots in the city. Henle also hired Thompson, which further solidified the university's commitment to providing opportunities to black people from inner-city Washington. Thompson then built Georgetown into a national basketball powerhouse with a 98 percent graduation rate among players, who were predominately black.[29] For the black Tiger players, seeing Thompson opened their eyes to the possibility of a black head coach at Memphis State.

The Tigers' black players turned to Sails and asked, "You mean he's the head coach?"[30] After Sails revealed that he was, they said, "We're all going to Murphy right now to tell 'the man' that we demand that you become our head coach."[31] Although flattered by the young men's enthusiasm, Sails and his wife Francine begged the young men not to go to Murphy. Sails applied his egalitarian ideology to himself as well as his players. At that moment, Sails was content with his position as an assistant coach. He expected that through his hard work and success, he would earn the head coach job at Memphis State. After this encounter in 1975, Thompson went on to be the first black head basketball coach to coach in the Final Four in 1982 and in 1984, and he was the first to win a national championship at the NCAA Division I level.

After the 1984 title game, Thompson told *Washington Post* reporter Ken Denlinger how he felt as the first African American coach to win the NCAA championship: "The biggest thing that leaps out in my mind is all of the people, particularly of my race, who I felt never had the opportunity to experience what I have."[32] Thompson mentioned fellow black coaches from Washington, D.C., who were never allowed to be head coaches at the Division I level. He also mentioned Smokey Gaines and John McLendon, who coached at historically black colleges. By 1984, Sails had been passed over for the head coaching job at Memphis State and was part of that list of black men who never received their opportunity. Like Thompson, Sails was successful at the high school level and was a proven recruiter. Unlike Thompson, Sails was never given the opportunity to be a head coach at the Division I level.

Sails also faced challenges on the court. Hired in 1974, many considered it a ploy to land Gunn and thought that Sails lacked the expertise to be a sideline coach. Many believed that Sails should know his role as an assistant and only actively get involved if there was a "racial" issue that needed attention. Assistants make suggestions during games, but the head coach makes the final decisions. Assistant coaches are subservient to head coaches. An incident with Tiger forward James Bradley during the final regular-season game of 1977 tested the working relationship between Yates and Sails. Bradley's on-court altercation led to a bench-clearing brawl. Sails had urged Yates to substitute Bradley out of the game before the altercation, but Yates chose to leave Bradley in.

On this night, Oklahoma City's (OCU) pressing defense created 29 Tiger turnovers in a very physical game. Bobby Hall, the *Commercial Appeal* beat writer, said the game was "more like a season-opening performance than a regular-season finale."[33] The fight began after Bradley fouled Oklahoma City's Calvin Montgomery late in the second half. The game's outcome was no longer an issue. OCU's Mark Gwatney took issue with the hard foul and exchanged words with Bradley. Bradley hit Gwatney. Both benches cleared, and Yates went on the court to restrain Bradley.[34]

Many other major college basketball programs had shied away from Bradley because of his temperament on the court at Melrose High. The most egregious incident transpired during his senior year, in the waning moments of a loss to Northside High in the Martin Luther King Tournament. Bradley spat on a Northside player, causing a fight that spread into the stands. Sails coached Bradley at Melrose and understood his disposition. After a one-year stint at Connors State Community College, Sails convinced Yates that Bradley's athletic talent outweighed his temper. During the Oklahoma City game, Sails warned Yates not to leave Bradley in the game, which the Tigers could not win at this point anyway. Yates dismissed Sails's plea, affirming his authority as head coach. If Yates had accepted Sails's suggestion, then the fight could have been avoided. When the fight broke out, Sails remained on the bench.[35]

The altercation that Bradley initiated further exposed the racial challenges that Sails faced. Tiger A.D. Bill Murphy was displeased with Coach Sails's response to the fight and made his feelings known unambiguously. The following Monday, Murphy ate lunch in the athletic dining hall. Sails, who was also in the hall, overheard Murphy's conversation: "When a fight breaks out, this man won't even participate." Murphy's voice carried unmistakably across the hall. Sails sat silently, ate his lunch, and listened to Murphy. After lunch, Sails followed Murphy back to the athletic offices in the Roane Field House to confront him. Sails told Murphy to treat him like a man. He reminded Murphy of his plea to Sails: "if you have any problems, see me directly and do not to go talking to everyone else."[36] Murphy had questioned Sails's manhood in front of everyone in South Hall. Murphy, the former football coach, expected his men to enter the fray in defense of brotherhood. But Murphy had missed the discussion between Sails and Yates when Yates ignored Sails. Sails was known to his players as the quiet in the storm. They also knew that if a player repeatedly did not follow his instructions, then that player would draw his ire. Sails would not tolerate "that mess."[37] When Sails had previously encountered racism, he had not run to the media or the NAACP but had respected Murphy's wishes and addressed the problem internally. He expected the same from Murphy. Sails also knew that if he had jumped off the bench, then he would have been chastised for not having the prerequisite level of respectability needed to be a coach at MSU. Sails had little control over the situation. In the face of racial injustice, he chose respectability.

Sails's calming demeanor, persistence, and understanding of the racial climate were vital during a period when Jim Crow attitudes still resonated throughout the city. As an assistant coach, Sails accepted the roles that Yates gave his former Melrose players, even when he disagreed. Sails believed that John Gunn's play in early practice sessions, for example, merited a starting spot, but Yates did not. When Gunn became frustrated with his role, Sails told him, "Son, all you can do is to go out there every day at practice and be the best player on both ends of the floor."[38] Sails maintained his egalitarian approach to the game, but as an assistant, he was relegated to a secondary role and had to acquiesce to Yates's coaching decisions. In Sails's first season, Yates relegated Sails to working with the second unit and placed M.K. Turk, the white, full-time assistant, in charge of the first team. He used his time coaching the second team to prove his value as a tactician. Gunn also had the opportunity to prove his abilities against the first team during team scrimmages. In these scrimmages, Sails employed an up-tempo style that destroyed zone defenses by beating the defense down the floor. In one of these early sessions, designed to work on zone offense and defense, Yates stopped the scrimmage and openly questioned Sails in front of the entire team. John Gunn yelled out, "Aww Yates, your boys are just getting beat and you can't stand it!"[39] Gunn stated, with bravado, what Sails knew but was not allowed to say because he was an assistant. The up-tempo style showcased Gunn's athletic ability, which eventually earned him a starting spot in the Tigers lineup.

Sails had tutored Gunn on and off the court since his freshman year at Melrose, and so he held a special place in Sails's heart. Sails watched Gunn blossom into one of the most heavily recruited high school post players in the country in his senior year—in a class that included Moses Malone. Sails continued to play a significant role in Gunn's growth as an athlete and a man at Memphis State. As evidenced by their relationship, Sails believed in his players and created a family atmosphere. His empathy for his players extended past the court. He had a personal attachment to each of his players. Gunn showed continued growth during his first two years as a Tiger, which gave Sails high hopes for the former high school All-American. At the beginning of Gunn's junior year, however, he was diagnosed with Stevens-Johnson Syndrome, a disease that affects the skin and mucous membranes. He struggled at practice before being hospitalized three games into the season. Gunn passed on December 21, 1976, while the Tigers were playing Ole Miss at the Coliseum. When Larry Finch made his way to the bench to notify him, Sails knew from the inflection in Finch's voice what he was about to hear.[40] When the announcer notified the crowd, the Mid-South Coliseum felt as if "an iceberg had passed through there."[41] Sails's heart stopped at that moment, just as a father's heart would.

Over the next two years, the Tiger program hovered in mediocrity because they lost Gunn. In the final weeks of the 1978–1979 season with only four games remaining, Yates resigned as head coach. He had been under heavy pressure to do so from discontented alumni and was being scrutinized by the media.[42] The team had been successful under Gene Bartow. Now, under Yates, the Tigers were losing, and fans questioned the direction the program had taken. The *Commercial Appeal* called Yates's resignation the byproduct of spectator pressures and player misfortunes. Problems for Yates had begun when Dennis Isbell dropped out of school after the 1977–1978 season. Yates lost another player when guard Buster Hancock quit the team after losing his starting job in December 1978. After an altercation in the Mid-South Coliseum parking lot, it became apparent that Yates could not rein in James Bradley's temper. Bradley broke bones in his hand during this incident and missed three weeks of the season. When the second semester began, Tony Rufus was academically ineligible to play. Problems continued to mount for Yates: Tommy Lowery quit school, and narcotics agents arrested redshirt freshman Steve Meachem.[43] Marred by a series of events that depleted the Tigers' bench depth, the administration decided that Yates had lost control of the program, and they pressured him into resigning.

Sails did not know that Yates had spoken to the administration about the future of the program or that Yates was going to resign. The resignation created confusion for the team and the coaching staff. Yates had released a statement and the university had announced his resignation shortly before the team arrived at the Roane Fieldhouse for practice on February 7. The press corps began questioning the coaching staff: Who would coach this Saturday against Louisville at the Coliseum? Had Yates suggested to any of his assistants that this was a possibility? Had the athletic department, the AD, or any booster made the staff aware that Yates was going to resign? Into this melee of media questions stepped a team and a coaching staff with questions of their own.[44] Yates held a brief closed-door team meeting and reiterated: "I was not fired. I resigned. There's not really anything else to say." The Tiger players and coaches were shocked by the sudden announcement. Freshman guard Otis Jackson recalled Sails being shocked. Sails looked on from the stands in the Roane Fieldhouse as the team began to stretch before practice. Visibly choked up,

Sails told the *Commercial Appeal*, "Coach Yates and I came here together. We lost some games, and we won some games, but we always did it together. Man, tell me this isn't happening." When asked about the remainder of the season, Sails replied, "Something like this can knock a team down. It's hard to tell. I think these young men will play as hard as they can. Coach Yates deserves that."[45]

The Tigers' archrival Louisville arrived in Memphis that Saturday for a critical Metro Conference game. With no word from the administration or Yates, the assistants continued to lead practices. Yates returned to practice on Friday and led the team to an emotional 60–53 win over Louisville.[46] James Bradley led the way with multiple blocks, including blocking one of Louisville's high-flying Darrell Griffith's dunk attempts. Otis Jackson's play from the guard position helped lead the Tigers to the win. Following the victory, the Tiger players presented Yates with a game ball signed by all the players.[47] After the emotional win over Louisville, the Tigers lost three of the next four games to finish at 13–15.[48] The Yates era was over, and the search for his replacement began.

By 1979 the Memphis State basketball program depended upon the talents of black basketball players to elevate its program. However, was the school ready for its first African American head coach? Sails had proven his worth as an assistant coach and hoped that this was his chance to become the head basketball coach at Memphis State. Yates's coaching resume had been similar when he was offered the job in 1974. During his tenure as an assistant, Sails had pleaded with his players to be patient and allow him the opportunity to earn the head job. If Finch had unified the city behind Tiger basketball in 1973, and if Sails' hiring a year later had been another step forward, then the next logical step would be to hire a qualified black man as head coach.

Yates told the Memphis State athletic department that Sails was "a highly qualified individual."[49] Even with Yates's endorsement, Sails knew that, as a black man, his chance of becoming the next head coach of the Tigers was slim. Shortly after the season ended, the administration sent word to Sails that his job as an assistant was safe for the upcoming season. They made it clear that he should not apply for the head coaching job.[50] This slight did not deter Sails. He believed he had earned an opportunity to become the next head coach. To avoid the political ramifications of going through the athletic department, he delivered his resume to President Billy Mac Jones. Sails understood the racial norms and climate on campus and knew that his best chance was to go around Murphy. As a member of the old guard, Murphy maintained the status quo of the white establishment. By bypassing the athletic director, Sails maneuvered through the complicated racial politics on campus. On his way back to the Roane Field House, Murphy greeted Sails. Murphy hugged Sails and thanked him for putting the resume on Jones's desk personally. Murphy was relieved that the NAACP, the *Press-Scimitar,* and the *Tri-State Defender* would not be able to blame him if Sails was not given the position.

Early in the search process, Sails's backers voiced their concerns about the legitimacy of the university's hiring process. Several Tiger basketball players and local high school coaches became concerned that, as a black man, he was not receiving the consideration he deserved. They felt that the final candidate pool should include Sails. Melrose coach Dorsey Sims told the *Commercial Appeal,* "a lot of people are concerned about whether he's going to get an equal opportunity for the job. He's not a 'nobody.' He's a viable candidate, and he has something to offer." The Memphis chapter of the NAACP recommended that President Jones name a black coach to replace Yates. Sails appreciated the support, but because he understood the racial dynamics on campus, he told the *Commercial Appeal that,* "we shouldn't put the buggy in front of the horse."[51] In the early stages of the search for a coach, black players openly wondered why Sails was not receiving serious consideration for the job. The white players also respected Sails and would have accepted him. According to former Tiger forward Hank McDowell, the white players believed that Sails was capable: "We would have accepted Sails as the next head coach without any problems."[52]

As the head coach search progressed, it became apparent that Sails was not going to be a serious candidate for the job. The Memphis Rebounders, the team's booster club, was initially caught off guard by Yates's resignation, and they sought to keep Yates. Jones and Murphy made it clear that they would search for a new head coach and that the booster club needed to accept the reality of Yates's resignation. They informed the Rebounders that Larry Brown and Dana Kirk were candidates and that Sails had applied for the job.[53] Brown eventually emerged as the lead candidate. The Tiger faithful were enthusiastic about Brown's coaching pedigree and his experience under Dean Smith at North Carolina. Dana Kirk's experience under Denny Crum at Louisville provided the pedigree he needed to be in the conversation for the Tigers' job. In the excitement surrounding the search, the *Commercial Appeal* raised very little concern that Sails was not being considered for the job. Except for mentioning that he had applied for the head job, the *Commercial Appeal* kept Sails's name out of the discussion. Black area high school coaches and members of the Memphis branch of the NAACP openly questioned the validity of a search that did not make Verties Sails a legitimate option. The city remained divided over the issue of race, which now played out in its search for Memphis State's next head basketball coach.

In the months that followed, the search committee officially narrowed the list to three finalists: Larry Brown, Dana Kirk, and Verties Sails. Sails's appearance as a finalist was a significant step forward for the black community. Sails believed that the new head coach should be selected by the same method he used to select starters: the best man wins the job. By including Sails on the list of finalists, the administration gave the impression that they valued him as a candidate. When the university evaluated Sails for the job, however, they did not give sufficient weight to the role he had played in their current recruiting cycle. Players commit to coaches more than to universities. If Memphis State had hired Sails in 1979, they would have had one of their best-recruiting classes in school history to date—Sails had already received verbal commitments from 6'6" Paul Thompson of Smyrna, Tennessee; 6'9" Kilpatrick Wells of Vidalia, Louisiana; and 6'2" Robert Williams of Katy, Texas.[54] The NBA eventually drafted all three of these recruits. When the university hired Kirk, these players all chose to go to different universities: Thompson went to Tulane University, Wells went to Mississippi State University, and Williams went to the University of Houston.[55] Sails had also been close to securing a commitment from Sam Bowie, a 7'1" All-American from Lebanon, Pennsylvania.[56] Sails never received a verbal commitment from Bowie, but Bowie's coach had told Sails, "Of all the coaches who have been up here, Sam's more impressed with you than anybody else."[57] When Sails was passed over, Bowie enrolled at the University of Kentucky where he starred under Joe B. Hall. In the 1984 NBA draft, he was drafted in front of Michael Jordan by the Portland Trailblazers. If the university had hired Sails in 1979, then the 1979 freshman class might have been one of the strongest in the entire nation.

Larry Brown was the most recognizable name among the finalists and was the frontrunner for the job until he dropped out. Rumor lingers around the university that Spook Murphy offered Brown the job but told him that he would have to hire Larry Finch as a full-time assistant coach if he accepted the offer. Finch had joined the staff of former Tiger coach Gene Bartow at the University of Alabama-Birmingham (UAB) for the 1977–78 season, but Murphy wanted to bring Finch home to Memphis. Murphy understood that Finch, because of his connections in Memphis, could recruit homegrown talent for Memphis

State. Brown, however, expected full control of the program, including the hiring of his assistants. Bubba Luckett, a 1979 graduate of Christian Brothers High School who was being recruited by both Finch (for UAB) and Sails, believed that Brown shied away from accepting the position because Murphy had already offered Finch an assistant's job.[58]

Once Brown removed his name from consideration, Kirk became the leading candidate for the job. Kirk, who had only three years of Division I head coaching experience, was willing to accept Murphy's mandate to hire Finch as an assistant. Once Murphy had hired Kirk and secured Finch as an assistant on Kirk's staff, Sails became expendable. With Finch and Sails on staff, Memphis now had two black assistant coaches, which was over the "acceptable" quota for black assistants at a school in the South. Murphy's backroom deal was another subtle, racist slight against Sails. Murphy's dealings brought Finch, a hometown hero, back the to the university, but his ploy also ensured that the school would not have to hire its first African American head coach. Sails had been left out of the discussion for the head coach position. Sails knew that his time at Memphis State was over and that it was time for him to move forward with his career. When the head coach position opened at Shelby State Community College, Memphis's local junior college, Sails applied for and was given the job.

Memphis sports columnists Geoff Calkins described Sails's unique place in Memphis's sports iconography: "An anachronism in the world of loud, look at me now coaches because it's never been about him, it's been about the work. It's about the players."[59] Coaches have the unique job of turning a group of individuals into a cohesive unit. Sails's persistence in the face of continued racism at Memphis State forged his character. His empathy for his players provides insight into the difficulties faced by black coaches during this era. This same empathy also solidified his relationship with those players. He cared for them as athletes and as young men. His authenticity was evident to his players; they saw him fight for himself, his players, and his family against the racial animus in the South. Finally, Sails's greatness can be measured by the knowledge that he gained while at Melrose, Memphis State, and Shelby State.[60] For the 33 years following the end of his tenure at Memphis State as an assistant coach, Sails remained a fixture in the basketball community.

Sails remained in close contact with Finch over the years and was both confidant and mentor to him. Sails spent many nights at the Finch household discussing strategy and breaking down Tigers game tape, all while he maintained his schedule as the head coach at Shelby State.[61] Sails never held a grudge against Memphis State. Instead, he focused on what he could control: the teams he coached at Shelby State. His career resulted in over 700 collegiate wins, sixteen Tennessee Community College Athletic Association championships, ten regional championships, and ten appearances in the National Junior College Athletic Association basketball tournament.[62] Respected by his players and his adversaries alike, Sails became a part of the city's collegiate basketball firmament.

Sails's time as the first full-time African American assistant coach at Memphis State paved the way for Finch, who returned to MSU as an assistant and then became head coach. Change in Memphis took time. Time caused Sails to miss out. The slowly shifting racial climate at Memphis State placated those in the community who feared change. As the years passed, Sails was able to look back upon his time at Memphis State and see the bigger picture: his protégé, Finch, became the school's first African American head coach. Sails placed it in Biblical terms, referring to himself as, "a Moses, who led his people out of Egypt and into the Wilderness, but never got to see the promised land. Joshua was the chosen one to lead his people into the promised land. Larry [Finch] became the Joshua for Memphis State basketball coaches."[63]

A Shakespearean Tragedy in Memphis

In 1979, the Memphis faithful were eager to find a coach who could once again elevate the Memphis State Tigers into the national discussion. After Larry Brown passed on Memphis State's offer, the Tigers turned to Dana Kirk. A relatively unknown name from Virginia Commonwealth University (VCU), Kirk had spent six years under Denny Crum at Louisville. He was tall, wavy-haired, handsome, and a natural extrovert. He had the handshake of a traveling salesman and the natural charm of "a grown-up Huck Finn wearing a necktie," according to *Commercial Appeal* columnist Al Dunning.[1] Kirk was an expert communicator who was able to convince talented players from Memphis to stay home and play for the hometown Tigers. He was eager to move up the coaching ladder and was willing to accept MSU's one stipulation: bring home-town hero Larry Finch on board as an assistant.

Kirk's tenure as the Tigers' head coach was plagued by a series of accusations, indictments, and investigations. His murky political situation mirrored Memphis's own. Politically, the city's old guard, white establishment was fighting to maintain the status quo while the black community was fighting for greater inclusion. Over the six years that Kirk coached at Memphis State, the basketball program was mired in corruption. The basketball program reflected the scandalous nature of politics in the city. MSU was no longer the "Dixie Darlings," and there was a desire to return the team to its 1973 glory. In 1973, politicians had pointed to MSU basketball as the emblem of a healing city. By the end of Kirk's tenure, basketball became a symbol of all that was wrong in the city.

Kirk catapulted the Tigers to a Number One ranking in the Associated Press (AP) basketball poll and returned the Tigers to the 1985 NCAA Final Four. However, the cost to the university and the city was high. In 1985, the Memphis branch of the NAACP claimed that Kirk was insensitive to the program's black players; it charged that since 1973, *no* black basketball players had graduated. Kirk resigned at the beginning of the 1986 season after recruiting violations led to an NCAA investigation. This investigation was followed by a federal grand jury indictment for point-shaving and game-fixing. The Tigers may have found an energetic and charismatic leader to resurrect their basketball program, but it came with a hefty price tag.

▲ ▼ ▲

By the 1980s, the Ford family's political machine was solidly entrenched. Wyeth Chandler was still mayor, but he was slowly losing popularity within the city government. Chandler survived a strike by both the police and fire departments, but his perception of himself as the "boss man" cost him the respect of both departments. At the same time, Willie Herenton emerged as the most popular non-elected black official in the city. Herenton, the city's first black superintendent, challenged the racial status quo and pushed for the city council and Mayor Chandler to increase the budget for the city schools. He claimed that the city council was not only irresponsible but were also mere puppets for Mayor Chandler.[2] Herenton, a life-long Memphian, grew up in poverty in South Memphis. As a graduate of Booker T. Washington High and LeMoyne-Owen College, he understood segregated Memphis.[3] Throughout the 1950s and 1960s, black Memphians had been told that if they trusted the system, worked hard, and became qualified, then they would be rewarded. Herenton epitomized this concept when he became the first black superintendent for the Memphis City Schools. Chandler's growing instability—exacerbated by Ford and Herenton's push for greater control of the city's political landscape—paralleled the instability in the basketball program led by Kirk.

▲ ▼ ▲

One of seven children, Dana Kirk grew up in a small town called Delbarton in the West Virginia coal-mining country. At age eight, his father died in a mining accident, and Dana now had to help make the family's ends meet.[4] By the time Kirk reached Burch High School at fourteen years old, he was long and gangly and was searching for himself. Sports were an outlet for expression and a way to succeed. He lettered in football, basketball, and baseball. By the time he graduated from high school in 1964, Kirk stood 6'7". Following a less than stellar academic career at Burch High School, Kirk signed a dual football/ basketball scholarship with Morris Harvey College in nearby Charleston, West Virginia. His academic struggles during his first year landed him on academic probation.[5] After his junior year, Morris Harvey disbanded the football program. Kirk transferred to Marshall University in Huntington, West Virginia, where he continued to play football and basketball. While at Marshall, Kirk met Ann Bew, who became his first wife. After he graduated from Marshall in 1958, the former athlete began a career as a high school coach.

Between his Marshall graduation to his hiring at Memphis State University, Kirk worked at three different high schools, held two collegiate head coaching positions, and was an assistant coach to Denny Crum at Louisville. Kirk began his career at the predominately Hispanic Jefferson High School in Tampa Bay, Florida. His success at Jefferson High School opened the door for his first big break into collegiate basketball at the University of Tampa in 1966. An NAIA school, Tampa played a schedule loaded with NCAA Division I foes to pay the bills. The university hired Kirk despite his lack of college-level experience. In 1971, when Tampa folded its athletic program, Kirk was offered an assistant coaching position under Denny Crum at Louisville. Kirk's and Crum's unique personalities complemented each, and they shared the drive to win. Crum was quiet and reserved; he enjoyed practices more than public appearances. Kirk's flamboyant personality suited him for public appearances. One year after the Louisville Cardinals' 1975 Final Four run, Kirk was fired. Louisville Athletic Director David Hart, not Crum, told Kirk that he was fired.[6] His dismissal at Louisville caused a rift between Kirk and Crum. In 1976, Virginia Commonwealth University in Richmond, Virginia, hired Kirk as its head coach. VCU showed improvement in Kirk's first year and earned a bid to the NIT in his second. Kirk led the VCU Rams to a 20–5 record in his third year, good enough to place him in the running for the Memphis job.

▲ ▼ ▲

In the 1980s, white flight shifted the racial demographics of the city. White flight intensified disparity in the city. In the 1950s, working-class white people moved just beyond the city's boundaries: first north to Frayser and south to Whitehaven, and then east to Germantown, Collierville, and Cordova. These new residents built roads, schools, shopping centers, and hospitals in these suburbs. The I-240 freeway loop, completed in 1984, directed commerce away from the urban core of Memphis and toward the suburbs. People with the highest concentrations of wealth, education, and the best paid jobs were on the eastern edge.[7] The 1980s also became known as the "Age of Indictment," as several local politicians served time for various financial violations.

Edgar Hardin Gillock, a Memphis attorney and state senator who had been indicted in 1972 and 1975 on charges of misconduct, was indicted again in the early 1980s. He is an example of the political corruption facing Memphis during this era. On June 14, 1982, a federal grand jury indicted Gillock under the Hobbs Act, which prohibits actual or attempted robbery or extortion affecting interstate or foreign commerce "in any way or degree."[8] Gillock had received $130,000 in a Shelby County deal with the Honeywell Corporation. Gillock was sentenced to three years in prison and fined $10,000.[9]

The Ford political machine was in and out of court during this same period. Harold Ford Sr. was implicated in an indictment of Edward Branch. The indictment claimed that Branch, working for Ford, intimidated and threatened several poll workers in the 1976 Congressional election. The case against Branch ended in an acquittal when eleven black jurors and one white juror found Branch not guilty on both charges.[10] As political jockeying for control of the city continued, the Justice Department opened a grand jury investigation into insurance fraud by Harold Ford's brother Emmitt. Emmitt Ford, riding the coattails of the family name, won the District 86 seat in the Tennessee state legislature in the fall of 1974—the same seat that his brother Harold vacated when he defeated Dan Kuykendall for the Eighth Congressional seat in the U.S. House of Representatives. In March of 1980, Emmitt Ford and his wife Earline Ford were both indicted on charges of insurance and mail fraud. The indictment stated that Emmitt and his wife staged an automobile accident in 1977 and then collected nearly $54,000 from twenty-nine insurance companies.[11] Emmitt used his political position to persuade the head of the police department's traffic division to change the original accident report. The original report listed no injuries. The amended report showed that his wife suffered serious injuries. Emmitt received a twenty-month sentence in prison and lost his legislative seat. His wife received a one-year suspended sentence and twenty months on probation.[12]

In the middle of the grand jury investigation into voter intimidation by Harold Ford Sr.'s 1976 campaign, the Ford political machine nominated Harold's brother John as a candidate for Shelby County Mayor in 1978. Shelby County Mayor Roy Nixon had announced that he was not seeking another term. This opened the door for the Ford machine to take more control in Shelby County. Mayor Wyeth Chandler held a back-room, whites-only meeting at the Coach and Four Motor Lodge on Lamar Avenue. The purpose of this meeting was to select a white candidate capable of defeating the growing Ford machine. Chandler vehemently denied that the meeting was racist: "It amazes me that anyone would make an accusation it was a racist meeting when at least 90 percent of the black population will be voting for a black [person] without regard to background or experience of any other candidate."[13]

Mayor Chandler's plantation mentality once again became transparent. He had no problem with black basketball players uniting a city, but he did have a problem with the Ford family infringing upon white political power. Historian John Hope Franklin argues that sport creates something of a mirage. It creates an exclusive opportunity for the black athlete while fostering the illusion that things are much better for black Americans than they are. Franklin went on to say, "there are always times when society could absorb a select number, a small number, which would be the exception that proved the rule."[14] Chandler embraced the athletic exploits of Finch and Robinson, but black people serving in political offices was too far. From Chandler's perspective, it was a privilege for black people to represent the city on the hardwood floor of the Mid-South Coliseum. It was not a black person's place, however, to represent the city in one of the highest political offices. In 1978, Bill Morris, the white candidate, defeated John Ford for Shelby County Mayor, and the old guard maintained the control to which it was desperately clinging.

▲▼▲

The Dana Kirk era began with a sub .500 performance during the 1979–80 season. The Tigers' fans had been enthusiastic about Kirk's arrival and hoped that he could quickly return the Tigers to post-season play. Instead, the new coach's quick temper and ultra-competitive demeanor on the sideline became the highlight of the season. In a game between the Tigers and Florida State

University, Kirk and referee Dan Wooldridge got into a heated argument after Wooldridge called a technical foul on the Memphis State bench. Kirk told Wooldridge that if the Florida Seminoles shoot the free throw for the technical foul, "We Quit!"[15] Kirk then walked his Tigers off the court. Wooldridge issued a forfeiture, which was upheld by Metro Conference commissioner Larry Albus. Albus blamed Kirk, as the head coach was responsible "for creating the circumstances" that led to the forfeiture. Kirk pled his case to the Assistant Coaches Club after this incident. Kirk redirected their focus away from this incident and the fans' anger to his plans to resurrect the program: "we are going on down the road, and we are going to win a national championship before it is over. . . . Dana Kirk promises right now to work a little harder toward achieving my goals."[16] To achieve these goals, Kirk needed to recruit higher caliber players. If the Tigers were going to win on the court, then Kirk had to win on the recruiting trail. He was a long way from having the talent he needed to compete for an NCAA championship.

Four starters returned for Kirk's 1980–81 Tigers team, and the future looked brighter. Otis Jackson, Hank McDowell, and Dennis Isbell, the Tigers three leading scorers from the previous season, were ready to lift the Tigers back to national prominence. Again, however, the Tigers fell below fan expectations and finished one game below .500 at 13–14. The Tigers lost in the first round of the Metro Conference Tournament, 72–66, to Virginia Tech.[17] The one high point was Kirk's first victory over Louisville in January at the Mid-South Coliseum. Against Louisville's noticeable size advantage, Kirk employed a series of zone defenses that kept the Cardinals from overpowering the Tigers on the inside. The zone forced the Cardinals to take more outside shots. The NCAA had not yet adopted the three-point line, but the temptation for Cardinal shooters to show off their range was too strong. They sank a few outside shots early, but as the game progressed, their shooting percentage dropped. Kirk relished the victory against his mentor and after the game told reporters, "I've got a lot of friends in Louisville who were looking and observing."[18]

Keith Lee, a 6'10" high school phenom from West Memphis, Arkansas, was in the crowd, as the Tigers defeated the Cardinals. Lee was committed to Arkansas State, but Kirk and his staff were working to convince him to de-committt from Arkansas State and committt to Memphis State. Three months later, Kirk secured his most significant recruiting victory: Lee committed to play with the Tigers. Kirk was at his finest in the news conference that he held after Lee signed with MSU. He reminded reporters that Lee "took his time in making up his mind. He thought it out thoroughly. He thought this was the best way for him to get a four-year education. I think I sold education harder than anyone else to him and his mother."[19] Kirk's polished sales pitch transformed the Tigers into a bright light in the recruiting world.

Once Keith Lee joined the Tigers, the Memphis team looked like they would be winners. The Tigers finished the 1981–1982 season 26–5 and held an impressive 18–0 record at the Mid-South Coliseum. The Tigers won both the regular season and the Metro Conference Tournament championships and ended the season ranked #9 in the AP Poll.[20] Keith Lee was a second-team AP All-American, the Metro Conference player of the year, and freshman of the year.[21] Rewarded with a #2 seed, the Tigers played in the NCAA East regional tournament, where they defeated Wake Forest University before falling to Villanova University in the East Regional Semi-Finals.[22] At the end of the season, Keith Lee decided to forego the NBA draft to stay with the Tigers, and Kirk landed another of the city's best players: Mitchell High School guard Andre Turner. Tiger fans were excited about the upcoming season.

▲▼▲

Political power shifted in Memphis in 1982. Mayor Wyeth Chandler, who sensed he was losing control in the city, asked governor Lamar Alexander to award him a judgeship and resigned his position as mayor. Richard Hackett, a relative newcomer to the political scene in Memphis, put together a grassroots movement that carried him into office. Hackett, a political novice who had gained limited experience under Wyeth Chandler, used racist rhetoric to win himself a spot in the runoff election. Hackett painted white Democrat Michael Cody, his most serious opponent, as a supporter of the ACLU and the NAACP as well as a political ally of Harold Ford Jr. He told white voters that Cody would be the puppet of the black political community. Hackett earned a spot in the runoff with 30 percent of the vote, finishing second behind the black candidate J.O. Patterson who won 41 percent. Hackett beat Michael Cody by only four percentage points. In the runoff election, Hackett claimed victory with 54 percent of the vote, approximately all of the white registered voters in the city. Although Hackett did not have a college degree or political experience, he was savvy enough to use the racial divide in the city to thrust himself into the mayor's office. Under Hackett, the problems facing the city and county continued to divide the city along racial lines. From 1980 to 1990, another five and a half percent of the city's white population fled to the eastern edges of Shelby County. They moved to avoid the shifting political atmosphere in city hall and the city's schools.[23] Perhaps Dana Kirk's Tigers could be a diversion from the issues facing the city? The 1982–83 season provided that distraction.

In September of 1982, Ira Murphy, a judge in Shelby County, became embroiled in a scandal. Ira Murphy first made a name for himself in 1960 as part of a group of eight black lawyers who challenged segregation in Memphis City Schools. The parents of eighteen black students filed suit in federal district court in Memphis. They accused the board of education of operating a biracial school district in violation of the Supreme Court's *Brown v. Board* ruling. Murphy joined Benjamin Hooks, Thurgood Marshall, and Russell Sugarmon in the *Deborah A. Norcross et. Al v. The Board of Education of the Memphis City Schools* case.[24] In 1969, Murphy began his career as a politician and was elected to the Tennessee state legislature.

The scandal in the 1980s involved Murphy, his associate Ronald Smith, and the Prince Hall Freemasons. The all-black Prince Hall Freemasons is a fraternal organization that confers an ideological bourgeoise status on its members. Since 1956, Whalum Lodge No. 373 in Memphis, has served as their state headquarters.[25] According to historian Martin Summers, Masons gave black men an imaginary claim to traditional and nineteenth-century notions of manhood. Through their collective and symbolic ownership of property, Freemasons invented a collective masculine self. They achieved this during a period when owning land, becoming a proprietor, or earning a living through skilled labor was difficult for most black men.[26] Murphy manipulated the political system by giving Ronald Smith a permit to operate a bingo hall as a tax-exempt 501(c)(3) organization at the Whalum Lodge. Murphy was convicted on eleven counts of mail fraud and one count of obstruction of justice. He was sentenced to five years in federal prison and fined $5,000. Just one more example of the scandalous nature of Memphis politics during this period.[27]

▲ ▼ ▲

Eleven games into Kirk's fourth season as head coach, the Tigers were first in the AP and UPI polls, undefeated, and winning by an average of 18 points per game.[28] The Tigers brought their 11–0 record to Cassell Coliseum at Virginia Tech, a challenging arena in which to play. The Tigers struggled with foul trouble and hobbled out of Blacksburg with their first loss of the season, 64–56.

The Tigers bounced back. They won at Cincinnati and eventual NCAA champion North Carolina State. They finished the season 21–6, which was only good enough for second place in the Metro Conference.[29] They also finished second to Louisville in the conference tournament but received a second straight bid to the NCAA tournament.[30] The Tigers received a first-round bye and waited on the winner of the Alcorn State University versus Georgetown University game.

The Georgetown Hoyas won. The Tigers and the Hoyas would now play each other, and this game would pit Keith Lee against one of the best big men in the country, Patrick Ewing. This game would also measure Lee's pro prospects and Memphis State's chances as a national power. Kirk assigned 6'9" Tiger Derrick Phillips to guard Ewing; Lee was able to save his energy for the offensive end of the floor because he did not have to guard the bigger Ewing in the post when Georgetown had possession. Lee owned the day with 28 points and 15 rebounds in the Tigers' 66–57 victory over Ewing's Hoyas.[31] Memphis State's reward for knocking off Georgetown was to play the Number One seed in the NCAA tournament, the Houston Cougars.

The University of Houston electrified the NCAA Final Four with three straight appearances from 1982–84. The Cougars transformed the game into an up-tempo, above-the-rim game that was more familiar on the concrete courts in America's inner cities, earning them the nickname "Phi Slamma Jamma."[32] Unfortunately for the Tigers, the game's biggest highlight came when Clyde Drexler jumped over 5'9" Andre Turner on the fast break. Drexler threw down one of the most memorable dunks in NCAA tournament history. Memphis State lost to Houston 70–63, and the Cougars went to the national championship game, where they were upset by North Carolina State. Back in Memphis, Kirk continued to recruit the best local talent. He signed 7'0" center William Bedford from state champion Melrose High, along with guard John Wilfong from state runner-up Briarcrest Christian High.[33] Kirk was perfecting his formula for recruiting from within the city's borders.

As Memphis State entered the new season, they aspired to return to the Final Four. All five starters returned to the Tiger lineup. (Four of these five starters would eventually score over 1,000 points in their playing careers.)[34] The Tigers opened the 1983–84 season ranked Number Five in the AP poll and won five of their first six games at home. In Los Angeles, in their first significant challenge of the season against the UCLA Bruins, however, the Tigers fell 65–51.

They lost again two weeks later, 73–66, to Iowa.[35] After they returned from the West Coast, the Tigers reeled off twelve straight wins. They improved to 19–3 and returned to the AP Poll at Number Eight.[36] During the win streak, Bobby Parks injured his knee in a 73–69 win over Florida State in Tallahassee. Derrick Phillips also spent time on the injured list, which further slowed the team's progress.[37]

Despite their injury problems, the Tigers won the Metro Conference regular-season title and hosted the conference tournament. They disposed of Southern Mississippi, Florida State, and Virginia Tech on their way to the Metro tournament championship and received their third straight NCAA tournament bid. The NCAA seeded the Tigers sixth in the Mid-West Region. Memphis State quickly disposed of Oral Roberts and Purdue University before running into the University of Houston for a second consecutive year in the Sweet Sixteen. The Cougars defeated the depleted Tigers 78–71, with Cougar Akeem Olajuwon recording 25 points and 13 rebounds.[38] Nevertheless, Kirk continued to land the city's most outstanding recruits back in Memphis. He signed the *Commercial Appeal's* Best of Preps winner Dwight Boyd from Kirby High School and Vincent Askew from Frayser High. The Tigers also added 6'9" Dewayne Bailey from Melrose High, who redshirted during the 1983–1984 season.

In 1985, the Tigers under Kirk finally reached the Final Four, Kirk's goal for the team since he first took over. Kirk strengthened the non-conference schedule. The team entered the season ranked Number Eight in the AP preseason poll and remained in the top ten for the entire season.[39] The media guide referred to Lee as "The Franchise," touting his All-American pedigree and his decision to forego the NBA draft.[40] The Tigers got off to a solid start with wins over UCLA and the University of Southern California at the Mid-South Coliseum. Victories over rivals Ole Miss and Mississippi State led to a 9–0 start. They dropped their first game to South Carolina in Columbia to open Metro Conference play. The Tigers then went on an eight-game win streak before losing to Kansas at Allen Field House. Kirk's team felt they were capable of reaching the Final Four. Memphis swept rival Louisville and won the Metro Conference tournament by knocking off Florida State.[41] Following a smooth regular season, the Tigers earned a second seed in the Midwest region of the 1985 NCAA tournament.

The Tigers began their road to the Final Four in Houston against Ivy League champion Penn. In 1985, the NCAA tournament expanded to 64 teams, which left the Tigers without an opening-round bye. Penn held Keith Lee to eight points thanks to its deliberate style of play, but the Tigers overmatched the Quakers and emerged with a 67–55 first-round victory. The Tigers then confronted their former coach Gene Bartow and the University of Alabama-Birmingham Blazers in the second round. Kirk's Tigers defeated Bartow's Blazers 67–66, with Keith Lee and Andre Turner scoring a combined 51 points. The Tigers advanced to the Sweet 16.[42] The team traveled to Dallas for their Sweet 16 matchup with Boston College at Reunion Arena, where they squeaked by Boston College 59–57 behind William Bedford's 23 points. In the Elite Eight, the University of Oklahoma provided another marquee matchup for Keith Lee against Waymon Tisdale. Lee once again shined the brightest, this time on the biggest stage, and against the best competition; he scored 23 points while holding Tisdale to only eleven.[43] With the 63–61 victory over the Sooners, Kirk delivered on his promise to carry the Tiger program back to the Final Four. The Yates years were now a distant memory, as were Kirk's first two years of sub .500 basketball. Memphis State headed to Lexington, Kentucky, for the Final Four.

Most of the basketball world was focused on three other teams there, all from the Big East. Curry Kirkpatrick of *Sports Illustrated* wrote, "Welcome to the return of the Big East Tournament, starring Georgetown, St. John's, and Villanova in their original roles and featuring Memphis State at Seton Hall." [44] In the Big East Conference's crowning moment the Tigers were given bottom billing. Patrick Ewing, Chris Mullins, and Ed Pinckney enjoyed the media's admiration heading into the Final Four, while the press mocked Andre Turner for his "southern Memphis soul stew" dialect. The media also praised Turner's shot-making heroics against Boston College and his ability to navigate the Sooner press in the regional finals. All-American candidate Keith Lee received scant coverage except for critiques of his post-season foul trouble, which had limited him in games against Penn and Boston College.[45]

Prognosticators hoped that Villanova's Wildcats would end up in the all-Big East national championship game. To get there, they first had to beat Memphis State. Villanova's deliberate pace and physical play in this semifinal game against Memphis mirrored the Tigers' game against Boston College. Villanova limited Lee's effectiveness with physical frontcourt play. Because his team was saddled by foul trouble, Kirk was forced to rely on his bench more than he wanted. Andre Turner matched Wildcat guard Gary McLain's play in the first half to keep the Tigers in the contest. At the half, the score was 23–23.[46] The game remained close throughout the second half. As time began to tick away, the Tigers had to foul. The Wildcats went to the foul line twenty-six times, while the Tigers shot only nine free throws. Lee's eleven points and Turner's ten points left the Tigers one game short of returning to the NCAA championship game. The disheartening 52–45 loss to Villanova marked the lowest point total for the Tigers all season.[47] They returned home at 31–4. Their fan base, despite the loss, celebrated the fact that Memphis State basketball had returned to the upper echelons of the basketball world. Their euphoria was short-lived. Kirk's tenure was about to take a tumultuous turn.

▲ ▼ ▲

Almost immediately after the painful Final Four loss to Villanova, Memphis State paid the price for hiring Dana Kirk. Kirk's problems started on his roster. Freshman guard Vincent Askew began an off-again, on-again relationship with Tiger basketball. Askew played in all 35 games, but he was not happy with his secondary role behind Lee. As the star player at Frayser High, Askew had been the center of attention, and he expected the same treatment from Kirk and the Tiger coaching staff. Many of his friends fueled his resentment when they wondered why he had not taken the open shots that had presented themselves against Villanova.[48] When his former high school coach, Al Perry, became an assistant on the Sycamores' staff, Askew considered moving to Indiana State. Less than a month after the Tigers lost to Villanova, Askew asked for his release. He claimed that his grandmother, who had raised him, was moving to Chicago, so the transfer to Indiana State was a family decision.[49] In reality, Askew was frustrated by Kirk's offense, which revolved around Keith Lee. Over the next three months, Askew wavered between transferring or staying. During the first week of August, Askew changed his mind again and decided to stay for the 1985–86 season.[50] The *Tri-State Defender*, wondered openly whether Askew had decided to stay at Memphis State on his own or whether some wealthy booster had "encouraged" him.

For almost three months, from the beginning of the Askew commotion until the late winter of 1988, Dana Kirk's actions off the court drew as much press attention as his on-court leadership. The month after Askew's feint toward Indiana State, three black basketball players at Memphis State enlisted the NAACP's help. They accused Kirk of using black athletes to win games but not caring about their academic or post-athletic careers. Local NAACP director

Maxine Smith claimed that "black [players] were being exploited" by the university. She called for Kirk's resignation, stating that he was insensitive to the issues that black players faced. She cited the low graduation rate for athletes at the university and the imbalance between "the time athletes spend in athletic events and make-up classes." Smith argued that Memphis State did not seem concerned about what happened to their players after they were ineligible to play for MSU or after they graduated. She cited the fact that the university did not have a program to help black athletes complete their education or to assist in job placement.[51] She recommended that the university increase the number of black employees in the athletic department and create a tutorial program that was not under the athletic department's control.[52] These allegations caught Kirk off guard and forced the university to address these issues.

A *Sports Illustrated* article revealed that only four of thirty-eight scholarship players (10.5 percent) in the Memphis State men's basketball program had graduated since 1973. All of them were white.[53] African American City Councilwoman Minerva Johnican joined the attack on the university. She condemned MSU's president Dr. Thomas Carpenter for trying to sweep the issue under the carpet by adding a single tutor. Johnican noted that the university prospered from its athletic revenue but was only willing to add one tutor. She told the *Tri-State Defender*, "Carpenter has become so wrapped up in basketball that he has ignored the academic needs of his students."[54] An NCAA investigation revealed that, between 1980 and 1984, Memphis State had overpaid student-athletes, both in men's basketball and in other sports, in Pell Grant funds to the tune of nearly $60,000.[55] Kirk did not appear to be involved in this violation.

In 1987, the NCAA pronounced the "death penalty" for Southern Methodist University's (SMU) football program. SMU was caught breaking NCAA rules regarding boosters seven times. An unnamed booster paid 13 Mustang players $61,000 from a slush fund with the approval of key members of the SMU athletic staff. The infractions occurred while the program was already on three years' probation for recruiting violations cited in 1985.[56] SMU was a small school in Texas outside of the Southwestern Conference, whose boosters were eager to compete with more prominent schools. These boosters became entrenched in the recruiting process. Former SMU football coach Bobby Collins attempted to justify the violations: "The problem is so many people love this university, and their competitive spirit just got out of hand."[57] Memphis State coach Dana

Kirk fell victim to this same competitive spirit. SMU's death penalty was not the first the NCAA had handed out. The organization shut down Kentucky's basketball program for the 1952–53 season because of booster payments to athletes. They suspended the basketball program at Southwestern Louisiana for two seasons (1973–75) because of more than 100 NCAA violations.[58] In 1985, after the Tigers lost to Villanova in the Final Four, the NCAA became aware of corruption in Memphis State's basketball program under Kirk.

During the spring of 1985, local media, particularly *Commercial Appeal* reporters Mike Fleming, Chuck Cook, and Otis Sanford, avidly pursued rumors that MSU boosters had paid basketball players. At the same time, a federal grand jury investigating sports gambling looked into rumors about Dana Kirk. Part of the coach's charm was his ability to rally people to support the Tiger basketball program. High-profile collegiate basketball coaches come into contact with hundreds, if not thousands, of fans and supporters every year, and Kirk was no exception. Two Memphians who actively supported Tiger basketball appeared in federal investigations and media scrutiny of the program. Nick Belisomo, a high-stakes gambler and pawnshop owner, and William Tanner, an advertising executive, were both under surveillance by the federal government for a variety of possible wrongdoings ranging from tax evasion to gambling. The Golden Tiger Club, which disbanded after the 1985 basketball season, was a booster club not officially associated with the university. The organization's founders included both Belisomo and Tanner. Following the 1981–1982 season, the Golden Tigers Club had presented various Memphis State leaders with cash rewards, including Kirk and his assistant coaches. Tanner was the driving force behind the Metro Conference television deal that was made during Kirk's tenure. This deal that brought in a lot of money for the MSU basketball program and undoubtedly benefitted Tanner too. By June of 1985, Tanner had been convicted of mail fraud and tax evasion, and he began serving a four-year sentence for those crimes. As the connection between the Tigers basketball program and these two indicted criminals became apparent, Kirk remained confident that the investigations would find no connection between himself and any illegal conduct.[59]

At the annual basketball banquet in 1985, Memphis State center William Bedford showed up in a flashy 1983 Jaguar, which he had borrowed from booster Ricky Allen.[60] Allen was a member of the exclusive Memphis State Super Tigers, a booster club that required a minimum yearly donation of $5,000.[61] The *Tri-State Defender* reported that Bedford had received three speeding tickets while driving Allen's Jaguar, compounding Bedford's woes. Kirk's association with another car dealership group, the Metro Ford Dealers Association, brought to light that dealers had furnished him with a car from 1982 to 1986. Giving a coach free use of a car did not violate the NCAA rules, but giving a player free use of a car did. Then there was the issue of a check Kirk received from the Winston Tires Company after the Tigers played in the Winston Tire Classic in Los Angeles in late December 1983.[62] Kirk had asked the tournament to send the program money, because of Keith Lee's notoriety, which appeared to be an NCAA violation.

In the summer of 1985, the most damning charges of financial impropriety in the basketball program surfaced. They involved Keith Lee's recruitment. Had his decision to attend Memphis been influenced by cash? In July, the *Commercial Appeal* published a tape-recorded conversation between "a former Tiger official" and a reporter:

> *Former Official*: Dana had come to me about a month after. He said, "You know I need some money to help get a basketball player." And I said, "What can I do to help out?" He said, "Well, if you could help me raise about $12,000 or $13,000." I said, "I'd be happy to. . . Of course, I went around to see some people. . . and then I went down to the bank and borrowed some money and gave it to him."
>
> *CA Reporter:* Just on your own?
>
> *Former Official:* Yeah.
>
> *CA Reporter:* You borrowed the money under your name?
>
> *Former Official:* Yeah. So, I gave him the money, and he said he was going to get the best basketball player he ever had.
>
> *CA Reporter:* Did he ever mention the name of the guy to you?
>
> *Former Official:* Yeah. He said when we were over in North Carolina one time: "You had more to do with him getting here than anybody will ever know."
>
> *CA Reporter:* Keith Lee? That's who he was?
>
> *Former Official:* Yeah
>
> *CA Reporter:* And he's never paid you back?
>
> *Former Official:* Lord no.
>
> *CA Reporter:* You asked him numerous times?
>
> *Former Official:* Oh, yes.
>
> *CA Reporter:* But, you handed him—what was it, a check from the bank?
>
> *Former Official:* No, no. Hell no. It was cash.[63]

Fifteen months later, in October 1986, testimony before the federal grand jury investigating Memphis sports betting shed further light on this telephone exchange. The MSU "former official" was former athletic director Bob Patterson.[64] The real source of the $12,000 loan was an unnamed booster. Keith Lee himself testified that Kirk gave him a "shoebox full of money" and, during his four years at Memphis State, a car, a color television, and a stereo.[65] Lee claimed that Kirk gave him cash payments of $400 or $600 a month and a 1975 Plymouth Duster during his senior year. The former Tiger star also told the grand jury that neither assistant coach Lee Fowler nor Larry Finch knew of his financial arrangement with Kirk.[66] Kirk alone was responsible for this scandal. Yet, two years later, in his self-published book, Kirk denied any wrongdoing.

Allegations of financial misdeeds were sufficiently shocking, but accusations also surfaced that Kirk and his celebrated 1985 team had been point-shaving. Point-shaving, making a game closer than it would otherwise be to help gamblers who bet large sums of money on point spreads, has bedeviled college basketball off and on since a wide-ranging scandal involving players at the City College of New York (CCNY) in 1951.[67] The accusations against Memphis State began almost immediately after the team's Final Four appearance in March of 1985. On April 4, a New Orleans grand jury indicted three Tulane basketball players for point-shaving. That case caused Tulane to drop its basketball program for several years. Dana Kirk testified on behalf of accused Tulane star John "Hot Rod" Williams. Williams was also accused of shaving points against Memphis during a February 20 game. Kirk defended Williams: "Tulane had led for much of the game, and it took some real effort to finally beat them in a close contest. Any suggestion that Wiliams, or any other Tulane player, had been trying to tamper with the game's result is just not based on reality."[68] Williams was acquitted of the charges and went on to a successful career in the National Basketball Association.

During the investigations, the jury discovered Kirk's gambling debts from numerous poker games at the Colonial Country Club exceeded $75,000. These gambling debts allegedly led Kirk to point-shaving at Memphis State. The federal district attorney's office investigated the possibility of point-shaving in the game between Memphis State and the University of Detroit on February 28, 1985, which the Tigers lost 71–66.[69] The grand jury concluded that the national betting trends indicated a high probability of point shaving. Bettors outside of Memphis favored Memphis State, and a large number of bettors from

Memphis had placed their wagers on the University of Detroit. Supposedly to clear his gambling debts, Kirk manipulated the final score by substituting players at critical points. The coach vehemently denied any connection between the Tigers' loss in Detroit and his gambling in Memphis. He explained that the game's outcome resulted from the team' situation coming into the game. The Tigers landed in Detroit with a record of 23–2 after having clinched the Metro Conference regular-season championship in Hattiesburg two days earlier. The Detroit game, a non-conference February game, was sandwiched between a road game with Southern Mississippi and a home game against the University of Louisville, slated for national television. Kirk argued that the loss was due to fatigue. He then went on to claim that the loss at Detroit motivated the Tigers against Louisville, and for the remainder of the season.[70] Both the grand jury and the NCAA eventually exonerated Kirk and Memphis State of all charges of point-shaving.

As the allegations swirled, the Memphis State fan base defended Kirk with a six-point plan that included a marketing blitz aimed at exonerating their embattled coach. David Hitzhusen, chair of the Assistant Coaches Club, held a press conference and began putting pro-Kirk messages on bumper stickers, billboards, and television ads.[71] Kirk's flamboyant style, endearing "Huckleberry" charm, and winning ways had won the loyalty of the Memphis State faithful, it seemed. That support, however, and the support of the university's administration, would prove to be short-lived.

Kirk testified before the Memphis grand jury in September 1986 and then returned to what he loved to do most: coach the Tigers. William Bedford became a symbol of the program's issues off the floor. During the 1985–1986 season, opposing teams' supporters jingled their keys as soon as they heard Bedford's name during player introductions.[72] Despite the distractions, the Tigers remained competitive during the regular season. They finished in second place in the Metro Conference with a record of 27–5, good enough to earn an NCAA bid for the fifth straight year. The Tigers defeated Ball State in an opening-round game before bowing out to Louisiana State University, 83–81, in the Round of 32 on March 15, 1986.[73]

Just as they had the year before, just weeks after the 1985–86 season ended, issues of wrongdoing surfaced. The Internal Revenue Service requested that Kirk's employers at WHBQ radio and WREG-TV both provide financial records of payments to Kirk. This request was part of the broader grand jury investigation into gambling.[74] As the grand jury continued its investigation,

Robert Ford and Alvin Shultz, both members of the Tigers Assistant Coaches Club, were subpoenaed to testify. Kirk again maintained his innocence, saying, "I am comfortable that there will be no finding of illegal conduct in connection with this."[75]Ominously, however, both Memphis State president Thomas Carpenter and athletic director Charles Cavagnaro remained silent throughout the grand jury investigation and the NCAA investigation into possible wrongdoing in the basketball program. When they did respond to media inquiries, they insisted that the grand jury's investigation was strictly an issue between the federal government and Dana Kirk.

Heading into the 1986–87 season, Kirk felt that the worst was behind him and that he could once again elevate the Tigers to the Final Four. He landed the services of three quality recruits: 6'6" forward Sylvester Gray from Bolton High School, 6'3" guard Cheyenne Gibson from Westwood High School, and 6'10" post player Ronnie McClain from Horn Lake, Mississippi.[76] However, the pressure was mounting, locally and nationally, to address the issues facing the basketball program. In May of 1986, the NCAA placed the Memphis State basketball program on two years' probation and banned the men's basketball program from playing in the post-season for one year. It also required the university to return 90% of the $700,000 that the university had made during its 1985–86 run to the Final Four.[77] The last time that President Carpenter and Kirk talked, Carpenter told Kirk that the "internal investigation" was continuing. On Wednesday, September 17, 1986, one week after that last discussion, Kirk returned to his basketball office to find a letter from Dr. Carpenter firing him immediately. President Carpenter cited a need for "new leadership."[78] After eighteen months of scrutiny by the federal government, the NCAA, and the university, Dana Kirk's tenure as the head basketball coach was over. Kirk felt betrayed by the university and its administration. He believed that they had allowed him to be the scapegoat for the university's problems in the athletic department.

Two months later, on November 20, 1986, Kirk was indicted by a federal grand jury on two counts of tax evasion, four counts of filing false tax returns, two counts of mail fraud, and three counts of obstruction of justice.[79] Kirk continued to sell himself, the program, and the job he had done: "Our basketball team last year [a participant in the NCAA's Final Four in 1985] was a credit to the university and this city and did the best it could to win every game it played."[80] The *Commercial Appeal* carried a political cartoon mocking Kirk. Kirk, portrayed as the fallen monarch from Shakespeare's *The Life and Death of King Richard II,* was on his knees, prostrate with a scepter in one hand, and a crown of basketballs upon his head. King Richard's words of despair were printed above the fallen Kirk: "O, that I was great as my grief, or lesser than my name, or that I can forget what I have done, or not remember what I must be now."[81] The king of Memphis hoops had fallen from his throne. Tigers' assistant and local hero Larry Finch took over control of the program. In this Memphis saga, Kirk was forced to defend himself in a court of law and suffer the consequences of his alleged actions.

As in any good Shakespearean tragedy, Kirk fought to the bitter end. Early in 1987, he filed libel lawsuits against the *Commercial Appeal* and *Sports Illustrated* for defamation of character.[82] In June, Kirk turned against two of his former assistants, Lee Fowler and Larry Finch. He accused Fowler of amending his tax returns with the help of IRS agent Alice Campbell, who was involved in prosecuting Kirk. He claimed that Fowler's attorney, Carl Langschmidt, amended Fowler's returns to show income received from working at MSU basketball camps. Kirk further claimed that Langschmidt then made additional adjustments before the feds and IRS questioned Kirk. Kirk levied the same claims against Larry Finch.[83] Kirk was in an all-out fight for survival, but he miscalculated when he attacked Larry Finch. Shortly after condemning Finch as an accomplice to the IRS take down, Kirk's libel suit against the *Commercial Appeal* reached Circuit Court Judge Wyeth Chandler. Fourteen years earlier, then-Mayor Chandler had proclaimed that Finch "unified the city like it has never been unified before."[84] Chandler threw Kirk's libel suit against the *Commercial Appeal* out of court.[85]

On November 15, 1988—almost two years after the grand jury lodged its indictments—Dana Kirk was convicted of five of the eleven charges against him. One count of tax evasion, three counts of filing false income tax returns, and one count obstruction of justice.[86] Three months later, on February 10, 1989, U.S. District Judge Odell Horton sentenced the former coach to one year and one day in jail, three years of probation, and a $275,000 fine. During sentencing, Kirk's attorney brought five witnesses forward to speak on his behalf, one of whom was former Tiger standout Otis Jackson. Despite the character witnesses' testimonies, Judge Horton issued this opinion: "While Coach Kirk is an outstanding citizen in this community, this does not excuse him from violating the tax and obstruction of justice laws of the Constitution on the United States."[87]

In March of 1989, Kirk entered the federal prison camp at Maxwell Air Force Base in Montgomery, Alabama.[88] Following his release, Kirk contacted President George H.W. Bush and requested a presidential pardon in his case. "George Steinbrenner just received a pardon from the president, right? Muhammad Ali, he was a draft dodger," Kirk said, "Why should it hurt me?"[89] Kirk sounded like he was back on the recruiting trail, trying to convince the next high school All-American to play basketball for him. He never received the pardon.

▲▼▲

Kirk was left wondering what happened to his dream of being a high-profile college coach. He remained in the Memphis suburb of Germantown, Tennessee. He spent time with his family. Kirk reemerged on the Memphis basketball scene as the general manager and coach of the Memphis franchise of the Global Basketball Association (GBA) in 1991–92. The Memphis Hotshots were a short-lived dream.[90] The GBA's short stay in Memphis gave Kirk his last opportunity to coach. In December of 1994, Kirk found his way onto the airwaves as the host of a weekly sports radio show on WMC-AM 79.

When Kirk died in 2010, he had been out of the spotlight for over twenty years. The *Commercial Appeal* ran two articles on Kirk: "Coaching Legacy" and "Always Game." Sports columnist Ron Higgins, who had covered Kirk's court case in the mid-1980s, memorialized Kirk as a man who had a passion for coaching. Higgins eulogized Kirk's successes. His former Tiger players defended their coach.[91] Andre Turner remembered Kirk as "fun to be around" and went on to say that "he didn't play favorites, and he made us play hard." John Wilfong praised Kirk's system and argued that if he had been given a second chance to coach, "he would have won a lot more games." Keith Lee, who was a central character in Kirk's downfall, remembered Kirk's ability to coach the Tigers in critical moments: "We always had confidence in him at the end of a tight game that he'd tell us the right thing to do."[92] In death, Kirk received the second chance that he had craved in life.

Kirk's downfall allowed Larry Finch to become Memphis State's first African American head basketball coach. The next chapter examines Finch's tenure as head coach at Memphis State and Finch's role was as a racial pioneer. The city's belief in his ability to mend its racial issues made Finch the right choice for many in the city. But just as Verties Sails Jr. faced racial hurdles throughout his tenure as the first black assistant coach at MSU, so too did Finch. By investigating Finch's time as the first black head basketball coach, we can gain a better understanding of how race and sport intersected in the city twenty years after Finch first led his Melrose High team against Overton High in the 1969 city basketball championship.

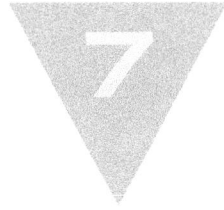

A Favorite Son

In the fall of 1986, following the Dana Kirk scandal, Larry Finch became the first African American head coach at Memphis State University. In the press release that announced Finch's promotion, athletic director Charles Cavagnaro hailed Finch as "the most recognized" player in the city's history. He claimed that "every move Finch ever made was done with the same class and integrity that we all know he will bring to the program."[1] Finch's reputation resonated throughout the entire Memphis community. The hero of Melrose's 1969 City Championship team, the star of Memphis State's 1973 NCAA runner-up team, and the face of Tiger basketball had elevated himself to basketball's highest position: head coach. The *Tri-State Defender* lauded his hire and said there was no time better to hire a black man as head basketball coach at the university.

Finch's promotion to head coach was not only a personal milestone but also a breakthrough for race relations in the city. Longtime beat writer for the *Tri-State Defender*, Bill Little, resonated with pride as he traced Finch's coaching lineage back to Verties Sails and William Collins at Melrose.[2] Finch's black coaching mentors never received the same opportunity and were relegated to lesser roles in the city's coaching fraternity. However, they laid the ground-work, with their success, professionalism, and respectability, for Finch to break through the racial barrier. Maxine Smith, local NAACP president and longtime advocate of racial equality at MSU, sent a letter to Memphis State University President Dr. Thomas Carpenter. She commended MSU for hiring a black coach but also urged the university to offer a compensation package similar to those received by white coaches. Finch was breaking barriers that many believed were permanent markers in the city's landscape. Larry Finch was a folk hero in Orange Mound and a symbol of hope for a city struggling to shake off its troubled, racist past.

▲▼▲

Throughout his career, Finch often returned to Orange Mound to help work with the community's younger kids at basketball camps. He attended Melrose High games during his collegiate playing career at Memphis State and while playing professionally for the Tams. So it was no surprise when he became the boys' basketball coach at Messick High School in 1976, after his brief professional career. When Memphis City Schools closed Messick the following summer, Finch's former coach, Gene Bartow, offered him a position as an assistant coach at the University of Alabama-Birmingham(UAB). He interviewed with the University of Tennessee at Knoxville for an assistant's position and Shelby State Community College for the head coaching position before accepting the position on Bartow's staff.[3] Two years later, eager to return home, Finch joined Kirk's staff. The *Commercial Appeal* lauded Finch's hire as Memphis State's head coach and listed the accolades he had received in his playing days. Just before he joined Kirk's staff at MSU in 1979, Bartow had offered him a $3,000 pay raise to stay at UAB.[4] Finch turned him down. Memphis was home. Billy 'Spook' Murphy, chair of the committee that hired Dana Kirk, recalled that "we couldn't let Larry Finch stay down there [at UAB with Bartow]. We had to get him back. It was very important to get him."[5] Murphy understood the importance of bringing the hometown hero home. He also understood the racial dynamics of the city. Finch was valuable to MSU because he would be able to recruit black players from Memphis. In Murphy's eyes, and the university's, Finch was a unifying force that could bring the city together behind basketball.

▲▼▲

Larry Finch was a product of a single-parent household in Orange Mound. He was an asset as a recruiter because he understood the way that many black families in Memphis operated. When trying to recruit Kenny Moody, for example, Larry Finch spoke to Moody's mother on the front porch of their house in South Memphis. Finch promised her that Moody would graduate if he came to MSU. Moody recalled that when he went into Coach Kirk's office to sign the papers, Finch stopped him and said, "Where's your momma? You need to go home and get your momma because you're not signing anything until she's here to watch."[6] Finch understood Memphis kids, but he also understood their families. On another home visit to recruit Mitchell point guard Andre Turner, Finch asked Turner's mother if he could speak with Andre outside. Finch sat Turner in the passenger seat of his car and told him that as a Memphis kid, he was going to Memphis State. No questions, he was going to Memphis State. Finch then went into Turner's house and told Turner's mom that he would take care of her son and that there was nothing to worry about.[7] Finch was not only their coach, but he was also a mentor, a man their mothers trusted, and a lifelong friend. These were valuable lessons he, himself had learned from men like Verties Sails during his playing career.

In 1983 Memphis's *Commercial Appeal* published a series of portraits of black men and women in the Mid-South called *Black Mosaics*. Finch was portrayed as a patient man who was waiting for his time as the first black head coach at a southern university. He recognized the position of older black coaches who had the qualifications but never received an opportunity to run a major college basketball program. For Finch, time was on his side, and the opportunity was within his reach, if he remained patient. Finch believed "that race was an issue since day one, but that if everybody would take the time to try to relate to one individual or group, race as a problem would be minimized." Finch proclaimed his simple formula for race relations: "treat people according to the way they treat me. I've learned to deal with people on an individual basis."[8] Finch believed that everybody had their way of fighting racism; for him, sports was the simplest of ways to combat racial issues in the city. *Commercial Appeal* reporter Leroy Williams reminded Memphians in his 1983 article that many black people in Orange Mound had counseled Finch not to attend Memphis State. Nevertheless, Finch decided to stay home and make his mark.[9]

In 1983, Finch loved his job as an assistant coach at Memphis State, and he knew that patience was vital if he was going to remain a unifying force. Patience in the face of segregation was the only response that the white establishment found acceptable. Patience allowed Finch to prevail upon Memphis's white society to abide by the doctrines of fair play and sportsmanship in his quest to be a head coach.

Three years later, when Dana Kirk was fired in September of 1986, Finch was named interim head coach. In the week that followed, the issue of race came to the forefront in the discussions about who would replace Kirk on a full-time basis. Was Memphis State University ready for its first African-American head basketball coach? When Memphis State fired Wayne Yates seven years earlier, Verties Sails received an obligatory interview. Sails had been among the three finalists, but he had never been a serious candidate for the job. Like Sails, Finch had recruited the majority of players on the Tigers' roster. Finch reminded the city that Sails should have had the opportunity to be a head coach at the major college level and that he never got the chance.[10] The university decided not to conduct a nationwide search. Compelled by the scandal and the fact that the fall term had already begun, the university announced on September 25 that Finch was the new head basketball coach. In so doing, Memphis State became the first school in the South to hire an African American as head coach. Gene Bartow, Verties Sails, and Melrose coach Dorsey Sims all praised his hiring. The local branch of the NAACP expressed its approval: "We are very pleased that Memphis State University has hired a black coach. We are sure Finch will be successful."[11] While the NAACP sang praises to the university for hiring Finch, they also diligently followed Finch's contract negotiations and urged Memphis State to pay Finch on the same scale that they had paid white coaches and to give him the same perks afforded previous coaches. The executive director of the local NAACP, Maxine Smith, met with Finch in late October to offer her support.[12] Smith, who earlier had chided the university for its treatment of its black basketball players, turned her attention to fighting for pay equity for the university's first black head basketball coach.

Larry Finch's position as the first black head coach in the South gave him a platform from which he could address some of the disparities in the coaching ranks. His standing as the hometown hero allowed him to break through the racial barrier in Memphis. After he was hired, he spoke openly of the lack of opportunities for black head coaches at major universities in the South. "I can't say why it happens. A lot of people say racism. That might have to be the basic reason, it probably is. But I hate to say that because I'm in a unique situation."[13] The SEC did not have a black head coach until the University of Tennessee hired Wade Houston in 1989. UT's location in the Upper South made it a somewhat less hostile environment for racial change, yet the university still moved slowly in this regard.[14] When Finch was hired as the head basketball coach at Memphis State, it opened the door for other black coaches in the South to join the ranks of collegiate head coaches.

One of the issues that black head coaches faced was that they received only one opportunity to be successful. When they failed, they were sent back to the ranks of assistant coach and left out of discussions for future head coaching positions. Fired white coaches are still considered viable head-coaching candidates. But fired black head coaches—once major white universities even hired black head coaches—could only later find assistant positions. Shortly after being hired, Finch said, "I know that if I fail, not only do I fail Larry Finch and Memphis State, but I fail for black people everywhere because the opportunities for other young black [coaches] will be diminished."[15] Finch was now in a unique situation. In Memphis, he was given an opportunity that he would not have received in other cities, but he now had a responsibility to his community and the black coaching community at large. The pressure of being the first black head coach at the university was significant, yet Finch felt that he was well-suited for success.

▲▼▲

Success came quickly for Finch. He was named the Metro Conference's Coach of the Year after the 1986–87 season. Even as the NCAA restrictions limited post-season play and left the university under NCAA scrutiny, Finch led the Tigers to a 23–8 regular-season record—the fourth-best record in school history.[16] Finch built his staff with local coaches by hiring Melrose's Dorsey Sims and Christian Brothers College's Dave Loos as assistants. Finch's patience, candor, and sincere approach changed how people viewed the program. Although the team started slow, they won 24 of their last 29 games. In their final game of the season, with the post-season not a possibility, they defeated rival Louisville 75–52 in the Metro Conference Championship game.[17] The sanctions levied by the NCAA meant that the Tigers could not play in the NCAA tournament, so the team relished their opportunity to win the conference championship against the rival Cardinals. Vincent Askew, who had considered transferring out of Kirk's program, shined for Finch throughout the season. He led the Tigers in scoring and was named First Team All-Metro. Sylvester Gray was named Metro Conference Freshman of the Year. It looked like Finch was guiding the Tigers out of the abyss back toward national prominence.[18] Shelby County Mayor Bill Morris praised Finch's success and reinvigorated the narrative that Finch was "a symbol of racial harmony, understanding, and civic pride."[19]

As the Tigers began their second season under Finch, Memphis felt a sense of relief as the NCAA reduced the post-season ban to one year, making the Tigers eligible for the 1988 NCAA tournament. Finch's second team confirmed that the Tigers were Memphis's hometown team: two-thirds of the roster were players from Memphis. Led by Dwight Boyd (from Kirby High), Sylvester Gray (from Bolton High), and Dewayne Bailey (from Melrose High), the team pushed through a sluggish start and advanced to the conference championship, where they lost to Louisville.[20] Their 20–12 record, the program's seventh straight twenty-win season, earned the Tigers a bid to the NCAA tournament. Placed in the Midwest bracket, the team traveled to South Bend, Indiana, where they defeated Baylor University in the first round before bowing out in the second round to Purdue.[21] Finch maintained the level of success that Tigers' fans expected. He ran a clean program, and he kept the roster full of local talent. After all of the issues the program had face during the Kirk years, the Memphis fanbase was once again reveling in the team's success.

While Tigers fans cheered, politics in the city remained racially charged. Scandal stood front and center. Rickey Peete, a black city councilman from the Seventh District, was indicted for violating the Hobbs Act. In October of 1988, Colonial Partners, a Memphis real estate developing company, applied for a permit to build the Pigeon Roost subdivision on Waring Road. Colonial Partners presented their project prospectus to the Memphis City Council's Land Use Board in January of 1989. It received approval and moved to the City Council for a final vote.[22] On February 9, 1990, Doug Dickens and Hank Hill of Colonial Partners met with Peete in his office at City Hall. After this meeting, Peete personally telephoned Hill and told him that for $2,000, Peete could secure the votes necessary to get approval in the City Council. Hill initially declined the offer and immediately telephoned his partner Dickens. Dickens then telephoned the United States District Attorney's office to report that Peete had solicited a bribe. Hill agreed to wear a wire and meet with Peete later that same afternoon. Hill offered Peete $1,000 before the vote and $1,000 after the vote, to which Peete agreed.[23] Peete's solicitation of $2,000 shows that graft was still prevalent in urban politics.

Peete's version of the meeting with Hill provides another look into racial tensions in the city at the time. Peete argued at his trial that the meeting with Hill had nothing to do with the Colonial Partner bid to develop the Pigeon Roost subdivision. He asserted that Hill was recruiting him to work with people who wanted to oust Mayor Richard Hackett from office. In Hill's testimony, he said that Peete had held one finger up to indicate that he was agreeing to the $1,000 bribe to garner the votes in the city council for the Pigeon Roost subdivision. Peete testified that he was holding up his middle finger to express his blunt opposition to the mayor as part of the recall effort. Instead of a bribe for the votes necessary for Pigeon Roost, Peete claimed that the money was a campaign contribution. The root of the problem, and his request for money from Hill, was financial. Peete was in arrears on an $18,000 loan and needed the money for personal reasons, not for his campaign fund. He told Hill, "It's not what you know, but who you know."[24] Peete accused the FBI of pursuing him because he had refused to aid in their investigation of Congressman Harold Ford Sr. Peete believed that the FBI was conspiring against himself and Ford because of their race.

The notion of racial unity through sport was absent in the war for political control of the city. Real estate developers Hill and Dickens were white insiders. Peete was a part of the black community's push for equitable representation. As a young, black city councilman, Peete was learning the harsh realities of politics in Memphis. His naiveté about how the white establishment conducted backroom deals cornered him into a position where they could, in turn, attack him for grievances of which they were also guilty. Peete helped his community in the same ways that the white establishment had been helping the white community for years, and white officials did not face legal reprisals for such actions. But as a young black politician, he could not commit those same sins without legal consequences. Although Peete helped to push through ordinances that helped the black community and put money in the pockets of black Memphians, Peete's participation in this scheme cost him two years in prison and six months in a halfway house.[25] White city councilman Tom Marshall believed that Peete "was often the glue that held the council together. He was the person many of us would go to in order to quash any kind of racial anxiety on any given issue. He always looked beyond race for the sake of expediency and the professional handling of issues."[26] In his attempt to look beyond race, Peete paid the price for the racial discord that permeated Memphis politics.

After Finch's first two seasons at the helm, the fanbase expected the team to return to national prominence and to the Final Four. Sophomore guard Elliot Perry led the Tigers in scoring and lived up to his accolades as a McDonald's All-American at Treadwell.[27] Freshman forward Ernie Smith and junior guard Cheyenne Gibson added scoring punch, but the Tigers did not have a legitimate post player to compete with the elite programs. Although the Tigers won twenty-one games in 1988–1989, they lost in the first round of the NCAA tournament to the University of DePaul. The optimism that fans had after the impressive 8–1 streak in February, which included wins over Florida State University and the University of Louisville, ended with an early exit from the NCAA tournament.[28] The following season, Finch's fourth, the team finished with less than twenty wins for the first time in nine years. The 1989–90 Tigers were never able to string together more than three wins in a row. The sub-par 18-win season ended with the Tigers losing to their in-state rival, the University of Tennessee, in the opening round of the NIT tournament at the Mid-South Coliseum.[29]

After his fourth season, fans began to question Finch's ability to lead the Tigers back to prominence. Many around the program began to wonder if Finch was as capable with the clipboard as he had been with the ball. Finch had been given a pass during his first two seasons. Now he was being held accountable for the recruits he was bringing on campus and for their performances in big games. One of the challenges Finch faced as a head coach was that many in the community still saw him as a young player whom they could advise and influence. They still expected him to take their advice as he had done as a player.[30] Finch faced scrutiny from the media, like his predecessors had. Bartow handled the media by pretending to listen to them but running the program his way regardless of the media's suggestions. Kirk did not even pretend to listen. He did the talking, and the media listened. Finch, as a young coach, was not as polished in front of the media.[31] He was kind to everyone in the community. When Finch made comments that rubbed some in the community the wrong way, he was chastised. It was his program, and, as a black man, he was asserting himself as the head coach in the same way his white predecessors had.

Heading into the 1990–91 season, Finch knew that the road ahead was going to be tough but that if the team could weather the storm, then they would soon return to prominence. In the spring of 1990, Finch landed Memphis State's biggest recruit since Finch himself had signed as a Tiger: Anfernee Hardaway. Hardaway, a local player out of Treadwell High, was the *Parade Magazine*'s High School Player of the Year and one of the most sought-after players in Memphis prep basketball history. Finch beat out local SEC power Arkansas and several other collegiate blue-bloods to sign Hardaway. Unfortunately for Finch, the NCAA's Proposition 48 forced Hardaway to take a red-shirt season because his academics did not meet increased NCAA standards.[32] Initiated in 1986, Proposition 48 was the NCAA's attempt to bolster the sagging academic performances of many student-athletes. It required incoming student-athletes to achieve an SAT score of 700 or an ACT score of 15 and to have a 2.0 high school grade-point average in 11 academic core courses in order to be eligible to play.[33] Coaches across the nation questioned the validity of these measurements as well as its racial bias against minority students. Prospective first-year student-athletes who did not meet all academic requirements lost eligibility in their first year. Partial qualifiers were not allowed to get athletic scholarships, although they could receive aid from a booster or other private or government sources. Georgetown University's John Thompson walked off the court before a game with Boston College in January of 1989 to protest Proposition 48's effect on minority student-athletes. Thompson told reporters after the game, "I will not coach in an NCAA sanctioned game until I am satisfied that something has been done to provide these student-athletes with appropriate opportunity and hope for access to college."[34]

Unlike Thompson, Finch remained quiet on the issue. He supported Hardaway in the classroom and accepted whatever fate his team would have without the Parade All-American. Finch grew up in a segregated Memphis; he realized that many things in life are not fair. His job was to figure out how to prosper in the face of adverse conditions, in the same way that he had prospered in the face of adversity as a young man in Orange Mound. If Finch played the race card like Thompson had, he would have damaged his reputation as a unifying force in the city. As the Tigers struggled, Hardaway sat. In April 1991, shortly after the season ended, Hardaway was shot in the foot in front of his cousin's house when four men held Hardaway and his cousin at gunpoint for their money, jewelry and shoes. Hardaway fractured three metatarsal bones in his foot but was quickly on his way to rehab after Finch chastised him privately. This was the only hiccup during his Prop 48 season. Hardaway had the bullet surgically removed and was back to full speed by the end of October, ready for his first season of eligibility.[35]

The Tigers' fanbase was excited as the 1991–1992 season approached. The Tigers prepared to move into the state-of-the-art Pyramid of America, located downtown along the Bluff. When the Tigers hosted Arkansas State University in the second round of the NIT on March 18, 1991, it became the last game the Tigers ever played in the Mid-South Coliseum. Emotionally, the building held a special place in the hearts of the Tiger faithful. Just before the Tigers' first game at the Pyramid, the political paradigm in the city shifted: Dr. Willie Herenton became the first African-American mayor in the city's history. He had claimed an improbable 142 vote victory over incumbent Richard Hackett.[36]

Herenton's victory over Hackett had seemed like a longshot. Just twelve months earlier A *Commercial Appeal* poll did not include Herenton as a candidate to respondents. Yet, many people in the black community believed that Herenton, the superintendent of the Memphis City Schools, was the most viable black candidate to defeat Hackett because of his growing political stature. When he announced his campaign in front of over a thousand supporters at the Peabody Hotel on July 3, 1991, he said, "I want to make it emphatically clear that the time is not four years from now. The time is now. We're saying to white Memphis to join hands with black Memphis. I firmly believe we are on our way. City hall, city hall, city hall."[37]

Herenton's political victory hinged upon his ability to unite the black vote and to convince the Ford political machine that he was the man to break the racial barrier. Earlier that year, in February, Shep Wilburn called for a "People's Convention," at which registered black voters would gather at the Mid-South Coliseum to vote for a consensus black mayoral candidate. In the eyes of the white establishment, the Coliseum, long celebrated as a space for black and white people to unite behind the Tigers, was now being used by the black community to further divide the city. White city councilwoman Pat Vander Schaaf tried to block their use of the arena, but the meeting still went forward as scheduled on April 27.[38] A consensus was harder to come by in the black community than Wilburn had expected. Six candidates were nominated that night, but Herenton received the largest percentage of votes. By the end of the night, there was still no one consensus candidate. Adding to the disputed outcome at the Mid-South Coliseum, Harold Ford Sr. denied the validity of the "People's Convention" and vowed to keep searching for a candidate. Five weeks later, Herenton forced Ford Sr.'s hand by resigning as Memphis City Schools Superintendent and filing the necessary paperwork to run for mayor. The black community would meet again to attempt to unify.

Reverend Ralph White offered his Bloomfield Baptist Church on South Parkway as a venue for a second political summit on Saturday, June 15. At this second summit, Ford Sr. had intended to announce Otis Higgs as his candidate for the mayoral seat. Yet when he arrived at the Bloomfield Baptist Church, Herenton's supporters had already packed the church to the rafters.[39] In a backroom deal, Ford met with Herenton and Higgs. Herenton's force of character persuaded Ford that Higgs could not win and that Herenton could. The black community was now united in its effort to win the 1991 mayoral election.

Herenton's quest was further aided by a 1991 judicial decision that changed the nature of mayoral elections in the city. Federal District Court Judge Jerome Turner banned runoffs in mayoral elections using the 1965 Voting Rights Act, Section 2, which bans voting practices that discriminate based on race, color, or membership in a language minority group.[40] In previous elections, white politicians used runoffs to divide and conquer. Hackett used this political strategy to win his first mayoral election in 1982. In the 1982 mayoral race Hackett campaigned against J.O. Patterson, a black city councilman, and Michael Cody, a white, liberal federal prosecutor. Hackett labeled Cody a divorcee and an ally of the ACLU, the NAACP, and Harold Ford Sr. In the eyes of the white establishment, this all meant that Cody was "black." Hackett discredited Cody in the white community, ensuring that he would win most of the white vote and thereby one of the two runoff spots. Patterson secured the second spot with most of the black vote. Hackett then relied upon the 54% of the city that was white to propel him past Patterson in the runoff election. Hackett made it quite clear that winning in Memphis politics required two things: "You need to know your numbers and your colors."[41] Turner's 1991 judicial decision meant that in the 1992 mayoral race, whoever could garner the most votes in November would become the mayor. The white establishment could no longer divide and conquer to maintain control of the mayor's office. Herenton's campaign for mayor also received a boost from an unexpected candidacy.

Prince Mongo's precipitous introduction on the ballot aided Herenton's campaign. Robert Hodges, better known by his self-styled moniker Prince Mongo, was a Memphis eccentric and minor political personality. He claimed to be the ambassador of the planet of Zambodia and to be 333 years old. Hodges's political fame in Memphis began in 1991 as an eccentric third candidate in the mayoral election. Infamous for his creative and bizarre public persona, Prince Mongo dressed in wildly stylized 1960s "Hippie" outfits. He often wore steampunk goggles, a long blonde wig, and various accessories, including a military bandolier loaded with tiny rubber chickens instead of bullets. He referred to everyone as "Spirit," and he "blessed" his followers by tossing white flour on them.[42] Independently wealthy, he had an affinity for politics in the city of Memphis. He owned several nightclubs in Memphis, including The Castle. The Castle, previously known as Ashlar Hall, was built by Robert Brinkley Snowden. Snowden's great-great-grandfather Colonel Robert C. Brinkley built the Peabody Hotel, and Snowden still owned the hotel during his lifetime. In 1960 the Brinkley family sold The Castle, and it was turned into a restaurant. Hodges bought The Castle in 1990 and converted it into a nightclub. Thus, Prince Mongo became associated with one of Memphis's founding families.[43]

This nightclub owner turned alien from Zambodia turned "righteous" political candidate, added a bizarre twist of political fate to Herenton's 142 vote mayoral victory in 1991. Prince Mongo's followers, a unique group of Bohemian eccentrics, cast 2,923 votes for Mongo, approximately 1.18% of the votes cast. If seventy-two of the voters who cast their ballot for Mongo had instead voted for Hackett, then Herenton would have lost.[44] Since the introduction of a commission form of government in the 1920s, the black community had felt that decisions in mayoral elections were mindboggling and irrational. When Prince Mongo entered into the 1991 mayoral election, irrationality allowed the black community in Memphis to gain what it had so long coveted: the mayor's office. Prince Mongo's presence does not diminish the political organization of the black community in the years and months leading up to this election. Yet without Prince Mongo's presence in this election, Herenton's slogan—"the time is now"—might have been empty words once again.

Hackett accepted the people's decision when the election commission issued the results; Herenton had won 122,596 votes, and Hackett had won 122,454 votes. Three hours later, Hackett told supporters: "a challenge (to the final tally) would not be appropriate despite irregularities in the vote." Amid the jubilation running rampant through black Memphis, pastor L. LaSimba Gray offered a call for political unity: "Brothers and sisters, it's healing time, a city that was once divided will now be brought together."[45] One month later, the Tigers opened the newly constructed Great American Pyramid in a game against 20th ranked DePaul University on November 29, which was televised by ESPN. The Tigers Media Guide referred to the 321 feet high, stainless steel edifice as "a cooperative effort of the city of Memphis, Shelby County, and Memphis State University that symbolizes a belief in the future."[46] Memphis was progressing forward with its first black mayor, a black hometown hero as the program's head coach, and another local black basketball phenom ready to take the Tigers back to national prominence.

Anfernee Hardaway's play impacted the program immediately; he helped the Tigers win twenty-three games. The team advanced to the Great Mid-West Conference championship game and returned to the NCAA tournament after a two-year hiatus. Hardaway averaged 17 points, 5.5 assists, and 7 rebounds as he led the program back to the Elite Eight. Hardaway became the face of the program, mirroring the popularity that Finch earned when he played. And with David Vaughn on the inside, the Tigers were poised to return to the upper tier of college basketball. An overtime win at Vanderbilt at the close of January brought the team together. After the Vanderbilt win, Finch proclaimed, "We knew that we could win on the road."[47] Although the Tigers lost to Cincinnati in the conference championship, they made the most of their six seed in the NCAA's Midwest Region.[48]

After defeating Pepperdine University in the first round by ten, the Tigers faced their regional foe, the University of Arkansas. Nolan Richardson's Hogs were not only one of the best teams in the nation, but they were also actively recruiting Memphis kids. Arkansas guard Todd Day was a McDonald's All-American out of Hamilton High. He left Memphis to play for Richardson at Arkansas.[49] This game meant more to both the Tiger faithful and Finch then most other games did. David Vaughn's winning shot with five seconds remaining in the game propelled the Tigers to a two-point upset over the favored Hogs. Finch needed the win to keep recruiting hometown talent. Finch's recruiting successes in the city were directly related to his playing days and the time he spent playing in community centers all over town. He knew every back street in the city.[50] This home court advantage became essential as outside programs began recruiting the city's best players. After Finch signed Hardaway and then defeated the Hogs in the NCAA tournament, Finch regained the momentum he needed to keep the city's best talent interested in playing for Memphis State.[51]

The overtime victory over the Razorbacks propelled the Tigers to the Sweet Sixteen against Georgia Tech. Billy Smith's running one-handed jumper as time expired forced overtime with the Yellow Jackets and saved the game for the Tigers, who had trailed the entire game. In the extra period, the Tigers gained control from the foul line and went on to post a four-point victory. The win over Bobby Cremins's team brought the Tigers back to the Elite Eight for the first time since 1985.[52] The Midwest bracket proved cruel to the Tigers. In the Elite 8, the Tigers were forced to play their conference nemesis the University of Cincinnati for the fourth time that season. Bob Huggins's Bearcats, led by Nick Van Exel's 22 points, polished off the Tigers and ended Memphis State's 1992 NCAA tournament.[53] Hardaway's play and the team's success during the season gave the Tiger faithful a renewed sense of hope moving forward.

Heading into the new season, Finch added assistant coach Tom Schuberth to bolster recruiting and to help land a point guard to complement Hardaway. As a recruiter for Northeastern Louisiana University, Schuberth became familiar with Memphis talent when he recruited some of Coach Verties Sails players from Shelby State. After a chance encounter with Schuberth on a flight to the 1986 Portsmouth Invitational, Finch decided to bring Schuberth on board to replace Jimmy Adams.[54] Local sports reporter Dennis Freeland succinctly challenged Finch's coaching ability in the *Memphis Flyer*: "when he has talent, he is a competent coach. Without talented players, he is lost."[55] Finch hired Schuberth with the expectation that the Tigers would be able to recruit better players. Schuberth recalls that when Finch hired him, Finch told him, "recruit them the right way. Do the best you can." Even as outside voices chimed in about Finch's inability as a strategist, he never wavered from his belief that things must be done the right way. He would not lure Tigers prospects with shoeboxes full of money. Finch prided himself on not jeopardizing his reputation, the school's reputation, or a kid's eligibility. If a player got away because another school was operating outside of the rules, that was out of Finch's control. Finch never played the game that way.[56]

Finch's goal of bringing a national championship back to Memphis seemed to be within his reach as the team looked forward to the 1992–1993 season. Hardaway was named a John Wooden Player of the Year candidate, and he adorned the Tigers media guide cover as a symbol of the hopes of Tigers fans. Hope turned to gloom during the home opener when David Vaughn suffered a season-ending injury. Before his injury in the opening moments of the second half, the Tigers had built a twenty-point lead against Arkansas. But without Vaughn in the post, the Razorbacks were able to knock off the Tigers. The second half proved to be a precursor to the season. The team sorely missed Vaughn's post presence.[57] The preseason Tigers had been ranked as high as #8 in the AP poll, but after their trip to the Maui Classic in Hawaii, the Tigers, now 3–4, dropped out of the AP Poll.[58] Hardaway and the Tigers righted the ship and finished the regular season at 8–2 in the Great Midwest Conference. The Tigers fell in the conference championship to Cincinnati but earned the school's fourteenth NCAA tournament bid and a #10 seed in the Southeast Regional. Hardaway's 17 points were not enough to push the Tigers past Western Kentucky in the opening round.[59] Following the disappointing loss, Hardaway declared for the upcoming NBA draft. Finch fought to keep the Tigers relevant nationally. He signed two highly recruited local players, McDonald's All-American guard Sylvester "Deuce" Ford Jr. from Fairley High and forward Cedric Henderson from East High. This signing class showed that Finch was still capable of keeping the best talent at home. It also gave the Tigers the number one ranked class in the country, according to recruiting expert Bob Gibbons.[60] With Hardaway's exodus, the Tigers would have to rely heavily upon this group of incoming freshmen.

Recruited to be Hardaway's heir apparent, "Deuce" Ford joined the Tigers as a highly-touted prospect. Ford had won the state championship at Fairley High with his father, Sylvester Ford Sr., at the helm. His father wanted him to leave Memphis to join the Fab Five at Michigan or play in the Southeastern Conference at Tennessee or Georgia. As a Memphis kid, Ford Jr. felt the allure and pull of playing for the hometown Tigers. He signed with Memphis State, hoping to follow in the footsteps of Finch and Hardaway. When "Deuce" arrived on campus that fall, he was still hampered by injuries. His drive and determination to win the state championship at Fairley had led him to play on stress fractures. After his senior season in high school, he had to have steel rods placed in both legs. When workouts began in the fall of 1993, it became apparent that Ford was not the same caliber of player that he had been before the surgery.[61] Unable to perform at the speed he had in high school, Ford soon fell out of favor with Finch. Midway through the season, he was out of the starting lineup. Fellow freshman point guard Chris Garner, from Treadwell High, sparked the Tigers defensively with 74 steals and shined in the backcourt. Sophomore David Vaughn returned to the Tiger lineup and posted 20 double-doubles (points and rebounds) to lead the way in the paint.[62] However, neither Vaughn's or Garner's play was enough to lead the Tigers to post-season play.

The Tigers finished under .500 for the second time in Finch's tenure at 13–16, and the losses began to take their toll on Finch. Finch remained adamant in his belief that he could not only return the Tigers to the Final Four but also bring home the national championship that they had been so close to winning in 1973. A local television station replayed the games each night after the local news. When Finch returned home after a game, he would watch it again at home. He was determined to find a way to win. Over the years, the more he lost, the heavier the weight became.[63] The skeptics began to reemerge after the sub .500 finish, but this time the skepticism came on the heels of one of the best recruiting classes in school history. The skeptics began to question Finch's ability to lead the Tigers back to the Final Four. He could recruit, but his ability to coach came under attack.

Over the next two seasons, the Tigers bounced back, and it looked as if Finch had once again righted the program's course. In the summer of 1994, President Lane Rawlings changed the name of the university from Memphis State to the

University of Memphis. As the university looked to move past its perception as a local state school, Finch brought in a recruiting class capable of lifting the Tigers to NCAA glory once again. His biggest recruiting coup came when he signed another McDonald's All-American, Lorenzen Wright, out of Booker T. Washington High.[64] Wright played for Finch's MSU teammate, Fred Horton, at Washington High and was the nephew of former Tiger guard Alvin Wright ('78). Wright told *Sports Illustrated* later that year, "I have known Coach Finch forever, and I came here because I knew he would do right by me."[65] Finch used his local connections again to sign Michael Wilson, a rising star from Shelby State Community College. After graduating from Melrose High, Wilson played at Shelby State for Verties Sails, who remained close to Finch. With high school All-American Wright, preseason All-American candidate David Vaughn, and conference Newcomer of the Year Cedric Henderson, the Tigers looked like they had one of the premier front lines in all of college basketball.[66]

The 1994–95 Tigers returned the program to national prominence with a Sweet Sixteen appearance. Eleven of the fourteen players on the roster had attended high school in Memphis. Finch was again on top, bringing the city together at the Pyramid to cheer on their Tigers. They reeled off thirteen wins in a fifteen-game span from December to February to solidify the team's NCAA chances and another twenty-win season.[67] The Tigers won the regular-season Great Midwest Conference title but lost to Cincinnati in the tournament semifinals. Disappointed by their conference tournament loss, a #6 seed in the NCAA's Mid-West Region reenergized the team.[68] They were greeted by their long-time rival Louisville in their first-round game but defeated the Cardinals by twenty-one points, the largest margin of loss for the Cardinals in the NCAA tournament. The team's win moved Finch's record against rival Louisville to 13–10 as both a player and coach.[69] T-shirts appeared around town with the slogan: "I'd rather be a Finch than a Cardinal."[70] In the second round, the Tigers survived a scare from Purdue in a dramatic two-point win as David Vaughn hit the game-winning basket at the buzzer.[71]

The win over Purdue advanced the Tigers to the Sweet Sixteen for the second time in Finch's tenure. Their reward was a matchup with local rival and defending national champion Arkansas. The Tigers were ahead by one with 14 seconds remaining when a "phantom call" on Tiger guard Chris Garner gave Razorback Corey Beck two foul shots. Beck, a Memphis product from Fairley High, hit one of the two and forced overtime. The Razorbacks opened with a 9–2 run in the extra period and ended the Tigers' hopes of advancing further in the tournament.[72] After the game, Finch criticized the officiating and was later fined by the NCAA for his comments.[73] Finch's critics returned and again pointed to his bench coaching as the reason for the team's failures. Local sports radio even predicted that Finch would have lost his job if he had lost to inter-state rival Tennessee earlier in the season. The Tigers won. They proceeded to win the conference, make the NCAA tournament, and advance to the Sweet Sixteen. Finch told reporters: "I was attacked personally, but you just have to keep believing in yourself. Everybody has an opinion."[74] Finch understood the dynamics of coaching in his hometown for the Tigers. The level of excellence he set as a player, became the expectation for him as a coach.

The 1995–1996 season brought another change to the Tiger program as it joined Conference USA (C-USA) for its inaugural season. C-USA was a twelve-team conference created with the sole purpose of increasing profits for its predominately basketball focused member schools. The league was created with a six-year $30 million contract from ESPN, which gave it financial stability and enabled early growth.[75] Tigers seniors Chris Garner, Michael Wilson, and Rodney Newsom returned, along with underclassmen Lorenzen Wright and Cedric Henderson. Preseason prognosticators believed they were ready to return to the NCAA tournament and make a deep run. They entered the season ranked #13 in the AP Poll and got off to a hot start, winning their first eight games. The team catapulted up to #3 in the AP Poll before losing by three points to John Calipari's top-ranked Minutemen from the University of Massachusetts.[76] Trouble soon followed when the Tigers lost to rival Louisville and then by over twenty points to Big East opponent Georgetown in a two-week span.[77] Although the Tigers never dropped out of the top 25 in the polls, they never reached the level that media and fans had expected for the team before the season began.

Finch remained as passionate as ever in practice. His consummate drive to be the best continued to inspire him to bring Memphis back to the Final Four. Players under Finch enjoyed his serious side, but they also appreciated that he could relate to them since he came from the neighborhood. As critics found more ways to criticize Finch, he remained focused. His system was a combination of styles from Bartow and Kirk. Yet the naysayers continued to question his coaching ability—something that the media had done far less often with his white predecessors. When his roster was laden with Memphis players, critics said he had too many Memphis kids. When he recruited players from outside of the city, they complained that he did not have enough Memphis players on his roster.[78] A city that once clamored to see Finch return to the university as coach now criticized his every move. Finch became the maligned hometown hero. Even as the city doubted him, Finch's love for the university and his city never waned.

Although Finch celebrated his 200th win in ten seasons when the Tigers won against Southern Mississippi University in late February, the critics remained perched to attack.[79] An early exit from the C-USA tournament in Memphis left the Tigers with a #5 seed in the NCAA's West region. The Tigers traveled to Albuquerque, New Mexico, where they met Drexel University, a #12 seed. Drexel thoroughly outplayed the Tigers in the opening half behind the play of their undersized post player Malik Rose. In the locker room at halftime, Finch did his best to convince the Tigers that they needed to improve their play. The Tigers were looking past Drexel in anticipation of playing Syracuse University in the next round.[80] When the Tigers came out in the second half, they watched as Drexel kept pounding it inside to Rose. When the Tigers collapsed on Rose, Jeff Meyers and Mike DeRocckis scorched the Tigers from behind the three-point line. Rose's 21 points and 15 rebounds spelled the end of the Tigers season. Finch felt the weight of another early exit from the NCAA tournament. Instead of a second-round matchup with Syracuse, the eventual national finalist, the Tigers limped home looking for answers. The Tigers were hard hit by graduation; they lost Garner, Newsome, Wilson, and Wright heading into the next season.

The Tigers opened the 1996–1997 campaign 1–4, which hastened the university's push to force Finch out as its head coach. The university first approached Finch after the December 18, 1996, game against the University of Louisiana-Monroe. He refused to accept their buyout on the spot. Instead, with the aid of longtime friend Reverend Bill Atkins, Finch asked for adequate compensation from the school before he agreed to a buyout.[81] The university did not offer Finch the appropriate compensation until he brought in legal counsel. After a 61–47 win over Oklahoma University at the Pyramid, the University of Memphis held a press conference and announced that Finch was resigning and would accept the school's buyout offer. Ironically, President Rawlins referred to Finch as "the most important figure in Memphis sports history."[82] Finch's attorney Ted Hansom, who had negotiated Finch's first head coaching contract in 1986, loudly proclaimed that "Finch is being made the scapegoat."[83] Finch's wife Vickie remembers "not know anything other than what I read in the newspapers about his firing."[84] Larry Finch Jr., who was a sophomore on the team, did not hear anything before his teammates did. "I heard the rumblings," he said, "but it wasn't anything I hadn't heard before."[85] If Finch knew anything about the firing, he kept it to himself to protect the ones he loved most. Finch prided himself on doing what was best for his family and his school.

Finch was at the center of the trope that basketball had healed the city, yet when the university felt the tug of the financial strain, they turned on Finch. Since he had been hired, many fans, alumni, and boosters had found it difficult to separate Finch as a player from Finch as a coach. As the seasons wore on, they became frustrated by their inability to influence him. They still saw him as the boy from Melrose High who would respectfully listen to their advice. But as their head coach and the man in charge, he listened less than he had as a player and made his own decisions. In the end, he, not those outside voices, was responsible for the wins and losses.[86] Publicly, Finch never spoke ill of the university, Rawlins, or Athletic Director R.C. Johnson. Memphis State basketball was his family. It had been the center of his life since 1969. As much pain as his removal caused, Finch never outwardly expressed his disappointment. What broke his heart more than anything was that he could not win a national championship for his alma mater. The university denied him the opportunity to reach this goal.[87]

Finch's position as head coach had been precarious from the onset of his tenure. His record was always questioned, even though he ran a clean program and graduated players. R.C. Johnson provided a vague five-point analysis of the criteria the athletic department used to evaluate Finch. The city's "most important figure in sports history" had been let go without anyone in the administration giving one clear reason for his dismissal. Melrose High principal LaVaughn Bridges called Finch "a man from Orange Mound, a model for the community."[88] Finch often spoke with the kids in Orange Mound. He told them, "You can be anything you want to be. But you have got to listen to the people that care about you. With that and the help of the Lord, you can do anything."[89] For years Larry Finch heeded the advice of Verties Sails, Gene Bartow, Ronnie Robinson, Herb Hilliard, and Dana Kirk as he forged a successful career. His career was marked by unparalleled success in the school's basketball history. The university's decision to move the Tigers from the Mid-South Coliseum to the Pyramid was the most significant factor in their decision to fire Finch. The 20,142 seat Pyramid required more season ticket holders, but when the university decided to air Tiger home games on live television, the number of people attending games in the arena went down.[90] By the 1990s, modern college basketball was becoming an economic juggernaut. This new paradigm meant that universities looked at economic impact figures, which were often outside a coach's control, rather than at a coach's record or abilities. Universities were not loyal to their coaches. Former Tiger head coach Dana Kirk, a sports talk show host on WMC-AM 79 at the time, painted an accurate picture of the situation: "When you're off in attendance you've got problems. The University of Memphis is the heartbeat of Memphis, Tennessee, and the athletic department is big business. If you're losing money, you've got to make corrections."[91]

If Memphis was to remain relevant in college basketball, the Great American Pyramid would need to play a vital role in this growth. Originally an $80 million-dollar project designed by Memphis real estate mogul Sidney Shlenker, former owner of the Denver Nuggets, the city was responsible for $56 million of its total cost.[92] By November 1991, the Pyramid stumbled to completion. The city fired Sidney Shlenker after he failed to raise $50 million in financing. Later, his management company sought protection in bankruptcy court for over $16 million.[93] The Pyramid was doomed financially from the start. It was initially designed to include shops, restaurants, and museums, but these never made the final plans. As a result, it served only as an arena for concerts and sporting events. The Tigers, its primary tenant, felt the financial pressure. Winning was supposed to bring fans downtown to spend money. When the Pyramid did not bring fans downtown, the entire downtown business district felt the impact. Without a museum or a theme park, the Tigers alone were responsible for attracting people to the downtown business district. The Pyramid's economic failure helped to bring down Finch.

The *Tri-State Defender* saw Finch's resignation in a different light. It argued that the university's all-time winningest coach lost his job because of "blatant racism."[94] Dr. L. Lasimba Gray, the pastor of the New Sardis Baptist Church, led the charge of Finch supporters who felt that the university had betrayed the black community. After Willie Herenton's 1991 mayoral victory, Gray urged the city to unite behind Herenton, but Finch's unexpected firing reminded Gray and black people throughout the community of the risks that black pioneers in Memphis faced. Many in the black community had urged Finch not to sign with Memphis State in 1969. After dedicating close to thirty years of his life to the university, he became the scapegoat for the financial fiasco of the Great American Pyramid. From the black community's perspective, the university had been uplifted by Finch's play, spirit, and long-term commitment to the university, and his reward was a forced resignation in the middle of the season.

Larry Finch handled the entire process with the dignity that had marked his tenure since his arrival on campus in 1969. On the night that Rawlins and R.C. Johnson announced his fate, Sunday Adebayo ran over and hugged Finch during player introductions. Finch's eyes welled up with tears. After the game, Finch said, "I won't ever forget Adebayo for that."[95] Finch referred to Lane Rawlins as a "class act" during the press conference announcing his resignation. Finch still held to one of Verties Sails life lessons: "If you can't say anything good, don't say anything at all."[96]

The Tigers won Finch's last game as head coach. Finch reflected, "the fans were just great, and I saw a group of young men really rise up to the occasion." Former players from Keith Lee to Rodney Douglas showed up to pay homage to their coach. Bartlett banker Harold Byrd epitomized the feelings of so many Memphis fans when he said, "we wanted national television to know what we think about him. He's the Jackie Robinson of basketball in Memphis. Larry did the bottom line right, with integrity, class, and no cheating." Following Finch's final game as coach, Tiger official scorer Jimmy Hayslip, who had worked every home game Finch attended as a player or coach, upheld the myth of Finch as a unifying figure: "I think he did more to solidify this city after Dr. King was killed than all the politicians combined. At that crucial time, he was the glue that held the city together."[97]

▲ ▼ ▲

Outside of the Mid-South Coliseum, Memphis was a very complicated place. School desegregation led to one of the largest exoduses in the history of public schools in the nation, creating one of the nation's largest private school communities. Harold Ford Sr. of Memphis became the first African American elected to the House of Representatives in the history of Tennessee. In the 1980s, both white and black political offices became targets of federal and state indictments. These scandals only further divided the city. The white establishment employed Larry Finch to quell the storm of political upheaval taking place before their own eyes. His position of leadership, as the university's head coach, was an acceptable middle ground for the white political establishment that struggled openly with the new racial paradigm in the city. For his part, Finch relished the role of unifier in the city. He remained apolitical during his basketball career and was adamant that, "If the world was like an athletic program—a winning team—It would be a lot better."[98] Unfortunately for Finch, the worlds of sport and politics collided in 1996 when he lost his head coaching job with the Tigers. For some lifelong Memphians, Finch had brought the city together behind basketball during one of the most turbulent times in the city's racist past. For others, the Tiger basketball program only masked the deeper racial wounds that remained present throughout Finch's basketball career.

Instead of signaling Memphis's arrival as a city in the New South, the most iconic basketball figure in the city's history paid the ultimate price. The local press looked back on bygone days with pride and joy, remembering not the failures but Finch's heroics as a player and as a coach. As a black man in the South, he was never afforded another opportunity to coach again. White Memphians remember the Coliseum as a space to cheer on their Tigers and see what racial equality might look like. However, after the games, they returned to a world that remained segregated by race. For black Memphians, many of whom had warned Finch against going to Memphis State, basketball provided hope that a shift in the cultural paradigm in the city was possible. But when the games were over, black Memphians still confronted the legacies and realities of Jim Crow in their daily lives. On the court, their native son, Finch, became a symbol of hope, even as his life revealed the barriers that remained.

From Finch's playing days at Melrose High through his coaching tenure at Memphis State, basketball was always at the center of his world. For Finch, basketball was a way to bring people together. Finch was born into a world governed by Jim Crow laws, in a city that leaned heavily on its old Southern culture. He came of age after one of the city's darkest moments and made a bold decision to go where others before him had not been allowed. His abilities on the basketball court allowed him to make inroads on Memphis State's campus as the school's first black basketball star. Accompanied by his high school running mate and high school sweetheart, he changed how many Memphians viewed young black men. Local politicians and journalists alike were drawn to his persona and began to present his success as an example of racial healing in the city. Unable to resolve the deep-seated racial issues present in this era, these men turned to Finch's story as a symbol of progress.

Outside of the Mid-South Coliseum, the city remained divided, when Finch graduated the university continued to struggle with racial progress. Across town, on the other side of the Belt Line, all-black LeMoyne-Owen College captured the city's first national championship. Hidden behind the veil of segregation, most white Memphians were oblivious to the school's basketball triumph. Later, when former Melrose prep coach Verties Sails Jr. became the first

African American full-time assistant basketball coach at Memphis State, the issue of race remained a stumbling block on campus and in the community. Sails made inroads in recruiting black athletes, helped defuse racial conflicts within the program, and supported his head coach, yet he still faced racism throughout his tenure. Denied an opportunity to be the head coach at Memphis State, Sails fell into near obscurity as Shelby State Community College's head basketball coach.

The ABA provided the city another opportunity to rally behind a hometown team. Instead, white Memphians resented the professional basketball players who made more money than them and actively defied acceptable cultural norms in the city. As a result, the league failed. The Mid-South Coliseum never reached a fevered pitch for the ABA as it had with the 1973 Tigers team. Neither Johnny Neumann or Larry Finch could resurrect the troubled franchise.

When Finch returned to Memphis as an assistant coach under Dana Kirk, the city once again embraced him. Finch's boss, Dana Kirk, set out to win at any cost and further exposed the racial discord within the city in the process. Accused of exploiting black players and funneling money to Tiger players, Kirk became a symbol of the ills of college basketball. Finch's ascension to the head chair in the university's basketball program was a byproduct of Kirk's failure and the timing of his demise. Many in the black community feared that their leading black candidate would get passed over again, as had Sails in 1979. Finch's position as head coach, once secured by contract, was tenuous. Many around the program continued to see him as the young boy who brought Memphis State fame in 1973, not a man capable of leading a major university's basketball program. His demise was a product of the city's poor economic planning and the changing climate of the collegiate game. Finch was still exalted as the city's favorite son, even in the hour of his demise.

Finch grew up in Boss Crump's segregated Memphis. Throughout his life, he witnessed the shifting racial dynamics in the city—from Crump to the city's first black mayor, Dr. Willie Herenton. Many of the same politicians and journalists who praised him and promulgated the myth that Finch was a racial unifier remained in the city throughout his basketball career. Memphians, and Memphis State basketball fans reveled in what Finch built: a basketball program with national acclaim. Nevertheless, in many ways, the city remained as divided along racial lines in 1997 as it had when Finch's Melrose team won the MIAA city championship in 1968 or when his Tigers team advanced to the NCAA finals against UCLA in 1973. Finch was a symbol of hope for a city torn by racial strife. The university, its fan base, and many in the city believed that one man could unify a city through sport. Finch understood the racial dynamics of his hometown and believed that his basketball career was one way he could make Memphis a better place. For a few short hours at a time throughout his basketball career, Finch united the city behind its love for basketball. However, once the fans left the arena, they returned to a city divided and struggling over race.

Epilogue

The year after Finch's forced resignation, he turned to local politics as a way to remain engaged with the city that he loved. Finch made a strong showing against Republican incumbent Guy Bates in the race for Shelby County Registrar. Finch's mother, Maple, suffered a heart attack on the eve of the election, and his heart immediately turned to caring for her. Bates won by 127 votes. Bates outspent Finch by a three-to-one margin. He also relied upon the white Republican majority in Shelby County to overcome Finch's popularity and retain his seat. Finch's respectability remained evident in his concession speech: "We didn't have the money of some of the well-oiled machines, but by the same token, we did the best with what we had and took our votes to the people."[1] Finch refused to bad mouth his opponent, a quality of his with which Memphians were familiar. Instead, he focused on how his campaign gave its best effort.

Three years after Finch's failed run for political office, the NBA awarded the city of Memphis a franchise. Following a unanimous vote by the NBA's relocation committee, the Vancouver Grizzlies announced their move to Memphis on June 29, 2001. Professional basketball was back in the city after a sixteen-year hiatus. They brought the Grizzlies name with them. Few basketball fans in the city remembered the Memphis Grizzlies from the 1970s World League of Football. When the Grizzlies' NBA management team polled the Memphis fans, they "overwhelmingly told us how much they loved the name."[2] The Grizzly name resonated with lifelong sports fans in the city. The city's pre-eminent sports journalist George Lapides celebrated the Grizzlies as ardently as he had the

Pros in the 1970s: "What [the Grizzlies] have done to reduce divisiveness in the community has been as good for this city as anything I can think of. It's great to sit in the stands and see a white guy and a black guy—who by chance happen to be sitting next to each other—high-five each other."[3] The Grizzlies offered the city's sports fans another opportunity to congregate together under one roof to support their hometown team.

"Grit and Grind" became the team's identity. The Grizzlies employed high-pressure on-ball defense, milked the clock offensively, and asserted their dominance physically on the opposition in the paint. The Grizzlies became the NBA franchise where castoff players like Zach Randolph were accepted. A former Michigan State player whose reputation in the NBA preceded him, Randolph became the embodiment of Grit and Grind in Memphis. Off the court, Randolph made an impact on the community by providing food baskets, Christmas gifts, and coats as well as $20,000 to the MIFA Emergency Services Plus-1 program. This program paid off past-due utility bills for 200 Memphis households on the verge of having their electricity and heating turned off.[4] Players like Randolph endeared themselves to Memphis fans, both black and white. Unlike the black professional players in the ABA who had faced racism and had not been accepted, the Grizzlies' players became part of the fabric of the community.

When Finch suffered a heart attack and two strokes in December of 2002, the health of the city's most iconic basketball legend concerned many in the community.[5] At age 51, he was left paralyzed on his left side and lost the ability to speak; his voice had been one of his most endearing character traits.[6] After Finch's forced resignation, the Tigers had struggled. At the time of his heart attack and strokes, they were on their third head coach in five years and were still looking for their first NCAA tournament bid since his departure. Finch's former player Ken Moody organized a benefit golf tournament to help pay the mounting costs of Finch's medical care. Moody brought the city together to support "Coach." Many people were reminded of how Finch had brought the city together for nearly thirty years. Moody told the crowd gathered at Galloway Golf Course: "Look at this crowd and its white [people] and black [people], males and females, young and old, and he has brought the city together again. There's no way the Lord would rain on this parade. This is one of his angels." Praising Finch, Pastor L. LaSimba Gray referred to him as "a builder of humanity."[7] The *Tri-State Defender* joined in the praise, but also echoed the sentiment in the black community that Finch had not been treated fairly by the university. Local black golf pro Charles Hudson, who helped to organize the event, reiterated that sentiment: "It wasn't right then, and now that he's in this predicament, those people he worked for need to step up to the plate and do the right thing."[8]

At the following year's golf benefit for Finch, the community was even more concerned as his health waned further. In the same year, new Tiger coach John Calipari received a $600,000 pay raise from the university to ensure that he remained in the city.[9] Calipari was a hired gun, a man who came into the city to resurrect the basketball program. Calipari returned the program to the NCAA championship game in 2009, where the Tigers lost to Kansas. Later that spring, Calipari departed for the University of Kentucky, to the outrage of many Memphians. The Tigers won and competed at the highest level nationally thanks to Finch. However, as Verties Sails told the *Commercial Appeal,* "a week or two after [Finch's] last game, people moved on to something else. Everybody forgot about Larry. But he didn't forget. He couldn't forget."[10]

The city opened the FedEx Forum for its NBA franchise in 2004. Located on Beale Street, the arena brought crowds downtown and revitalized the Beale Street district when it opened. The FedEx Forum cost $250 million in taxpayer money, but the city once again had a venue to serve as a central meeting place. Billboards around town hailed the arena because it offered something for everyone. The phrase "The Thrill is On," an adaption of the B.B. King song "The Thrill is Gone," was plastered on these billboards. The Forum used this cultural symbol to sell the Grizzlies and fabricate feelings of excitement and authenticity for visitors and residents in the "home of the blues."[11] The Forum sits on the edge of Beale Street in downtown Memphis: an intersection of the white and black communities. Its accessible location for all Memphians marks a decided advantage over the Pyramid. The FedEx Forum, like the Mid-South Coliseum once did, brings white and black people together on common ground to cheer on Memphis basketball.

On April 2, 2011, Larry Finch succumbed to the health issues that had plagued him for the previous ten years. The front page of the *Commercial Appeal* published a picture of Finch smiling and shaking hands after a 1997 victory over the Houston Cougars at the Pyramid. Below that was a black and white picture of Finch, in tears, being comforted by Coach Gene Bartow after the 1973 NCAA Finals loss to UCLA. Six full pages of stories and pictures memorialized the man who brought Memphis together like no other man in the history of the city. Columnist Geoff Calkins reminded the city how Finch had chosen Memphis State over other suitors, even over the objection of many people in Orange Mound. Finch, along with Ronnie Robinson, "brought black and white together, carried Memphis State to the Final Four in 1973 and caused a city driven by racial hatred to see past its differences."[12] For Memphians, Finch was a native son who broke down the color barrier for the best black basketball players in the city. He became a symbol of hope for the white political establishment after the 1968 Sanitation Workers Strike. Finch spurned the NBA to remain at home and play for his hometown's ABA team, the Tams. The university turned to him to bring respectability back to Tiger basketball as its head coach, and he did. Larry Finch embodied the best that the city and university had to offer.

Off the court, the city remained as divided as it had in 1973 over schooling. In 2013, the Memphis City Schools rescinded their charter and forced the predominately white Shelby County Schools to incorporate their system. Within one calendar year, the incorporated communities of Collierville, Germantown, Arlington, Lakeland, and Millington opened their "special" districts. The 1973 busing dilemma still echoes through the city's social fabric. Shelby County Schools remain underfunded and predominately black, as they had been under the umbrella of the Memphis City Schools. White parents placed their trust in these new municipal schools instead of the Shelby County Schools. The disparities between the districts remain evident in amount of funding schools in each district receive and the state of their facilities. The racial composition of these new municipal districts shows how solidly white flight has impacted the city of Memphis and Shelby County. Even as racial animus remains prevalent in the issue of schooling, basketball in the city still provides hope and a place for the city to gather united behind a singular cause.

In the spring of 2018, the university hired Anfernee "Penny" Hardaway to resurrect its basketball program. Hardaway is the school's most storied player after Finch. In his two seasons as a Tiger, Hardaway led the team to a 43–23 record—including eight wins over nationally ranked schools—and directed the Tigers to two NCAA Tournament appearances, including an Elite Eight trip in 1992. A two-time All-American and two-time Great Midwest Conference Player of the Year, Hardaway averaged 22.8 points, 8.5 rebounds, 6.4 assists, and 2.4 steals in 1992–93. After his junior year, Hardaway declared for the NBA Draft. Following his last season in a Tigers uniform, Hardaway secured a role in the movie *Blue Chips* starring Nick Nolte and Shaquille O'Neal. The introverted Hardaway developed an on-court relationship with O'Neal during filming, which led O'Neal to lobby the Orlando Magic to acquire Hardaway that summer through the draft.[13] Hardaway began a 14-year pro career with the Orlando Magic.[14] The pair became the organization's foundation and brought the franchise to its first NBA Finals in 1995.

Because of Hardway's early success in the NBA, Nike tabbed him as their next superstar pitchman. However, His quiet demeanor and unassuming way needed a boost. Enter Lil Penny. Lil Penny became Hardaway's trash-talking alter-ego in a series of Nike advertisements. Voiced by Chris Rock, Lil Penny said things Anfernee never said. Stacy Wall, creative director for the campaign, created a character full of ego, full of brash, funny, and unafraid to say that Penny was the best player in the NBA.[15] Memphis's hometown hero was now front and center as part of one of the most extensive ad campaigns in Nike history. Lil Penny became a cultural icon of the 1990s and embedded Hardaway as a basketball cultural icon in turn. On the court, Hardaway came into his own. The 1994–1995 Magic team won the NBA's Atlantic Division as Hardaway and O'Neal teamed to create one of the most dynamic duos in the league. Hardaway's 20.9 points and 7.2 assists per game complimented O'Neal's 29.3 points and 11.4 rebounds per game. The Magic danced to the NBA Finals.[16]

The Houston Rockets swept the Magic in the 1995 NBA Finals. The following season, Michael Jordan's Chicago Bulls swept the Magic in the Eastern Conference Finals, and O'Neal left Orlando in the off-season. Hardaway remained with the Magic for the next three seasons, carrying the bulwark of the load as the team's central figure. In August 1999, after a series of injuries, the Magic traded Hardaway to the Phoenix Suns for Danny Manning, Pat Garrity, and two first-round picks. Suns owner Jerry Colangelo said it "ranked up there with any acquisition we've ever made."[17] Hardaway averaged 20 points and five assists in the playoffs for the Suns in 2000 as they knocked off the Spurs before losing to O'Neal's Lakers in the 2nd round. After off-season microfracture surgery, Penny was never the same again. Although he remained in Phoenix for the next two and a half seasons, he never again soared as high as he had in Orlando.[18] After fifteen years in the league, Hardaway retired from the game and came home as the most decorated Memphis State basketball alum.

Like Finch, Hardaway returned home and began investing in the community where he grew up, Binghamton. One of Hardaway's closest friends from his youth was Desmond "Dez" Middleton. Penny and "Dez" had played together in middle school at Lester before Penny went to Treadwell High and "Dez" went to East High. When Hardaway returned, "Dez" asked Hardaway to help him coach their old Lester Middle School team.[19] The Memphis City Schools originally built Lester in 1955, one year after *Brown v. Board.* It was a remnant of a segregated past when white and black students were not allowed to attend the same schools. Judge McCrae's busing ruling forced Lester High students to integrate with white students at East High during the 1973–1974 school year.[20] Today both Lester and East High are populated by predominately black students. Both serve as examples of *de facto* segregation in 2018. Penny's return to his neighborhood to help coach Lester echoes the heart and empathy Finch showed Orange Mound. Hardaway followed Middleton over to East High in 2014 as an assistant. He eventually took over the Mustang basketball program when Middleton succumbed to colon cancer in February 2015. From 2015 to 2018, Hardaway's East High Mustangs completed a three-peat of high school basketball state championships in the AAA classification [largest classification] in Tennessee.

While Hardaway's East Mustangs were garnering national attention, the University of Memphis men's basketball program was floundering under Tubby Smith. Over 200 people, including Vickie Finch, crowded into the Laurie-Walton practice facility on the South Campus of the University of Memphis to see Hardaway announced as the school's next head coach on March 17, 2018. She said her husband "would be incredibly proud of his former player. Larry would be smiling."[21] Memphians longed to return to the glory days of Finch and Robinson, Lee and Turner, and Hardaway and Vaughn. Former Tiger players, city dignitaries, and even Finch's widow were all on hand to see Hardaway announced as head coach. In a city that remains divided racially over issues such as public schools, Hardaway creates an illusion of unity behind Tigers basketball. Although much has changed in the Bluff City, much has stayed the same. Memphis Tiger basketball remains one of a few places were white and black people can come together as one, if only for a moment.

On June 18, 2018, the LeMoyne-Owen community gathered at the Holiday Inn on the University of Memphis campus for Coach Jerry Johnson's 100th birthday. Many of Johnson's players from his over forty years of coaching at LeMoyne-Owen attended, including many from his 1975 NCAA national championship team. Anfernee Hardaway, who had just been hired as head coach at the University of Memphis, was the keynote speaker for the night. The event was held to help raise funds to support athletics at LeMoyne-Owen College. Most of the attendees at this event were black; very few white Memphians came. The veil of segregation remained firmly in place as the black community celebrated its most successful coach. Hardaway, the city's hope for basketball success at the University of Memphis, paid homage to a legend from the other side of the tracks. He acknowledged a coaching tree that starts with James Naismith and extends down through Jerry Johnson, Verties Sails, and Larry Finch.

The city of Memphis continues to look at basketball as a unifying and redemptive force. Professional wrestling only visits the city periodically at the FedEx Forum, and professional football franchises continually fail to survive in the city. The city's best run at professional football came in 1984 and 1985. Led by former Alabama quarterback Walter Lewis and former University of Tennessee defensive lineman Reggie White, the United States Football League's (USFL) Memphis Showboats were a success. The team ranked in the top tier in league attendance, selling out the Liberty Bowl, a stadium the media referred to as "crumbling and antiquated."[22] However, when the USFL moved its season to the fall in 1986, the Showboats folded with the remainder of the league. The Canadian Football League made a brief one-year appearance in Memphis in 1995 as the Memphis Mad Dogs. After failing to land a bid for its own NFL franchise in the early 1990s, the city played host to the former Houston Oilers in 1997. Attendance was so weak at the Liberty Bowl that owner Bud Adams broke his lease and moved to Nashville a year earlier than expected. Vince McMahon from World Wrestling Entertainment then brought the XFL to Memphis in 2001. The entire league folded after the 2001 season. In 2019 the Alliance of American Football brought the Memphis Express to the city, but they too folded. They did not even complete their season.

Once again, the city's hope rises and falls with the Grizzlies and the Tigers. The LeMoyne-Owen Magicians remain hidden away on Walker Avenue. Former Magician shooting guard Clint Jackson is the school's athletic director now. His running mate from the 1975 championship team, Robert Newman, still meets him periodically at the Four Way restaurant for lunch. LeMoyne-Owen alum William Anderson coaches their men's basketball team, which competes in the NCAA's Division II SIAC conference. Ironically, the once historically black SIAC recently admitted predominately white Spring Hill College (Mobile, Alabama) into its fold. While ESPN chronicles the 2019–2020 season for the Tigers with their series "The Harder Way" on ESPN +, the Magicians marketing reaches approximately 450 followers on Instagram. LeMoyne-Owen remains an aberration for most white Memphians. The city still gathers together for Tigers games, only now the location is a gentrified Beale Street where Memphis's soul can be marketed and sold. The university's iconic hero, Penny Hardaway, will be judged as harshly as Finch once was.

Nevertheless, Hardaway's love for the university stems from the love that Finch showed him as a coach and mentor. This love reaches back to Verties Sails's love for Finch and even further back to Jerry Johnson's love for Verties Sails. These black men faced the racist realities of Memphis during their eras, and they jumped through hoops to uplift the black community in the Bluff City through the game of basketball.

Notes

INTRODUCTION

1. Michael Honey, *Going Down Jericho Road: The Memphis Strike, Martin Luther King's Last Campaign* (New York: W.W. Norton & Company, 2007), 500.

2. "Finch Strives for the Ultimate," *Commercial Appeal,* March 15, 1973.

3. Aram Goudsouzian, "Back to One City, The 1973 Memphis State Tigers, and Myths of Race and Sport," March 21, 2016, http://southernstudies.olemiss.edu.

4. Beverly Bond and Janann Sherman, *Memphis in Black and White* (Chicago: Arcadia Publishing, 2003), 140.

5. Harry Edwards, *The Revolt of the Black Athlete* (Urbana: University of Illinois Press, 1969). Edwards's foundational work challenged the theory that athletics brought together men of all races and nationalities on equal footing. Arguing that although white people may begrudgingly admit a black man's prowess as an athlete, he will not acknowledge his equality as a human being. Jack Olsen's *The Black Athlete: A Shameful Story,* examines further the dehumanization, exploitation, and abandoned state of the black collegiate athlete. Finch's career as a basketball player spans this same period of black athletic resistance taking place nationally.

6. Dave Zirin, *What's My Name, Fool? Sports and Resistance in the United States* (Chicago: Haymarket Books, 2005), 21.

7. Randy Roberts, *Joe Louis* (New Haven: Yale University Press, 2010), xi, xii.

8. Jules Tygiel, *Baseball's Great Experiment: Jackie Robinson and His Legacy* (Oxford: Oxford University Press, 2008), 344.

9. Zirin, *What's My Name, Fool?,* 53, 63.

10. David Wiggins, *Glory Bound: Black Athletes in a White America* (Syracuse: Syracuse University Press, 1997), 215.

11. William C. Rhoden, *Forty Million Dollar Slaves: The Rise, Fall and Redemption of the Black Athlete* (New York: Three Rivers Press, 2006). Rhoden's assertion that black sporting life reflects the main currents of black life in America allows for a more nuanced understanding of the treatment of black athletes. He questions the preparedness of black athletes at big-time college universities to deal with those racial realities. Seeing black athletes as commodities and not as human beings created tensions that he argues are easily masked by the celebrity and benefits black athletes received.

12. Adam Criblez, *Tall Tales and Short Shorts: Dr. J., Pistol Pete, and the Birth of the Modern NBA* (New York: Rowman and Littlefield, 2017). Criblez asserts that the modern NBA is a product of the black aesthetic found in the ABA. Pete Axthelm, *The City Game* (Lincoln: University of Nebraska Press, 1970), Rick Telander, *Heaven is a Playground* (New York: Sports Publishing, 2013), and Vincent Mallozzi, *Asphalt Gods: An Oral History of the Rucker* (New York: Doubleday Publishing, 2003). These three works illustrate the unique black aesthetic found in inner-city basketball, and the culture of inner-city basketball. Although both describe basketball in New York City, the introduction of the black aesthetic to Memphis basketball began with the onset of the MIAA city basketball championship. Finch became an iconic figure in Memphis State lore because of his role as one of the first black players who starred at Memphis State whose play embodied the black aesthetic.

13. Barry Jacobs, *Across the Line: Profiles in Courage, Tales of the First Black Players in the ACC and SEC* (Guilford: Lyons Press, 2008), xvi–xviii.

14. Shirletta Kinchen, *Black Power in the Bluff City: African American Youth and Student Activism in Memphis, 1965–1975* (Knoxville: University of Tennessee Press, 2016), 22–23.

15. Ibid., 153.

16. Ibid., 159.

17. Ibid., 164.

18. Ibid., 158, 159, 171.

19. Ibid., 173.

20. Stanley Cohen, *The Game They Played* (New York: Carroll and Graf Publishers, 1977), ix.

CHAPTER 1

1. Bill McAfee, "Catholic Defeats Bertrand," *Press-Scimitar*, September 16, 1965.

2. Andrew Maraniss, *Strong Inside: Perry Wallace and the Collision of Race and Sports in the South* (Nashville: Vanderbilt University Press, 2014), 81, 86. Although Finch was not the first black person to play at MSU, the era in which he played collegiate basketball was dominated black men who became the first to play at

southern universities. Charles Martin's *Benching Jim Crow* and Barry Jacobs' *Across the Line* chronicle the narratives of the black men who broke the color barrier in the SEC and ACC. Finch's role as an iconic hero in Memphis places him alongside these same pioneering black athletes.

3. David K. Wiggins and Patrick B. Miller, *The Unlevel Playing Field: A Documentary History of the African American Experience in Sport* (Urbana: University of Illinois Press, 2003), 205.

4. Michael Kelley, "Memphis City Schools: A District Born amid Segregation, Yellow Fever Fades into History," *Commercial Appeal,* June 28, 2013.

5. Keith Wood, "CBHS Football Game vs. Melrose Helped to Bring City Together," *Purple and Gold* (Spring Summer 2016): 46–47.

6. Keith Gentry, *2015–2016 Shelby Metro High School Basketball* (Memphis: Gentry's Statistical Service, 2015), 95.

7. Linda T. Wynn, *Profiles of African Americans in Tennessee,* pdf, Nashville: Tennessee State University, March 2007.

8. Verties Sails Sr., interview by author, July 9, 2019.

9. Ibid.

10. Ed Odeven, "Documentary on former hoop star Neumann's life provides a cautionary tale," *Japan Times,* July 19, 2017.

11. Honey, *Going Down Jericho Road,* 1–2.

12. Michael Honey, "Labor and Civil Rights Movements at the Crossroads: Martin Luther King, the black Workers, and the Memphis Sanitation Strike," *West Tennessee Historical Society Papers,* vol. no. 57 (2003): 25–26.

13. Richard Lentz, "Committee Gives in to Sit-In of Strikers, But Loeb Holds Firm," *Commercial Appeal,* February 23, 1968.

14. Allegra Turner, *Except by Grace: The Life of Jesse H. Turner* (Jonesboro: Four G Publishers, 2004), 92.

15. Ibid., 94.

16. Joseph Sweatt, "Action is Rebuff: 700 Workers, Friends Push into Chamber; Council to Meet Today," *Commercial Appeal,* February 23, 1968.

17. David Tucker, *Memphis Since Crump: Bossism, Blacks and Civic Reformers* (Knoxville: University of Tennessee Press, 1980), 55.

18. Roger Biles, "Ed Crump Versus the Unions: The Labor Movement in Memphis during the 1930s," *Labor History,* vol. 25, no. 4 (1984), 533.

19. Larry Rea, "Bevel Gives Spark to Frayser," *Commercial Appeal,* February 19, 1968.

20. Gentry, *2015–2016 Shelby Metro High School Basketball,* 95.

21. United States, Department of Commerce Economic Development Administration, Regional Economic Development Center, *Memphis Retail Potential Study: South Memphis,* by Luchy Burrell (Memphis, Tennessee: University of Memphis, 1998), 8–11.

22. David Waters, "Good People Still Call Riverview Home; Once it was a Kinder Place," *Commercial Appeal*, March 20, 1994.

23. Gary Waters, "Carver High Ends as it Began, in a Segregated City," *Commercial Appeal*, June 12, 2016.

24. David Vincent, "In Spite of Attacks, Carver Rates," *Commercial Appeal*, May 30, 1968.

25. Waters, "Good People Still Call Riverview Home."

26. Steve Pike, "Blair T. Hunt," WKNO FM, July 9, 2013, http://wknofm.org.

27. Jenni Carlson, "L.C. Gordon thankful to be a trailblazer at Oklahoma State," *NewsOK.com*, October 16, 2013, http://newsok.com.

28. Bill Burk, "L.C. Gordon Aiming for State Title," *Press-Scimitar*, February 16, 1968.

29. Ibid.

30. Community LIFT, Frayser Snapshot (Memphis, TN: City of Memphis, 2010), http://www.communitylift.org.

31. Ibid.

32. Gentry, *2015–2016 Shelby Metro High School Basketball*, 95.

33. Burk, "L.C. Gordon Aiming for State Title."

34. Ibid.

35. Honey, "Labor and Civil Rights Movements at the Crossroads," 27.

36. Ibid.

37. Ibid., 28.

38. Honey, *Going Down Jericho Road*, 410.

39. Martin Luther King Jr., "I've Been to the Mountaintop" (speech, Mason Temple COGIC, Memphis, April 3, 1968).

40. Honey, *Going Down Jericho Road*, 490.

41. Ibid., 489.

42. Otis Sanford, *From Boss Crump to King Willie: How Race Changed Memphis Politics* (Knoxville: University of Tennessee Press, 2017), 116–117.

43. Marcus Pohlmann, *Opportunity Lost: Race and Poverty in the Memphis City Schools* (Knoxville: University of Tennessee Press, 2008), 78.

44. Ibid., 85.

45. Richard Hunter, "The Administration of Court-Ordered School Desegregation in Urban School Districts: The
Law and Experience," *The Journal of Negro Education*, vol. 73 no. 3 (Summer 2004): 220–221.

46. Pohlmann, *Opportunity Lost*, 66–67.

47. Charles Williams, *African American Life, and Culture in Orange Mound: Case study of a Black community in Memphis, Tennessee, 1890–1980* (New York: Lexington Books, 2013), 13–14.

48. Ibid., 24 and 34.

49. "History of Orange Mound," Memphis Melrose High School Historical Yearbook Website, accessed December 20, 2017, http://www.melroseyearbooks.com.

50. *U.S. Social Security Applications and Claims Index, 1936–2007*, accessed February 3, 2018, www.Ancestry.com.

51. Interment Control Forms, 1928–1962, Interment Control Forms, A1 2110-B, Records of the Office of the Quartermaster General, 1774–1985, Record Group 92, *National Archives at College Park*, accessed February 3, 2018, www.Ancestry.com.

52. Miriam DeCosta-Willis, *Notable Black Memphians* (Amherst: Cambria Press, 2008), 119–120.

53. Vickie S. Finch, interview by author, February 7, 2018.

54. Ibid.

55. Williams, *African American Life, and Culture in Orange Mound*, 26.

56. Geoff Calkins, "He loved his city; Memphis reciprocated," *Commercial Appeal*, April 3, 2011.

57. Larry Finch Jr., interview by author, January 31, 2018.

58. Dale L. Stephens, *Funeral Program Larry Onis Finch* (Memphis: Stephens Signs and Design, 2011).

59. Williams, *African American Life, and Culture in Orange Mound*, 77.

60. Michael Messner, *Power Play: Sports and the Problem of Masculinity* (Boston: Beacon Press, 1992), 102.

61. Leonard Draper, interview by author, December 21, 2017.

62. Vickie S. Finch, interview by author, February 7, 2018.

63. Ibid.

64. Williams, *African American Life, and Culture in Orange Mound*, 82.

65. Ibid., 84.

66. Vickie S. Finch, interview by author, February 7, 2018.

67. Ibid.

68. Ibid.

69. Ibid.

70. Ron Higgins, "Larry's Journey," *Commercial Appeal*, March 4, 2007.

71. Leonard Draper, interview by author, December 21, 2017.

72. Vickie S. Finch, interview by author, February 7, 2018.

73. Larry Rea, "Farewell to Finch," *Commercial Appeal*, March 1, 1997.

74. Vickie S. Finch, interview by author, February 7, 2018.

75. Randy Roberts, *Papa Jack: Jack Johnson and the Era of White Hopes* (New York: Free Press, 1983),68.

76. Vickie S. Finch, interview by author, February 7, 2018.

77. "Tigers basketball coach Larry Finch passes away," WMC Action News 5—Memphis, Tennessee, April 02, 2011, http://www.wmcactionnews5.com.

78. *The Rebel*, directed by Paul Carruthers (SEC Storied: May 2017), https://www
.amazon.com.

79. Nelson George, *Elevating the Game: Black Men and Basketball* (Lincoln:
Nebraska UP, 1992), xi–xii.

80. Gena Caponi-Tabery, "Jump For Joy: Jump Blues, Dance, and Basketball in
1930s African America," found in *Sports Matters: Race, Recreation and Culture* (New
York: New York University Press, 2002). Tabery argues that the "jump" was part of
the black aesthetic in the 1930s and made its way into mainstream culture through
music and sport during the 1930s. Like jazz music, the jump shot was part of the
improvisation as soloists but was still considered part of the collaborative element of
the ensemble. Tabery refutes the historical introduction of the jump shot by white
players Luisetti but instead points to the free-flowing style of the African American
game from the 1930s.

81. Ibid., xiv–xvi.

82. Pete Axthelm, *The City Game* (Lincoln: University of Nebraska Press, 1970),
xv–xvi.

83. Vincent Mallozzi, *Asphalt Gods: An Oral History of the Rucker Tournament*
(New York: Doubleday Publishing, 2003), 3.

84. Gentry, *2015–2016 Shelby Metro High School Basketball*, 86.

85. Zach McMillan, "Memphis State: Quite a Commitment," *Commercial Appeal*,
March 30, 2003.

86. B. Holland, Find a Grave database, April 26, 2015, https://www.findagrave.com.

87. Aharon N. Varady, *Bond Hill: Origin and Transformation of a 19th Century
Cincinnati Railroad Suburb*, report, 9th ed. (Cincinnati: Henry Watkins Press, 2005).

88. *The Rebel*, dir. Paul Carruthers.

89. Memphis State Men's Basketball Media Guide, 1963–1964.

90. *The Rebel*, dir. Paul Carruthers.

91. Ibid.

92. Ibid.

93. "Hewlett Helped Get Overton High Started," *Commercial Appeal*, December 23,
1965.

94. George Lapides, "Overton's Coach Successful Even Before Neumann," *Press-
Scimitar*, February 20, 1969.

95. Odeven, "Documentary on former hoop star Neumann's life provides a
cautionary tale."

96. Frank Fitzpatrick, *And the Walls Came Tumbling Down: Kentucky, Texas
Western and the game that changed American sports* (New York: Simon and Schuster,
1999), 130.

97. Aram Goudsouzian, *King of the Court: Bill Russell and the Basketball Revolution*
(Berkeley: University of California Press, 2010), 225.

98. Ibid.

99. Gentry, *2015–2016 Shelby Metro High School Basketball*, 88.

100. Vickie S. Finch, interview by author, February 7, 2018.

101. "1968–69 Memphis Tigers Schedule and Results," College Basketball at Sports -Reference.com, accessed October 16, 2017, https://www.sports-reference.com.

102. Andy Edson, "It's Neumann vs Finch Tomorrow Night," *Press-Scimitar,* February 20, 1969.

103. Larry Rea, "Melrose Challenges Overton Friday," *Commercial Appeal,* February 18, 1969.

104. Larry Rea, "The 380th Game Will Decide It," *Commercial Appeal,* February 21, 1969.

105. *The Rebel,* dir. Paul Carruthers.

106. Larry, Rea, "Melrose Ends Overton's Streak," *Commercial Appeal,* February 22, 1969.

107. Andy Edson, "Melrose too Much for Spunky Overton," *Press-Scimitar,* February 21, 1969.

108. *The Rebel,* dir. Paul Carruthers.

109. Rea, "Melrose Ends Overton's Streak."

110. Odeven, "Documentary on former hoop star Neumann's life provides a cautionary tale."

111. Rea, "Melrose Ends Overton's Streak."

112. Ibid.

113. Clint Jackson, interview by author, July 13, 2016.

114. Vickie S. Finch, interview by author, February 17, 2018.

115. Leonard Draper, interview by author, December 21, 2017.

116. Rea, "Farewell to Finch."

117. Leonard Draper, interview by author, December 21, 2017.

118. Verties Sails Sr., Interview by author, March 28, 2016.

119. Al Harvin, "People in Sports," *New York Times,* July 09, 1975.

120. Terry Pluto, *Loose Balls: The Short, Wild Life of the ABA* (New York: Simon & Schuster, 1990),235.

121. Gary West, *Kentucky Colonels of the ABA: The Real Story of a Team Left Behind* (Morley: Acclaim Press, 2011), 305.

122. Zandria Robinson, *This Ain't Chicago: Race, Class, and Regional Identity in the Post-Soul South* (Chapel Hill: University of North Carolina Press, 2014), 4.

123. Seth Davis, *When March Went Mad: The Game that Transformed Basketball* (New York: Holt, 2010), 4.

124. Ken Rappaport and Barry Wilner, *The Big Dance: The Story of the NCAA Basketball Tournament* (New York: Taylor Trade Publishing, 2012), 68–70.

125. Davis, *When March Went Mad,* 9.

126. *The Rebel*, dir. Paul Carruthers.

127. Davis, *When March Went Mad*, 19–20.

128. Ibid., 23.

CHAPTER 2

1. University of Memphis Men's Basketball Media Guide, 2015–2016.

2. Rappaport and Wilner, *The Big Dance*, 100.

3. "Tigers to Honor Herb Hilliard," University of Memphis Athletics, February 24, 2017, http://www.gotigersgo.com.

4. Trey Heath, "Finch shined during era of racial tension," *Daily Helmsman*, March 5, 2005.

5. Ibid., 333.

6. Maraniss, *Strong Inside*, 201, 310.

7. Rhoden, *Forty Million Dollar Slaves*, 2.

8. Ibid., 3.

9. Ibid., 333.

10. Zach McMillin, "Finch was Memphis' Unifier," *Commercial Appeal*, April 4, 2011.

11. Hunter, "The Administration of Court-Ordered School Desegregation in Urban School Districts," 220–221.

12. Tygiel, *Baseball's Great Experiment*, 36.

13. Barbara Lapides, interview by author, July 9, 2019.

14. Harold Byrd, interview by author, July 9, 2019.

15. George Lapides, "Never-to-Forget Weekend Dulled Only by Score," *Press-Scimitar*, March 13, 1972.

16. George Lapides, "Mayor Sees Some Good in Memphis State Loss," *Press-Scimitar*, March 13, 1972.

17. Ibid.

18. Wayne Chastain, "New Disorders at Westwood," *Press-Scimitar*, March 3, 1972.

19. Sanford, *From Boss Crump to King Willie*, 157.

20. Ron Higgins, "Farewell to Finch." *Commercial Appeal*, March 1, 1997.

21. Ibid.

22. "1970–71 Memphis Tigers Schedule and Results," College Basketball at Sports-Reference.com, accessed May 22, 2017, http://www.sports-reference.com.

23. Ibid.

24. Messner, *Power at Play*, 102.

25. Tom Miller, interview by author, December 26, 2017.

26. Goudsouzian, "Back to One City."

27. Buck Patton, "Who's the Best? Only Time Will Tell," *Press-Scimitar*, February 29, 1972.

28. Bond and Sherman, *Memphis in Black and White*, 140.

29. John Branston, *Rowdy Memphis: The South Unscripted* (Nashville: Cold Tree Press, 2004), 117. An editor and writer for *The Memphis Flyer,* Branston uses stories he crafted over the course of his career and brings them together in this unique construction of the history of Memphis. His grassroots accounts of the individuals who made Memphis "rowdy" allowed for a much more nuanced understanding of the city's construction of southern identity.

30. Bond and Sherman, *Memphis in Black and White*, 141.

31. Sanford, *From Boss Crump to King Willie*, 120.

32. Virginia Duke, "To Disturb the People as Little as Possible: The Desegregation of the Memphis City Schools," (master's thesis, University of Tennessee at Knoxville, 2005), 37.

33. Sanford, *From Boss Crump to King Willie*, 124.

34. Ibid.

35. Ibid., 38.

36. Ibid, 39.

37. "History of Briarcrest School," Briarcrest Christian School, accessed October 07, 2017, https://www.briarcrest.com.

38. Ibid.

39. "History SBEC," Northpoint Christian School, accessed October 07, 2017, http://ncstrojans.com.

40. Bond and Sherman, *Memphis in Black and White*, 140.

41. Tim Church, "Tigers Eye NCAA Title as cage Season Begins," *The Helmsman,* December 1, 1972.

42. Ibid.

43. Jeff Weinberger, "Finch, Robinson Reflect on new Season, Future," *The Helmsman,* December 5, 1972.

44. Bob Jones, "Tigers Paint an Early Sellout Sign," *Commercial Appeal,* August 8, 1972.

45. Goudsouzian, "Back to One City."

46. "Student decries Conduct at Basketball Games," *The Helmsman,* January 16, 1973.

47. Tim Church, "Sports Talk on a Variety of Themes," *The Helmsman,* January 19, 1973.

48. Vickie S. Finch, interview by author, February 7, 2018.

49. Maraniss, *Strong Inside*, 270.

50. Vickie S. Finch, interview by author, February 7, 2018.

51. Ibid.

52. Zach McMillan, "Valley Goal: The Tigers' talent, tenacity were essential to winning title," *Commercial Appeal,* April 3, 2003.

53. Jeff Weinberger, "Kenon-Finch Ready for ABA Battle," *The Helmsman*, November 13, 1974.

54. Bobby Hall, "'73 Tigers Recall Highs, Slow Start," *Commercial Appeal*, February 12, 1994.

55. Tim Church, "MSU Blows Past Fla. Tech, Looks to Billikens Saturday," *The Helmsman*, January 12, 1973.

56. Bobby Hall, "Finch Captures Scoring record as Tigers Romp," *Commercial Appeal*, January 21, 1973.

57. Goudsouzian, "Back to One City."

58. Duke, "To Disturb the People as Little as Possible," 41.

59. "Bussing Underway," *Tri-State Defender*, January 27, 2013.

60. Branston, *Rowdy Memphis*, 118–119.

61. Tim Church, "MSU Record Marred by Louisville Victory," *The Helmsman*, February 13, 1973.

62. Tim Church, "MSU Seniors Bow Out in One-Sided Victory," *The Helmsman*, February 16, 1973.

63. George Lapides, "A Moment that Will Live Forever," *Press-Scimitar*, February 19, 1973.

64. "Kenon, Robinson and Finch Win MVC Honors," *The Helmsman*, March 16, 1973.

65. Sanford, *From Boss Crump to King Willie*, 148–149.

66. Zach McMillan, "All the way: Tigers didn't waltz into UCLA meeting." *Commercial Appeal*, April 4, 2003.

67. Tim Church, "Regional Victories Send Tigers to NCAA Finals," *The Helmsman*, March 20, 1973.

68. Ron Huggins, "From Melrose to Tigers, Finch was Self-made Star," *Commercial Appeal*, April 3, 2011.

69. McMillan, "All the way."

70. Tim Church, "Victorious Tigers Return Home to Jubilant Homecoming," *The Helmsman*, March 20, 1973.

71. Bill Little, "Road to St. Louis for Memphis State Tigers 'Easy'," *Tri-State Defender*, March 24, 1973.

72. McMillan, "All the way."

73. Robert Gordon, *Respect Yourself: Stax Records and the Soul Explosion* (New York: Bloomsbury, 2013), 237–238. Stax Studios was another bridge in the city of Memphis that united white and black people. The Stax sound became the soundtrack for black liberation, the song of triumph, and the sound of the path toward freedom. The black aesthetic was firmly entrenched in the soulful sounds emanating from this South Memphis studio. Gordon wraps the studio's story around its struggle for

success, which brought out the city's best and the city's worst. Like Finch, the studio was praised and lifted as an iconic symbol of hope in the city.

74. Ibid., 264.

75. Ibid., 258.

76. Joe Jares, "Mad for Marvin B. and Ernie D.," *Sports Illustrated,* February 14, 1972.

77. Mike Carey, *Bad News* (New York: Sports Publishing, 2016), 27–28.

78. Jares, "Mad for Marvin B. and Ernie D."

79. McMillan, "All the way."

80. Buck Patton, "MSU Prepares for Act of Providence," *Press-Scimitar,* March 23, 1973.

81. Carey, *Bad News,* 26.

82. Ibid., 33–34.

83. Goudsouzian, "Back to One City."

84. Carey, *Bad News,* 44 and 48.

85. Goudsouzian, "Back to One City."

86. Peter Farrelly, "Me and Ernie D The Popular Filmmaker on his—and his home state's—love of Providence hoops," *Sports Illustrated,* July 14, 2013.

87. Patton, "MSU Prepares for Act of Providence."

88. Carey, *Bad News,* 54.

89. Goudsouzian, "Back to One City."

90. Carey, *Bad News,* 55.

91. Patton, "MSU Prepares for Act of Providence."

92. Goudsouzian, "Back to One City."

93. Peter Farrelly, "Me and Ernie D."

94. "Laurie 'Underestimated' Ernie D," *The Helmsman,* March 28, 1973.

95. Basil Brooks, "Tall-Walking, Jubilant Tigers of MSU Hurl Challenging Growl at UCLA," *Commercial Appeal,* March 25, 1973.

96. John Matthew Smith, *The Sons of Westwood: John Wooden, UCLA, and the Dynasty that Changed College Basketball* (Urbana: University of Illinois Press, 2013), 219.

97. Rappaport and Wilner, *The Big Dance,* 39.

98. Ibid., 220.

99. Ibid., 223.

100. Goudsouzian, "Back to One City."

101. Smith, *The Sons of Westwood,* 223.

102. Bob Jones, "Mighty UCLA Ends MSU Dream Season," *Commercial Appeal,* March 27, 1973.

103. Smith, *The Sons of Westwood,* 224.

104. Jones, "Mighty UCLA Ends MSU Dream Season."

105. Jeff Weinberger, "Tigers' Effort Refutes Press," *The Helmsman,* March 30, 1973.

106. Bruce Patton, "Tigers High in Their Praise of Bruins," *Press-Scimitar,* March 27, 1973.

107. Larry Finch Jr., interview by author, January 31, 2018.

108. "A Grateful City Greets Its Team," *Press-Scimitar*, March 27, 1973.

109. Keith Easterwood, interview by author, October 10, 2017.

110. Ibid.

111. "It Was a Great Homecoming for Tigers," *Tri-State Defender*, March 31, 1973.

112. Tim Church, "Crowd of 6,000 Greets History-Making Tigers," *The Helmsman*, March 30, 1973.

113. Bob Jones, "MSU Can Savor Sweet Spoils of NCAA Success," *Commercial Appeal*, March 28, 1973.

114. Bob Jones, "Tiger Duo Named First to Star List," *Commercial Appeal*, February 2, 1973.

115. Zack McMillan, "Spirit of '73," *Commercial Appeal*, April 6, 2003.

116. Goudsouzian, "Back to One City."

117. Calkins, "He Loved his City."

118. Goudsouzian, "Back to One City."

119. Tracie Church Guzzio, "Race and Basketball in the Works of John Edgar Wideman," in *In the Game: Race, Identity and Sports in the Twentieth Century*, ed. Amy Bass (New York: MacMillan, 2005), 224.

120. Tim Church, "Form of Memphis Unity Remains to be Seen," *The Helmsman*, March 28, 1973.

121. Paula Wooldridge, interview by author, October 11, 2017.

CHAPTER 3

1. Pluto, *Loose Balls*, 44.

2. Mark Montieth, *Reborn: The Pacers and the Return of Pro Basketball to Indianapolis* (Indianapolis: Halfcourt Press, 2017), 92.

3. Pluto, *Loose Balls*, 244–245.

4. "1967–68 New Orleans Buccaneers," Basketball-Reference.com, accessed August 3, 2016. http://www.basketball-reference.com.

5. Thomas Aiello, "Sambo's Boys: The Rise and Fall of the New Orleans Jazz, 1974–1979," *Journal of Sport History*, vol. 45, no. 3 (Fall 2018): 281.

6. Bill Burk, "Pros Owner Stays Busy," *Press-Scimitar*, September 2, 1970.

7. Bill Burk, "Memphis Pros Await League OK," *Press-Scimitar*, September 1, 1970.

8. "Loeb Helps Pros Launch Season Ticket Sale," *Press-Scimitar*, September 29, 1970.

9. Bob Phillips, "Memphis Rolls Out ABA Red Carpet," *Press-Scimitar*, September 22, 1970.

10. Ibid.

11. Ibid.

12. Richard Coleman, interview by author, November 23, 2018.

13. George Lapides, "Pros Trade Butler to Utah," *Press-Scimitar,* September 11, 1970.

14. Kyle Veazey, *Champions for Change: How the Mississippi State Bulldogs and Their Bold Coach Defied Segregation* (Charleston: The History Press, 2012), 100.

15. Russell Henderson, "The 1963 Mississippi State University Basketball Controversy and the Repeal of the Unwritten Law: 'Something more than the game will be lost,'" *Journal of Southern History,* vol.63, no. 4 (Nov., 1997): 854.

16. Pluto, *Loose Balls,* 239.

17. "Remember the ABA: Memphis Pros," Remember the ABA: Memphis Pros. Accessed August 03, 2016. http://www.remembertheaba.com.

18. "Knick, Bullets Here Tomorrow," *Press-Scimitar,* September 28, 1970.

19. Bob Phillips, "Memphis Steps Into Big Leagues Tonight," *Press-Scimitar,* October 20, 1970.

20. Pluto, *Loose Balls,* 267.

21. Jim O'Brien, "Remember the ABA: Wendell Ladner Biography," Accessed August 04, 2016. http://www.remembertheaba.com.

22. Mark Montieth, *Reborn,* 347.

23. Criblez, *Tall Tales and Short Shorts,* 202.

24. Ibid., 191.

25. Pluto, *Loose Balls,* 215–216.

26. Ibid., 268.

27. Montieth, *Reborn,* 114–115.

28. "Memphis Pros/Tams/Sounds," NBA Hoops Online, accessed November 24, 2017, http://nbahoopsonline.com.

29. "1972–73 Memphis Tams Roster and Stats," Basketball-Reference.com, accessed November 16, 2017, https://www.basketball-reference.com.

30. Ibid.

31. Ibid.

32. Jimmy Gentry, "Memphis Group Purchases the Pros' Franchise," *Commercial Appeal,* February 13, 1971.

33. *The Rebel,* dir. Paul Carruthers.

34. Ibid.

35. Woodrow Paige, "Kerner Cites 'Uncertainties' in Rejecting Pros' Offer," *Commercial Appeal,* April 25, 1972.

36. Woodrow Paige, "Sinking Pros Grab a Dallas Lifeline," *Commercial Appeal,* June 12, 1972.

37. Bob Phillips, "Pros Case Goes to 'Jury,'" *Press-Scimitar,* June 12, 1972.

38. Bob Phillips, "Hectic Week Ends with Pros in Memphis," *Press-Scimitar,* June 17, 1972.

39. Michael Green and Roger D. Launius, *Charlie Finley: The Outrageous Story of Baseball's Super Showman* (New York: Walker & Company, 2010), 2.

40. Woodrow Paige, "Franchise to Finley," *Commercial Appeal,* July 7, 1972.

41. Woodrow Paige, "Search for Nickname Begins," *Commercial Appeal,* June 28, 1972.

42. "Mid-South, Greet Your New ABA Team: The Tams," *Commercial Appeal,* July 16, 1972.

43. Green and Launius, *Charlie Finley,* 166.

44. Pluto, *Loose Balls,* 240.

45. Woodrow Paige, "Baron Will Direct Memphis March," *Commercial Appeal,* July 16, 1972.

46. Fitzpatrick, *And the Walls Came Tumbling Down,* 224.

47. George Lapides, "Missing Opener Necessary for Charlie Finley," *Press-Scimitar,* October 5, 1972.

48. "Tams Endorse Moustaches," *Commercial Appeal,* December 24, 1972.

49. Woodrow Paige "Tans Send Ladner to the Colonels," *Commercial Appeal,* January 20, 1973.

50. Woodrow Paige, "Tams' Secret Choices are Kenon, Lewis," *Commercial Appeal,* April 5, 1973.

51. Mich Recht, ed., *ABA Official Guide 1973–74* (St. Louis: The Sporting News, 1973), 37.

52. Bill Young, "Carlson Ducks as Kenon Plot Thickens," *Commercial Appeal,* May 2, 1973.

53. Wood, "CBHS Football Game vs. Melrose Helped to Bring City Together," vi.

54. Woodrow Paige, "Tams Take Positive Step, Sign Larry Finch," *Commercial Appeal,* September 11, 1973.

55. Pluto, *Loose Balls,* 272.

56. Ron Cobb, "Finch finds Himself in Unusual Position," *Commercial Appeal,* November 30, 1974.

57. *The Rebel,* dir. Paul Carruthers.

58. Sharon Mazor, *Professional Wrestling: Sport and Spectacle* (Oxford: University Mississippi Press, 1998), 6–8.

59. *It Happened at the Mid-South Coliseum: Monday Nights,* perf. Andy Kauffman, Andre the Giant, Jerry Lawler, Ric Flair (70s-TV.com), DVD.

60. Randy Covitz, "December-It Was the Worst Month yet for the Tams," *Press-Scimitar,* January 2, 1974.

61. "ABA Meetings Include Review of Tams' Future," *Commercial Appeal,* January 27, 1974.

62. Gordon, *Respect Yourself,* 306, 315.

63. "Stax Poised with Large Eraser," *Press-Scimitar,* March 6, 1974.

64. Gordon, *Respect Yourself,* 337, 339.

65. Woodrow Paige, "Stax Says Snags Cleared from Path to Tams Sale," *Commercial Appeal,* March 6, 1974.

66. "Finley Heeds Doctor's Advice," *Press-Scimitar,* January 10, 1974.

67. Woodrow Paige, "Lady Luck Snubs the Tams," *Commercial Appeal,* March 26, 1974.

68. Ray Jordan, "Storen Resigns ABA Post to Purchase Tams," *Commercial Appeal,* July 15, 1974.

69. Montieth, *Reborn,* 39–41.

70. West, *Kentucky Colonels of the ABA,* 74.

71. Ray Jordan, "'Sounds' is New Nickname," *Commercial Appeal,* July 25, 1974.

72. Gordon, *Respect Yourself,* 339.

73. West, *Kentucky Colonels of the ABA,* 120.

74. Ray Jordan, "Mullaney Awaits Word from Sounds," *Commercial Appeal,* August 13, 1974.

75. George Lapides "Tams Acquire Mel Daniels, Freddie Lewis," *Press-Scimitar,* July 23, 1974; and Pluto, *Loose Balls,* 245.

76. "Sounds Key '74–'75 Card to Weekend," *Commercial Appeal,* August 27, 1974.

77. "City Unveils Ticket Plan," *Press-Scimitar,* September 19, 1974.

78. George Lapides, "Sounds Woes Give ABA No Choice," *Press-Scimitar,* April 15, 1975.

79. Ron Cobb, "Its Either Memphis or Nowhere for the Sounds," *Press-Scimitar,* April 15, 1975.

80. Randy Covitz, "WFL Announces it Will 'Play Ball' in 1975," *Press-Scimitar,* April 16, 1975.

81. George Lapides, "McVay Overjoyed with 'Big Three,'" *Press-Scimitar,* April 16, 1975.

82. Mike Fleming, "Bassett Offers His Organization to Help Sounds," *Commercial Appeal,* August 25, 1975.

83. Ray Jordan, "Sounds' Farewell Expected Today," *Commercial Appeal,* August 28, 1975.

84. George Lapides, "A Sad Ending for Memphis' Pro Basketball," *Press-Scimitar,* July 17, 1975.

CHAPTER 4

1. Charles Martin, *Benching Jim Crow: The Rise and Fall of the Color Line in Southern College Sports, 1890–1980* (Urbana: University of Illinois Press, 2010), 18.

2. Patrick Miller, "To Bring the Race Along Rapidly: Sport, Student Culture, and Educational Mission at Historically Black Colleges during the Interwar Years," in *The Sporting World of the Modern South* (Urbana: University of Illinois Press, 2002), 136. Also in *The Sporting World of the Modern South*, Rita Liberti discusses the role of women's basketball at historically black universities in "We Were Ladies, We Just

Played Like Boys: African American Women and Competitive Basketball at Bennett College, 1928–1942." Liberti discusses the varying views on the role of women's athletics at HBCUs and further nuances the role of athletics at HBCUs. Whereas leaders at some HBCUs contended that athletics ran counter to the middle-class feminine ideal grounded in refinement and respectability, others, like those at Bennett College, balanced and negotiated various understandings of class, race, and gender arrangements as they supported women's basketball. LOC did not have a women's basketball team in 1974–1975, but by discussing the intersection of gender and athletics at HBCUs we can better understand the overall role of athletics and respectability in the black community.

3. David K. Wiggins, ed., *Separate Games: African American Sport behind the Walls of Segregation* (Fayetteville: University of Arkansas Press, 2016), xiii–xiv.

4. William Rhodes, *Forty Million Dollar Slaves: The Rise, Fall, and Redemption of the Black Athlete* (New York: Three Rivers Press, 2006), 137.

5. Derrick E. White, *Blood, Sweat and Tears: Jake Gaither, Florida A&M, and the history of Black College Football* (Chapel Hill: University of North Carolina Press, 2019), 8.

6. Kinchen, *Black Power in the Bluff City*, 119.

7. George Lapides, "One phase of basketball ends," *Press-Scimitar,* March 17, 1975.

8. *NCAA Division III Basketball Championship Program* (Reading: Albright College, 1975), 35.

9. Martin, *Benching Jim Crow*, 254.

10. "SIAC History," SIAC, accessed April 26, 2018, http://www.thesiac.com.

11. Jerry Johnson, interview by author, March 29,2018.

12. George Curry, "An Unsolved Murder case in a College in Knoxville," *The Harvard Crimson* (July 1968) http://www.thecrimson.com.

13. Jerry Johnson, interview by author, March 29, 2018.

14. Ibram Rogers, *The Black Campus Movement: Black Students and the Racial Reconstitution of Higher Education, 1965–1972* (New York: MacMillan, 2012), 67. Rogers has changed his name to Ibram Kendi. During the late 1960s and early 1970s, LOC was confronted by the changing political environment on campus precipitated by the black campus movement. As a historically black college, LOC leaned heavily on its black middle-class bourgeoisie status in the community. In this period LOC changed presidents three times and struggled with the changing construction of racial politics in its community. Black student activism on campus forced the administration and trustees at LOC to reevaluate itself. Martha Biondi's *The Black Revolution on Campus* chronicles how the BCM forced change on college campuses across the country. She contends that the BCM successfully pressured universities to embrace black studies programs and draw stronger connections with their black students' cultural roots.

15. Ibid., 3.

16. Kinchen, *Black Power in the Bluff City*, 130.

17. Rogers, *The Black Campus Movement*, 5.

18. Kinchen, *Black Power in the Bluff City*, 125–138.

19. Harry Edwards, *Sociology of Sport* (Homewood: Dorsey Press, 1973), 148–151.

20. Richard Sandomir, "Civil Rights on the Basketball Court," *New York Times*, March 15, 2008.

21. White, *Blood, Sweat and Tears*, 194.

22. "East Texas Oilfield Discovery," American Oil & Gas Historical Society, February 14, 2018, https://aoghs.org; and Jerry Johnson, interview by author, March 29, 2018.

23. Ibid.

24. "Wiley College History," Wiley College, accessed June 27, 2016. https://https.wileyc.edu.

25. "The 93rd Birthday Celebration for the Legendary Coach Jerry C. Johnson," RSS, accessed June 27, 2016, http://athletics.loc.edu.

26. Roger Saylor, "Fayetteville State University Football Historical Data," Fayetteville State University, accessed April 03, 2018, http://www.fsubroncos.com.

27. Milton Katz, *Breaking Through: John B. McLendon, Basketball Legend and Civil Rights Pioneer* (Fayetteville: University of Arkansas Press, 2007), 33 and 46.

28. Jerry Johnson, interview by author, March 29, 2018.

29. "Volunteer State Athletic Conference," BR Bullpen, accessed November 17, 2019, https://www.baseball-reference.com.

30. Katz, *Breaking Through*, 79 and 82.

31. Milton Stephens, interview by author, July 17, 2018.

32. Jon Morse, "1974 NAIA Men's Basketball District Regionals," Varsity Pride, May 26, 2018, http://www.jonfmorse.com.

33. "NAIA Div. I Men's Basketball Championship History," NAIA, accessed November 16, 2019, http://grfx.cstv.com/photos/schools/naia/sports/m-baskbl/auto_pdf/MBBDIChampionshipHistory1223.pdf.

34. Ben Little, "Sports Horizons," *Tri-State Defender*, March 1, 1975.

35. Ray Jordan, "Unbeaten Hamilton Claims First City Championship," *Commercial Appeal*, February 20, 1971.

36. Robert Newman, interview by author, June 27, 2016.

37. Clint Jackson, interview by author, June 21, 2016.

38. Robert Newman, interview by author, June 27, 2016.

39. Jerry McNeal, interview by author, July 17, 2018.

40. Willie Parr, interview by author, July 1, 2018.

41. Ibid.

42. Carla Parker, "Trinity High Alums Remember Athletic Success," *The Champion*, June 19, 2015.

43. Jerry McNeal, interview by author, July 17, 2018.

44. Denise Dillon, "Trophy from 1969 Championship Game Replaced," WAGA, January 11, 2018, http://www.fox5atlanta.com.

45. "Latest News," *Decatur Bulldog Basketball,* January 17, 2014.

46. Jerry McNeal, interview by author, July 17, 2018.

47. Ibid.

48. Leonard Moore, "The School Desegregation Crisis of Cleveland, Ohio, 1963–1964: The Catalyst for Black Political Power in a Northern City," *Journal of Urban History* (January 2002): 135. Moore's article analyzes the racial issues that faced Cleveland during the desegregation of its schools. Memphis would be faced by similar racial issues ten years later with the advent of Plan Z. Milton Stephen decided to attend LOC, where he felt safer surrounded by a black community he was more comfortable around.

49. Milton Stephens, interview by author, July 17, 2018.

50. Ibid.

51. Ibid.

52. George, *Elevating the Game,*76.

53. Ibid., 134.

54. Clint Jackson, interview by author, June 21, 2016.

55. Ibid.

56. Robert Newman, interview by author, June 27, 2016.

57. Jerry McNeal, interview by author, July 17, 2018.

58. Milton Stephens, interview by author, July 17, 2018.

59. Stevenson Bratcher, interview by author, July 31, 2018.

60. 2008–2009 Morgan State University Men's Basketball Media Guide (Baltimore: Morgan State, 2008), 91.

61. Ken Murray, "Record Setting Morgan State Player Marvin Webster Dies," *Baltimore Sun,* April 8, 2009.

62. Mike Conklin, "Magicians in Finals Today of Cage Meet," *Chicago Tribune,* December 29,1973.

63. "1974 Maryland-Eastern Shore Hawks," College Basketball at Sports-Reference. com, accessed June 23, 2016. http://www.sports-reference.com.

64. Clint Jackson, interview by author by e-mail, June 23, 2016.

65. Robert Newman, interview by author, June27, 2016.

66. Milton Stephens, interview by author, July 17, 2018.

67. Stevenson Bratcher, interview by author, July 31, 2018.

68. Jerry McNeal, interview by author, July 17, 2018.

69. Milton Stephens, interview by author, July 17, 2018.

70. Robert Newman, interview by author, June 27,2016.

71. Ibid.

72. Stevenson Bratcher, interview by author, July 31, 2018.

73. "Four Way Restaurant Owner Willie Earl Bates Dies," WMC Action News 5—Memphis, Tennessee, May 20, 2016, http://www.wmcactionnews5.com.

74. Jerry McNeal, interview by author, July 17, 2018.

75. Milton Stephens, interview by author, July 17, 2018.

76. Earl Lewis, *In Their Own Interests: Race, Class, and Power in Twentieth-Century Norfolk, Virginia* (Berkeley: University of California Press, 1991), 90.

77. Chad Carlson, *Making March Madness: The Early Years of the NCAA, NIT and College Basketball Championships* (Fayetteville: University of Arkansas Press, 2017), 53, 58, 88.

78. Ibid., 147–148.

79. Ibid., 158, 240.

80. Ibid., 253.

81. Ibid., 232.

82. Ibid., 251, 301.

83. Randy Covitz, "No Pressure on Magicians," *Press-Scimitar,* February 27, 1975.

84. "Magicians Will Host Tourney," *Press-Scimitar,* February 19, 1975.

85. Jerry McNeal, interview by author, July 17, 2018.

86. Ibid.

87. "Magicians Win Cage Title," *Tri-State Defender,* March 15, 1975.

88. "Magicians Will be Shooting in the dark," *Press-Scimitar,* March 7, 1975.

89. Ken Jones, "Only Miles Stands in Magicians Way," *Press-Scimitar,* March 8, 1975.

90. Clint Jackson, interview by author, June 21, 2016.

91. "Strong Bench Lifts LeMoyne," *Press-Scimitar,* February 10, 1975.

92. Lee Sanders, interview by author, July 5, 2018.

93. "Strong Bench Lifts LeMoyne."

94. Randy Covitz, "Like Magic, L-O Makes NCAA Semis," *Press-Scimitar,* March 12, 1975.

95. Ibid.

96. Andrew Ramsey, "The Skies Refused to Fall: Crispus Attucks High School and Indiana Basketball," in *The Unlevel Playing Field: A Documentary History of the African American Experience in Sport* (Chicago: University of Illinois Press, 2003), 254–257.

97. Jerry McNeal, interview by author, July 17, 2018.

98. Clint Jackson, interview by author, June 21, 2016.

99. Robert Newman, interview by author, June 27, 2016.

100. Ken Jones, "Magicians Smell NCAA Championship," *Press-Scimitar,* March 15, 1975.

101. Bobby Ervin, "LeMoyne's Victory is No Magic," *Commercial Appeal,* March 15, 1975.

102. Jones, 'Magicians Smell NCAA Championship."

103. Jerry McNeal, interview by author, July 17, 2018.

104. *NCAA Division III Basketball Championship Program*, 18, 24, 26, and 30.

105. Bobby Erving, "Determined Magicians Claim National Title," *Commercial Appeal*, March 15, 1975.

106. Jerry McNeal, interview by author, July 17, 2018.

107. Ibid.; and Jerry Johnson, interview by author, March 29, 2018.

108. Robert Newman, interview by author, June 27, 2016.

109. Jerry McNeal, interview by author, July 17, 2018.

CHAPTER 5

1. Linda Moore, "Former Students gather in North Shelby County for Woodstock High School Centennial," *Commercial Appeal*, October 05, 2013.

2. Ibid.

3. Gentry, *2015–2016 Shelby Metro High School Basketball*, 91.

4. Verties Sails Sr., interview by author, March 28, 2016.

5. Sandomir, "Civil Rights on the Basketball Court."

6. "Magicians Take on Fisk U. Bulldogs Monday Night in Annual Homecoming Battle," *Memphis World*, February 9, 1963.

7. Gentry, *2015–2016 Shelby Metro High School Basketball*, 91.

8. Ray Jordan "Melrose Wins Heated Final," *Commercial Appeal*, February 23, 1974; and Gentry, *2015–2016 Shelby Metro High School Basketball*, 91.

9. *Memphis State University Men's Basketball Media Guide*, 1974–1975.

10. Verties Sails Sr., interview by author, March 28, 2016.

11. "Sails Jr., Verties," Tennessee Sports Hall of Fame, Accessed March 30, 2016, http://tshf.net.

12. Verties Sails Sr., interview by author, March 28, 2016.

13. Ibid.

14. 1973–1974 *University of Memphis Men's Basketball Media Guide*, 9.

15. Verties Sails Sr., interview by author, March 28, 2016.

16. Michael Lollar, "Memphis Civil Rights Legend Maxine Smith Dies at 83," *Commercial Appeal*, April 26, 2013.

17. Verties Sails Sr., interview by author, March 28, 2016.

18. Ibid.

19. Wiggins, *Glory Bound*, 123–124.

20. Verties Sails Sr., interview by author, March 28, 2016.

21. Little, "Sports Horizons." *Tri-State Defender*, February 15, 1975.

22. Wiggins, *Glory Bound*, 124.

23. Bill Little, "Sports Horizons," *Tri-State Defender*, February 15, 1975.

24. Verties Sails Sr., interview by author, March 28, 2016.

25. Bill Little, "Sports Horizon," *Tri-State Defender,* Feb 22, 1975.

26. Verties Sails Sr., interview by author, March 28, 2016.

27. Leonard Shapiro, *Big Man on Campus: John Thompson and the Georgetown Hoyas* (New York: Holt and Company, 1991), 88.

28. Ibid., 73.

29. Ibid., 9.

30. Verties Sails Sr., interview by author, March 28, 2016.

31. Ibid.

32. Shapiro, *Big Man on Campus,* 222.

33. Bobby Hall, "Tigers Must Face Metro Action with Memories of Chief Defeat," *Commercial Appeal,* February 27, 1977.

34. Ibid.

35. Verties Sails Sr., interview by author, March 28, 2016.

36. Ibid.

37. Hank McDowell, interview by author, April 13, 2016.

38. Verties Sails Sr., interview by author, March 28, 2016.

39. Ibid.

40. John Varlas, "Former Tiger John Gunn's Star Shines 40 Years Later," *Commercial Appeal,* December 21, 2016.

41. Ibid.

42. Bobby Hall, "Emotional Memphis State Shocks Louisville," *Commercial Appeal,* February 18, 1979.

43. Al Dunning, "Yates Quits MSU Post: Cites Unity," *Commercial Appeal,* February 8, 1979.

44. Ibid.

45. Mike Fleming, "Yates Shocks His Squad," *Commercial Appeal,* February 8, 1979.

46. "1979 Louisville Cardinals," College Basketball at Sports-Reference.com, accessed April 10, 2016, http://www.sports-reference.com.

47. Hall, "Emotional Memphis State Shocks Louisville."

48. "1979 Memphis Tigers," College Basketball at Sports-Reference.com, accessed April 10, 2016, http://www.sports-reference.com.

49. Dunning, "Yates Quits MSU Post; Cites Unity."

50. Verties Sails Sr., interview by author, March 28, 2016.

51. "Sails Backers Voice Concern," *Commercial Appeal,* February 18, 1979.

52. Hank McDowell, interview by author, April 13, 2016.

53. Bobby Hall, "Yates Decision to Resign is Final," *Commercial Appeal,* February 20, 1979.

54. Verties Sails, interview by Geoff Calkins, *Sports Files with Geoff Calkins WKNO,* July 2012, https://www.youtube.com.

55. "NBA," Kilpatrick Wells Player Profile, Mississippi State, NCAA Stats, Awards, accessed May 27, 2016, http://basketball.realgm.com.

56. "NBA." Sam Bowie Player Profile, Los Angeles Lakers, Stats, NCAA Stats, Game Logs, Bests, Awards, accessed May 27, 2016, http://basketball.realgm.com.

57. Verties Sails Sr., interview by author, March 28, 2016.

58. Bubba Luckett, interview by author, August 22, 2017.

59. Verties Sails, interview by Geoff Calkins, *Sports Files with Geoff Calkins WKNO*.

60. Seth Davis, *Getting to Us: How Great Coaches Make Great Teams* (New York: Penguin Books Inc., 2018), 2–5.

61. Vickie S. Finch, interview by author, February 7, 2018.

62. Marlon Morgan, "After 33 seasons of junior college coaching, Verties Sails is ready to relax," *Commercial Appeal*, accessed April 6, 2016, http://www.commercialappeal.com.

63. Verties Sails Sr., interview by author, March 28, 2016.

CHAPTER 6

1. Al Dunning, "Kirk: From Pigeon Creek to 'Top 10' Mainstream," *Commercial Appeal*, February 28, 1982.

2. Sanford, *From Boss Crump to King Willie*, 214.

3. Ibid., 203.

4. Dunning, "Kirk: From Pigeon Creek to 'Top 10' Mainstream."

5. Dana Kirk, *Simply Amazing: The Dana Kirk Story* (United States of America, 1988), 17. Following his indictment by a federal grand jury, Kirk set out to salvage his name. Kirk personally paid for the publication of his autobiography to clarify his side of the story. The book was distributed mainly to local Walgreen's pharmacies and never made waves nationally.

6. Ibid., 37–47.

7. Preston Lauterbach, "Memphis Burning," *Places Journal*, March 2016, https://placesjournal.org.

8. *Hobbs Act*, U.S. Code, vol. 18, section 371 (1946).

9. *United States v. Bobby, Gillock, Ayers, 752 F. 2d 1116 (6th Circuit. 1985)*.

10. Sanford, *From Boss Crump to King Willie*, 176–178.

11. "Fraud Charges Levied Against Emmitt Fords," *Commercial Appeal.* March 28, 1980.

12. Sanford, *From Boss Crump to King Willie*, 179.

13. "Ford, Farris Patch Up Fight on Mayor Race; Withdrawals Expected," *Commercial Appeal*, May 9, 1978.

14. Rhoden, *Forty Million Dollar Slaves*, 269.

15. "Tape is Inconclusive," *Commercial Appeal*, February 10, 1980.

16. Bobby Hall, "Kirk Offers Apologies as Tigers Meet Tulane," *Commercial Appeal,* February 12, 1980.

17. "1980–81 Memphis Tigers Schedule and Results," College Basketball at Sports -Reference.com, accessed June 23, 2017, https://www.sports-reference.com.

18. John Stamm, "Kirk Masks Feelings—Almost," *Press-Scimitar,* January 23, 1981.

19. Bobby Hall, "Tigers Land Prize Recruit," *Commercial Appeal,* April 28, 1981.

20. "1981–82 Memphis Tigers Schedule and Results." College Basketball at Sports -Reference.com, accessed June 23, 2017, http://www.sports-reference.com.

21. Kirk, *Simply Amazing,* 90.

22. "1981–1982 Memphis Tigers Schedule and Results."

23. Branston, *Rowdy Memphis,* 39–41.

24. Sanford, *From Boss Crump to King Willie,* 120–121.

25. *United States of America v. Ira Henderson Murphy,* 836 F.2d 248 (6th Circuit, 1988).

26. Summers, 27.

27. *Ira Murphy v. Board of Professional Responsibility.* 02-S-01-9503-CH-00031 (Sup. Ct. TN. 1996).

28. "1982–83 Memphis Tigers Schedule and Results," College Basketball at Sports -Reference.com, accessed June 23, 2017, http://www.sports-reference.com.

29. Kirk, *Simply Amazing,* 101.

30. "1982–83 Memphis Tigers Schedule and Results."

31. University of Memphis Men's Basketball Fact Book, 2012–13, https://issuu.com.

32. "Phi Slama Jama—ESPN Films: 30 for 30," *ESPN,* accessed June 24, 2017, http://www.espn.com.

33. Kirk, *Simply Amazing,* 106–107.

34. University of Memphis Men's Basketball Media Guide, 2015–2016, 72.

35. Kirk, *Simply Amazing,* 111.

36. "1983–84 Memphis Tigers Schedule and Results," College Basketball at Sports-Reference.com, accessed June 24, 2017, http://www.sports-reference.com.

37. Kirk, *Simply Amazing,* 112.

38. *University of Memphis Men's Basketball Media Guide, 2015–2016,* 93.

39. "1984–85 Memphis Tigers Schedule and Results," College Basketball at Sports -Reference.com, accessed June 24, 2017, http://www.sports-reference.com.

40. *Memphis State University Men's Basketball Media Guide,* 1984–1985, 24.

41. "1984–85 Memphis Tigers Schedule and Results."

42. Kirk, *Simply Amazing,* 128.

43. University of Memphis Men's Basketball Media Guide, 2015–2016, 93–94.

44. Curry Kirkpatrick, "Looking back at Villanova's magical run to the 1985 NCAA title 'The Gang's All Here.'" *Sports Illustrated,* April 1, 1985.

45. Alexander Wolff, "A Little Tiger Turner-bout," *Sports Illustrated,* April 1, 1985.

46. Kirk, *Simply Amazing,* 144–145.

47. University of Memphis Men's basketball Guide, 2015–2016, 95; and "1984–85 Memphis Tigers Schedule and Results."

48. Bill Little, "Kirk's Days Are Numbered," *Tri-State Defender,* July 20, 1985.

49. Bobby Hall, "Askew to ask for release from Tigers," *Commercial Appeal,* April 29, 1985.

50. Bill Little, "A Frustrated Askew Returns," *Tri-State Defender,* August 3, 1985.

51. "Smith Nudges Kirk: Resign," *Tri-State Defender,* May 18, 1985.

52. Maxine A. Smith, "1986 Annual Report of Executive Secretary," Folder 26, Box 1, Maxine A. Smith NAACP Collection, Memphis/Shelby County Public Library.

53. Douglas S. Looney, "Trouble Times at Memphis State," *Sports Illustrated,* June 24, 1985.

54. "Smith Nudges Kirk: Resign."

55. Otis Sanford, "Kirk confirms finances under question: Kirk says finances grand jury's target," *Commercial Appeal,* August 1, 1985.

56. Robert Sullivan, "Shame on You, SMU," *Sports Illustrated,* March 9, 1987.

57. Douglass Looney, "Deception in the Heart of Texas," *Sports Illustrated,* September 30, 1985.

58. Sullivan, "Shame on You, SMU."

59. Otis Sanford, "Kirk confirms finances under question: Kirk says finances grand jury's target," *Commercial Appeal,* September 26, 1985.

60. Bill Little, "MSU cage program receives a jolt," *Tri-State Defender,* May 8, 1985.

61. "Bedford has wreck in Tiger fan's auto," *Commercial Appeal,* April 26, 1985.

62. Mike Fleming, "IRS looking at Kirk's car connection," *Commercial Appeal,* September 3, 1986.

63. Mike Fleming and Chuck Cook, "Kirk Given Loan Funds, Source Says," *Commercial Appeal,* July 14, 1985.

64. Mike Fleming and Otis Sanford, "Grand jury set to call Keith Lee in Kirk case," *Commercial Appeal,* October 8, 1986.

65. Shirley Downing and Anita Houk, "Lee testifies Kirk gave him cash, car for playing," *Commercial Appeal,* September 30, 1988.

66. Ibid.

67. Cohen, *The Game They Played,* x.

68. Kirk, *Simply Amazing,* 154–155.

69. Lela Garlington, "Kirk attorneys link probe to allegations: Documents say jury told points shaved," *Commercial Appeal,* May 8, 1987.

70. Kirk, *Simply Amazing,* 126–127.

71. "Group launches Kirk campaign," *Commercial Appeal,* July 27, 1985.

72. Kirk, *Simply Amazing,* 164.

73. "1985–86 Memphis Tigers Roster and Stats," College Basketball at Sports-Reference.com, accessed May 27, 2017, http://www.sports-reference.com; and

"1985–86 Men's Basketball Schedule," University of Memphis Athletics—1985–86 Men's Basketball Schedule, accessed May 27, 2017, http://www.gotigersgo.com.

74. Mike Fleming and Chuck Cook, "Federal agents tune in Kirk shows," *Commercial Appeal*, March 25, 1986.

75. Mike Fleming, "MSU booster club members testify," *Commercial Appeal*, June 27, 1986.

76. Kirk, *Simply Amazing*, 201.

77. Ibid., 203.

78. Ibid., 206–7.

79. Mike Fleming and Lela Garlington, "Kirk Indicted on 11 counts," *Commercial Appeal*, November 21, 1986.

80. Mike Fleming, "Grand Jury Turned Talkative Kirk Quiet," *Commercial Appeal*, November 21, 1986.

81. Scott Stantis, cartoon of Dana Kirk, in *Commercial Appeal* (Memphis, TN, November 23, 1986).

82. John Branston, "Kirk Files Three Libel Suits Against Newspaper, Others," *Commercial Appeal*, January 24, 1987.

83. Lela Garlington, "Dana Kirk Contends Tax Case Selective," *Commercial Appeal*, June 3, 1987; and Lela Garlington, "Kirk Points Finger at Finch's Tax Return," *Commercial Appeal*, June 20, 1987.

84. Goudsouzian, "Back to One City."

85. James Chisum, "Libel suits from Kirk dismissed," *Commercial Appeal*, June 24, 1987.

86. Shirley Downing and Anita Houk, "'I am not a criminal,' ex-MSU coach insists," *Commercial Appeal*, November 16, 1988.

87. Anita Houk, "Kirk handed 1-year term, $20,000 fine," *Commercial Appeal*, February 11, 1989.

88. Shirley Downing, "Kirk ordered to prison in Alabama," *Commercial Appeal*, March 10, 1989.

89. Steve Wieberg, "Eliminating distress, Kirk seeks a presidential pardon," *USA Today*, August 15, 1989.

90. Andy Crossley, "Global Basketball Association (1991–1992) Fun While It Lasted," November 22, 2012, http://www.funwhileitlasted.net.

91. Ron Higgins, "Always game," *Commercial Appeal*, February 16, 2010; and Dan Wolken, "Coaching Legacy," *Commercial Appeal*, February 16, 2010.

92. Ibid.

CHAPTER 7

1. Bobby Hall, "Finch signs a three-year pact, takes MSU basketball reins," *Commercial Appeal*, September 9, 1986.

2. Bill Little, "MSU names first black coach," *Tri-State Defender,* September 27, 1986.

3. Randy Covitz, "Larry Finch joins Bartow at Birmingham," *Press-Scimitar,* July 14, 1977.

4. "Finch Joins Memphis State's Staff," *Commercial Appeal,* March 25, 1979.

5. Ron Higgins, "Farewell to Finch," *Commercial Appeal,* March 1, 1997.

6. Geoff Calkins, "Finch, City's Basketball Soul, Needs an Assist," *Commercial Appeal,* April 16, 2006.

7. Vickie S. Finch, interview by author, February 7, 2018.

8. Leroy Williams Jr., "Patient Finch Sees Time as Being on His Side," *Commercial Appeal,* September 27, 1983.

9. Ibid.

10. Bobby Hall, "Finch see his situation as 'unique,'" *Commercial Appeal,* February 1, 1987.

11. Ron Higgins, "Booster Gets Emotional over Hiring," *Commercial Appeal,* September 26, 1986.

12. Maxine A. Smith, "Report of Executive Secretary," 3 September–7 October 1986, box 1, folder 26, Maxine A. Smith NAACP Collection, Memphis/Shelby County Public Library.

13. Bobby Hall, "Finch Sees His Situation as 'Unique,'" *Commercial Appeal,* February 1, 1987.

14. Martin, *Benching Jim Crow,* 237–240.

15. Hall, "Finch see his situation as 'unique.'"

16. "Finch Beats the Odds," *Commercial Appeal,* March 6, 1987.

17. Memphis State University Men's Basketball Media Guide, 1987–88, 55.

18. Memphis State University Men's Basketball Media Guide, 1987–88, 57 and 59.

19. Michael Lollar, "Coach Larry Finch Calls the Plays His Own Way," *Commercial Appeal,* January 17, 1988.

20. Memphis State University Men's Basketball Media Guide, 1988–89, 54.

21. "1987–88 Memphis Tigers Schedule and Results," College Basketball at Sports -Reference.com, accessed July 10, 2017, http://www.sports-reference.com.

22. *United States v. Peete,* 919 F. 2d 1168 (6th Circuit. 1990)

23. Ibid.

24. Ibid.

25. John Branston, "On Rickey Peete: 'An Indictment Against Us All,'" *Memphis Flyer,* June 21, 2007.

26. Ibid.

27. Memphis State University Men's Basketball Media Guide, 1988–89, 41.

28. "1988–89 Memphis Tigers Schedule and Results," College Basketball at Sports -Reference.com, accessed July 11, 2017, http://www.sports-reference.com.

29. "1989–90 Memphis Tigers Schedule and Results," College Basketball at Sports -Reference.com, accessed July 11, 2017, http://www.sports-reference.com.

30. Vickie S. Finch, interview by author, February 7, 2018.

31. Harold Byrd, interview by author, July 9, 2019.

32. Memphis State University Men's Basketball Media Guide, 1991–92, 31.

33. Gary Brown, "NCAA Graduation Rates: A Quarter-Century of Tracking Academic Success," NCAA.org—The Official Site of the NCAA, October 28, 2014, http://www.ncaa.org.

34. William Rhoden, "Big East; Thompson's Protest Intensifies Debate," *New York Times,* January 16, 1989.

35. Memphis State University Men's Basketball Media Guide, 1992–93, 41.

36. Branston, *Rowdy Memphis,* 37.

37. Sanford, *From Boss Crump to King Willie,* 231–232.

38. Ibid., 224–226.

39. Ibid., 228.

40. John Branston, "Majority Rules: Should the Runoff be Brought Back in Mayoral and Citywide Elections?" *Memphis Flyer,* March 15, 2007.

41. Branston, *Rowdy Memphis,* 38–40.

42. Walter Arnold, "Prince Mongo's Castle—Ashlar Hall—Memphis, TN," The Art of Abandonment, January 13, 2016, https://artofabandonment.com.

43. Ibid.

44. Branston, *Rowdy Memphis,* 37

45. Sanford, *From Boss Crump to King Willie,* 242.

46. Memphis State University Men's Basketball Media Guide, 1991–92, 5.

47. Memphis State University Men's Basketball Media Guide, 1992–92, 41, 59, 60

48. "1991–92 Memphis Tigers Schedule and Results," College Basketball at Sports -Reference.com, accessed July 11, 2017, http://www.sports-reference.com/cbb/schools /memphis/1992-schedule.html.

49. Gentry, *2015–2016 Shelby Metro High School Basketball,* 128.

50. Larry Finch Jr., interview by author, January 31, 2018.

51. Gentry, *2015–2016 Shelby Metro High School Basketball,* 83–84.

52. Memphis State University Men's Basketball Media Guide, 1992–93, 59.

53. Ibid., 60.

54. Tom Schuberth, interview by author, July 9, 2019.

55. Dennis Freeland. "Freefall: There's no light at the end of the Memphis Tiger basketball tunnel," *Memphis Flyer.* December 1996.

56. Tom Schuberth, interview by author, July 9, 2019.

57. Memphis State Men's Basketball Media Guide, 1993–94, 53.

58. "1992–93 Memphis Tigers Schedule and Results," College Basketball at Sports -Reference.com, accessed July 13, 2017, http://www.sports-reference.com.

59. Memphis State University Men's Basketball Media Guide, 1993–94, 64.

60. Ibid., 17.

61. Mark Bialek, "Deuce's Downfall: The Former McDonald's All-American Never Lived up to Expectations," *Memphis Flyer*, July 29,1998

62. Memphis State University Men's Basketball Media Guide, 1994–95, 72.

63. Larry Finch Jr., interview by author, January 31, 2018.

64. Ibid., 62.

65. Kelly Whiteside, "7 Memphis," *Sports Illustrated*, October 24, 1995.

66. University of Memphis Men's Basketball Media Guide, 1994–1995, 23.

67. "1994–95 Memphis Tigers Schedule and Results," College Basketball at Sports-Reference.com, accessed July 13, 2017, http://www.sports-reference.com.

68. Ibid.

69. Congress, House of Representatives, Representative Steve Cohen of Tennessee Honoring the life of Memphis State basketball player and coach, Larry Finch. 112th Congress, 1st Session, (6 April 2011): 5367.

70. Larry Finch Jr., interview by author, January 31, 2018.

71. Dennis Freeland, "Tiger Basketball in the Nineties: A Decade of Decline," *Memphis Flyer*, December 16, 1999.

72. Memphis State University Men's Basketball Media Guide, 1995–96, 64.

73. Memphis State University Men's Basketball Media Guide, 1995–1996, 87.

74. Kelly Whiteside, "7 Memphis," *Sports Illustrated*, October 24, 1995.

75. Gerry Callahan, "USA! USA! Born Out of the All-American Desire to Increase Profits, the New Conference USA is an Instant Power," *Sports Illustrated*, October 24, 1995.

76. University of Memphis Men's Basketball Media Guide 1996–1997, 49.

77. "1995–96 Memphis Tigers Schedule and Results," College Basketball at Sports-Reference.com, accessed August 1, 2017, https://www.sports-reference.com.

78. Tom Schuberth, interview by author, July 9, 2019.

79. University of Memphis Men's Basketball Media Guide, 1996–1997, 50.

80. Larry Finch Jr., interview by author, January 31, 2018.

81. Dennis Freeland, "Dead Man Walking," *Memphis Flyer*, February 12, 1997.

82. Phil Stukenborg, "Finch Resigns; Buyout Ends Tiger era," *Commercial Appeal*, January 31, 1997.

83. Thomas Harding, "Finch is 'scapegoat,' Attorney says," *Commercial Appeal*, January 30, 1997.

84. Vickie S. Finch, interview by author, February 7, 2018.

85. Larry Finch Jr., interview by author, January 31, 2018.

86. Vickie S. Finch, interview by author, February 7, 2018.

87. Ibid.

88. Kevin Robbins, "Community Where it All Began Feels for Finch," *Commercial Appeal*, January 30, 1997.

89. Ibid.

90. Harding, "Finch is 'scapegoat,' Attorney says."

91. Ron Higgins, "Kirk Takes to Airwaves at Full Speed," *Commercial Appeal*, December 27, 1994.

92. Woody Baird, "Memphis Will Celebrate," *Reading Eagle*, September 15, 1989.

93. Woody Baird, "Big Pyramid, Little Wonder," *The Fredericksburg Free Lance-Star*, November 9, 1991.

94. Bill Little, "Larry Finch Accepts Fate," *Tri-State Defender*, February 8, 1997.

95. Bobby Hall, "Finch, Tiger icon, coaches home finale," *Commercial Appeal*, March 1, 1997.

96. Michael Lollar, "Coach Larry Finch calls the plays his own way," *Commercial Appeal*, January 17, 1988.

97. Bobby Hall, "With an Emotional Finale, Finch Leaves his Home Court a Winner," *Commercial Appeal*, March 2, 1997.

98. "Finch Strives for the Ultimate."

EPILOGUE

1. Kriste Goad, "Slim loss is the least of Finch's concerns," *Commercial Appeal*, August 8, 1998.

2. "Behind the Name—Memphis," NBA.com, March 12, 2006, https://www.nba.com.

3. Geoff Calkins, "George Lapides reflects on a lifetime of sports in the city he loves," *Commercial Appeal*, June 8, 2016.

4. Michael Wallace, "Z-Bo's Holiday Outreach Lands NBA's Community Assist Award," NBA.com, February 28, 2017, https://www.nba.com.

5. John Buehler, "Memphis Grizzlies: 15 Players Who Defined Grit and Grind," Fansided, accessed November 24, 2019, https://bealestreetbears.com.

6. Zack McMillan, "Family and Friends Help Coach Finch Reach for His Biggest-ever Rebound," *Commercial Appeal*, December 15, 2002.

7. Zack McMillan, "In Illness, Finch still a unifier," *Commercial Appeal*, April 30, 2005.

8. Wiley Henry, "Golf Tourney funds to benefit Finch," *Tri-State Defender*, April 23, 2005.

9. Geoff Calkins, "Finch, city's basketball soul, needs an assist," *Commercial Appeal*, April 16, 2006.

10. Higgins, "Larry's Journey."

11. Wanda Rushing, *Memphis and the Paradox of Race: Globalization in the American South* (Chapel Hill: University of North Carolina Press, 2009), 144.

12. Calkins, "He Loved His City."

13. Drew Hill, "'Blue Chips' 25th anniversary: Penny Hardaway's movie role was a dream come true," *Commercial Appeal*, February 18, 2019.

14. "Anfernee 'Penny' Hardaway—Men's Basketball Coaching Staff," University of Memphis Athletics, accessed November 24, 2019, https://gotigersgo.com.

15. Philip Rossman-Reich, "The Glorious History of Lil Penny," Fansided, accessed November 24, 2019, https://orlandomagicdaily.com.

16. "1994–1995 Orlando Magic Roster and Stats," Basketball Reference, accessed November 24, 2019, https://www.basketball-reference.com.

17. Scott Howard, "Throwback Thursday: Backcourt 2000," SB Nation: Bright Side of the Sun, January 31, 2014, https://www.brightsideofthesun.com.

18. Ibid.

19. Kelly D Evans and Sharon Brown, "Penny Hardaway's Prep High School Team Wins Again," The Undefeated, March 27, 2016, https://theundefeated.com.

20. Marcus Pohlman, *Opportunity Lost: Race and Poverty in the Memphis City Schools* (Knoxville: University of Tennessee Press, 2008), 76.

21. Geoff Calkins, "Hardaway Reminds a City What Tiger Basketball Can Be," *Commercial Appeal*, March 20, 2018.

22. Jeff Pearlman, "New USFL Book highlights Memphis Showboats' crazy times and Reggie White." *Commercial Appeal*, October 8, 2018.

Selected Bibliography

ARCHIVAL SOURCES

College Park, Maryland
  National Archives at College Park
Jackson, Mississippi
  Mississippi Sports Hall of Fame and Museum
Memphis, Tennessee
  Lemoyne-Owen College, Hollis Price Library Special Collections
  Memphis and Shelby County Room, Benjamin L. Hooks Public Library
    ABA Pro Basketball in Memphis
      Chandler Collection
      Dana Kirk Folder
      Larry Finch Folder
    Maxine A. Smith NAACP Collection
  Mississippi Valley Collection, Ned R. McWherther Library, Univ. of Memphis
    University of Memphis Basketball Archive

PERIODICALS

Baltimore Sun
Chicago Tribune
Cleveland Plain-Dealer
Daily Helmsman (Memphis State)
Fredericksburg Free Lance Star
Harvard Crimson

Japan Times
Journal of Negro Education
Journal of Southern History
Labor History
Las Vegas Sun
Lawrence Daily Journal World
Memphis Commercial Appeal
Memphis Daily News
Memphis Flyer
Memphis Press-Scimitar
Memphis Tri-State Defender
New York Times
Oklahoman
Places Journal
Purple and Gold Christian Brothers Memphis
Reading Eagle
Sports Illustrated
Tuscaloosa News
Tuscaloosa Times
USA Today
Washington Post
West Tennessee Historical Society Papers

BOOKS

Ash, Stephen. *A Massacre in Memphis: The Race Riots That Shook the Nation One Year after the Civil War*. New York, Hill and Wang, 2013.

Axthelm, Pete. *The City Game*. Lincoln: University of Nebraska Press, 1970.

Ayers, Edward. *The Promise of the New South: Life After Reconstruction*. Oxford: Oxford University Press, 2007.

Biondi, Martha. *The Black Revolution on Campus*. Berkeley: University of California Press, 2012.

Bond, Beverly and Janann Sherman. *Memphis in Black and White*. Chicago: Arcadia Publishing, 2003.

Boyd, Todd. *Young, Black, Rich, and Famous*. Lincoln: University of Nebraska Press, 2003.

Branston, John. *Rowdy Memphis: The South Unscripted*. Nashville: Cold Tree Press, 2004.

Capers, Gerald. *The Biography of a River Town*. New Orleans: Tulane University Press, 1966.

Carey, Mike. *Bad News.* New York: Sports Publishing, 2016.

Cohen, Stanley. *The Game They Played.* New York: Carroll and Graf Publishers, 1977.

Criblez, Adam. *Tall Tales and Short Shorts: Dr. J., Pistol Pete, and the Birth of the Modern NBA.* New York: Rowman and Littlefield, 2017.

Davis, Seth. *Getting to Us: How Great Coaches Make Great Teams.* New York: Penguin Books Inc., 2018.

Davis, Seth. *When March Went Mad: The Game that Transformed Basketball.* New York: Holt, 2010.

DeCosta-Willis, Miriam. *Notable Black Memphians.* Amherst: Cambria Press, 2008.

Dowdy, Wayne. *Mayor Crump Don't Like It.* Jackson: University of Mississippi Press, 2006.

Edwards, Harry. *The Revolt of the Black Athlete.* Urbana: University of Illinois Press, 1969.

Edwards, Harry. *Sociology of Sport.* Homewood: Dorsey Press, 1973.

Estes, Steve. *I am a Man: Race, Manhood, and the Civil Rights Movement.* Chapel Hill: University of North Carolina Press, 2005.

Fitzpatrick, Frank. *And the Walls Came Tumbling Down: Kentucky, Texas Western and the Game that Changed American Sports.* New York: Simon and Schuster, 1999.

Ford Jr., Harold. *More Davids Than Goliaths.* New York: Crown Publishers, 2010.

Gentry, Keith. *2015–2016 Shelby Metro High School Basketball.* Memphis: Gentry's Statistical Service, 2015.

George, Nelson. *Elevating the Game: Black Men and Basketball.* Lincoln: University of Nebraska Press, 1992.

Gordon, Robert. *Respect Yourself: Stax records and the Soul Explosion.* New York: Bloomsbury, 2013.

Green, Laurie. *Battling the Plantation Mentality: Memphis and the Black Freedom Struggle.* Chapel Hill: University of North Carolina Press, 2007.

Green, Michael and Roger D. Launius. *Charlie Finley: The Outrageous Story of Baseball's Super Showman.* New York: Walker & Company, 2010.

Gritter, Elizabeth. *River of Hope: Black Politics and the Memphis Freedom Movement, 1865–1975* Lexington: University of Kentucky Press, 2014.

Goudsouzian, Aram. *King of the Court: Bill Russell and the Basketball Revolution.* Berkeley: University of California Press, 2010.

Guzzio, Tracie Church. "Race and Basketball in the Works of John Edgar Wideman," in *In the Game: Race, Identity, and Sports in the Twentieth Century,* edited by Amy Bass, 221–36. New York: MacMillan, 2005.

Harkins, John. *Metropolis of the American Nile: Memphis and Shelby County.* Oxford: Guild Bindery Press, 1982.

Honey, Michael. *Going Down Jericho Road: The Memphis Strike, MLK's Last Campaign.* New York: W.W. Norton & Co., 2007.

Jacobs, Berry. *Across the Lines: Profiles in Courage: Tales of the First Black Players in the ACC and SEC*. New York: Lyons Press, 2007.

Katz, Milton. *Breaking Through: John B. McLendon, Basketball Legend and Civil Rights Pioneer*. Fayetteville: University of Arkansas Press, 2007.

Kinchen, Shirletta. *Black Power in the Bluff City: African American Youth and Student Activism in Memphis, 1965–1975*. Knoxville: University of Tennessee Press, 2016.

Kirk, Dana. *Simply Amazing: The Dana Kirk Story*. United States of America, 1988.

Kriegel, Mark. *Pistol: The Life of Pete Maravich*. New York: Free Press, 2008.

Lewis, Earl. *In Their Own Interests: Race, Class, and Power in Twentieth-Century Norfolk, Virginia*. Berkeley: University of California Press, 1991.

Litwack, Leon. *Trouble in Mind: Black Southerners in the Age of Jim Crow*. New York: Vintage Books, 1999.

Mallozzi, Vincent. *Asphalt Gods: An Oral History of the Rucker Tournament*. New York: Doubleday Publishing, 2003.

Maraniss, Andrew. *Strong Inside: Perry Wallace and the Collision of Race and Sports in the South*. Nashville: Vanderbilt Press, 2014.

Martin, Charles. *Benching Jim Crow: The Rise and fall of the Color Line in Southern College Sports, 1890 - 1980*. Urbana: University of Illinois Press, 2010.

Mazor, Sharon. *Professional Wrestling: Sport and Spectacle*. Oxford, MS: University of Mississippi Press, 1998.

Messner, Michael. *Power Play: Sports and the Problem of Masculinity*. Boston: Beacon Press, 1992.

Montieth, Mark. *Reborn: The Pacers and the Return of Pro Basketball to Indianapolis*. Indianapolis: Halfcourt Press, 2017.

Olsen, Jack. *The Black Athlete: A Shameful Story*. New York: Time Life Publishing, 1968.

Pluto, Terry. *Loose Balls: The Short, Wild Life of the ABA*. New York: Simon & Schuster, 1990.

Pohlman, Marcus. *Opportunity Lost: Race & Poverty in the Memphis City Schools*. Knoxville: University of Tennessee Press, 2008.

Rappaport, Ken and Barry Wilner. *The Big Dance: The Story of the NCAA Basketball Tournament*. New York: Taylor Trade Publishing, 2012.

Recht, Michael, ed. *ABA Official Guide 1973–74*. St. Louis: The Sporting News, 1973.

Rhoden, William C. *Forty Million Dollar Slaves: The Rise, Fall, and Redemption of the Black Athlete*. New York: Three Rivers Press, 2006.

Roberts, Randy. *Papa Jack: Jack Johnson and the Era of White Hopes*. New York: Free Press, 1983.

Robinson, Zandria. *This Ain't Chicago: Race, Class, and Regional Identity in the Post-Soul South*. Chapel Hill: University of North Carolina Press, 2014.

Rogers, Ibram. *The Black Campus Movement: Black Student and the Racial Reconstitution of Higher Education, 1965–1972.* New York: MacMillan, 2012.

Ruck, Rob. *Sandlot Seasons: Sport in Black Pittsburgh.* Urbana: University of Illinois Press, 1993.

Sanford, Otis. *From Boss Crump to King Willie: How Race Changed Memphis Politics.* Knoxville: University of Tennessee Press,2017.

Shapiro, Leonard. *Big Man on Campus: John Thompson and the Georgetown Hoyas.* New York: Holt and Company, 1991.

Smith, John Matthew. *Sons of Westwood: John Wooden, UCLA, and the Dynasty That Changed College Basketball (Sport and Society).* Urbana: University of Illinois Press, 2013.

Telander, Rick. *Heaven is a Playground.* Lincoln, NE: Bison Books, 1995.

Tucker, David. *Memphis Since Crump: Bossism, Blacks, and Civic Reformers.* Knoxville: University of Tennessee Press, 1980.

Turner, Allegra. *Except by Grace: The Life of Jesse H. Turner.* Jonesboro, AR: Four G Publishers, 2004.

Tygiel, Jules. *Baseball's Great Experiment: Jackie Robinson and his Legacy.* Oxford: Oxford University Press, 1983.

Varady, Aharon N. Bond Hill: *Origin and Transformation of a 19th Century Cincinnati Railroad Suburb,* report, 9th ed. Cincinnati: Henry Watkins Press, 2005.

Veazey, Kyle. *Champions for Change: How the Mississippi State Bulldogs and their Bold Coach Defied Segregation.* Charleston, SC: The History Press, 2012.

West, Gary. *Kentucky Colonels of the ABA: The Real Story of a Team Left Behind.* Morley, MO: Acclaim Press, 2011.

White, Derrick E. *Blood, Sweat, and Tears: Jake Gaither, Florida A&M, and the History of Black College Football.* Chapel Hill: University of North Carolina Press, 2019.

Wiggins, David. *Glory Bound Black Athletes in a White America.* Syracuse, NY: Syracuse University Press, 1997.

Wiggins, David. *Separate Games: African American Sport behind the Walls of Segregation.* Fayetteville: University of Arkansas Press, 2016.

Wiggins, David K. and Patrick B. Miller. *The Unlevel Playing Field: A Documentary History of the African American Experience in Sport.* Chicago: University of Illinois Press, 2003.

Williams, Charles. *African American Life and Culture in Orange Mound: Case Study of a Black Community in Memphis, Tennessee, 1890–1980.* New York: Lexington Books, 2013.

Bratcher, Stevenson. Interview by author. Memphis, TN., July 31, 2018.

Byrd, Harold. Interview by author. Memphis, TN., July 9, 2019.

Coleman, Richard. Interview by author. Memphis, TN., April 23, 2017, and November 23, 2018.

Draper, Leonard. Interview by author. Memphis, TN., December 21, 2017.

Easterwood, Keith. Phone interview by author. October 10, 2017.

Finch, Larry Jr. Interview by author. Memphis, TN., January 31, 2018.

Finch, Vickie S. Interview by author. Memphis, TN., February 7, 2018.

Jackson, Clint. Interview by author. Memphis, TN., June 21, 2016; June 23, 2016; and July 13, 2016.

Johnson, Jerry. Interview by author. Memphis, TN., March 29, 2018.

Lapides, Barbara. Interview by author. Memphis, TN., July 9, 2019.

Luckett, Bubba. Interview by author. Memphis, TN., August 22, 2017.

McDowell, Hank. Interview by author. Memphis, TN., April 13, 2016.

McNeal, Jerry. Interview by author. Memphis, TN., July 17, 2018.

Miller, Tom. Phone interview by author. December 26, 2017.

Newman, Robert. Interview by author. Memphis, TN., June 27, 2016.

Parr, Willie. Phone interview by author. July 1, 2018.

Sails, Verties Sr. Interview by author. Memphis, TN., March 28, 2016, and February 15, 2018.

Sails, Verties Sr. Interview by Geoff Calkins, Sports Files with Geoff Calkins WKNO, July 2012.

Sanders, Lee. Phone interview by author. July 5, 2018.

Schuberth, Tom. Phone interview by author. June 26, 2019.

Stephens, Milton. Phone interview by author. July 17, 2018.

Index

www.ingramcontent.com/pod-product-compliance
Lightning Source LLC
Chambersburg PA
CBHW031121020426
42333CB00012B/178